PROMOTING MORAL GROWTH

PROMOTING MORAL GROWTH

From Piaget to Kohlberg

Richard H. Hersh
University of Oregon

Diana Pritchard Paolitto
Boston College

Joseph Reimer
Boston College

LONGMAN
New York and London

PROMOTING MORAL GROWTH
From Piaget to Kohlberg

Longman Inc., New York
Associated companies, branches, and representatives throughout the world.

Developmental Editor: Nicole Benevento
Editorial and Design Supervisor: Linda Salmonson
Interior Design: Pencils Portfolio, Inc.
Cover Design: Tim McKeen
Manufacturing and Production Supervisor: Louis Gaber
Composition: Book Composition Services

Library of Congress Cataloging in Publication Data

Hersh, Richard.
    Promoting moral growth.

    Includes bibliographical references and index.
    1. Moral education. 2. Kohlberg, Lawrence,
1927–   3. Piaget, Jean, 1896–
4. Child Development. I. Paolitto, Diana Pritchard,
joint author. II. Reimer, Joseph, joint author.
III. Title.
LC268.H47   370.11′4   78-23963
ISBN 0-582-28057-5 pbk.

Manufactured in the United States of America
9 8 7 6 5 4 3 2

To Lawrence Kohlberg

Contents

Contents

Foreword

by Lawrence Kohlberg

I was pleased to be asked to write a foreword to this book, not only because the authors are friends and colleagues of mine, but also because it is the best introduction to the cognitive-developmental approach to moral education of Piaget or myself currently available. Because the book is written for the classroom teacher, the authors have taken pains to present the theory clearly, as well as to relate theory to practice with concrete and insightful examples. Though clear and concrete, the book makes no intellectual compromises. It presents my theories and those of Piaget with integrity and with a balanced statement of the evidence in terms of research findings and the experience of teachers. I plan to use this book in a graduate course in moral education at Harvard University.[1]

One merit of the book, then, is its clarity as an introduction to the theory. More important to me is the fact that this work is the only current statement of the theory of moral education that has what I feel is a sound perspective on the relation of psychological theory to educational practice. I emphasize this because I myself initially adopted an incorrect perspective on this issue and have corrected my perspective only over the last five years

---

1. A useful accompaniment is Peter Scharf's collection of reprinted articles on this approach. See Peter Scharf, *Readings in Moral Education* (Minneapolis: Winston Press, 1978).

of actual day-to-day involvement in moral education in the Cluster alternative school at the Cambridge public high school.

When I started working in the schools, I attempted to deduce practices the teacher should use from my research-based psychological theory. In this attempt I related theory to educational practice in the same way as B. F. Skinner and other psychologist colleagues had done. I thought Piaget's cognitive-developmental theory a better theory than Skinner's behavioristic, or operant, theory, but I still believed that good educational practice involved teaching teachers an existing theory and providing a manual of teacher practices deduced from it. I now view the way of relating theory to practice followed by Skinner, and by me when I started, as the psychologist's fallacy.

The "psychologist's fallacy" assumes that the variables important for psychologists to research are the important variables for teachers to think about, or that laws or generalizations which are valid conclusions about research should be the foundation of valid teacher thinking about educational practice. This assumption lay behind the construction of behavior-modification programs in education. Before constructing these programs, Skinner and his colleagues had made important and valid generalizations about research on the relations between behavior and rewarding consequences; they had constructed a valid psychological theory for summarizing and explaining research findings. Though valid for explaining many research findings, Skinner's theory is not a valid educational theory in the sense of being a basis for good educational practices, a good theory for teachers to learn and follow. Skinner may dispense with ideas of freedom and dignity to arrive at a theory valid for explaining studies of reward in animals and children. A theory "beyond freedom and dignity" must, however, have serious flaws as a guide to teacher behavior. A theory that ignores freedom and dignity in the learning process leads to the practice of constructing "teacher-proof" materials. It also leads to kits designed to be "student proof," that is, to modify the student's behavior without his understanding or assent to the theory and methods applied to him.

The present book does not make Skinner's mistake of short-circuiting the teacher's point of view to prescribe teacher-proof practices. It assumes that only if a theory can be genuinely accepted by teachers in terms of their own autonomous thinking, and not from the prestige or authority of "science," can it form a valid basis for practice. If an educational theory is too complicated, too far from the teacher's common sense and observation, the fault lies not in the teachers but in the theory. If this book demonstrates respect for the teacher's point of view, it perhaps does not do enough to indicate the ways the theory may be presented to students so that moral education may go on with informed consent, rather than through student-proof techniques.

Underlying the mistaken efforts at teacher-proof and student-proof approaches is the assumption that a psychological theory can prescribe values to teachers and students. In this aspect, the psychologist's fallacy is "the fallacy that one can derive conclusions about what human values and desires ought to be from psychological research, about what human values and desires are, sliding over the distinction between what is *desired* and what is *desirable*." Skinner makes this fallacy, called by philosophers "the naturalistic fallacy," in calling the good for children "reinforcement" or "gaining reinforcement." In my early work in education I realized that it was not sufficient to jump from the psychological findings of a moral-stage sequence to the philosophic conclusion that attaining a higher stage should be the aim of moral education. Accordingly, I attempted to demonstrate philosophically John Dewey's first educational assumption, that development is the fundamental aim of education and that a later moral stage is a better or more adequate stage from a moral philosopher's standpoint. Our philosophic assumption about higher stages is tested in educational practice by student preferences for thinking above his or her own stage.

The theory assumes that the child or the adolescent is a natural philosopher and hence prefers the philosophically challenging and the philosophically better. Were this assumption unfounded, our approach would have little circulation among educators. It is the interest that hypothetical moral dilemmas arouse in classrooms and in teacher workshops that primarily accounts for the popularity of the cognitive-developmental approach to moral education. Our hypothetical dilemmas arouse interest not because of the usual "psychological principles" that dictate same-age, same-sex heroes but because they set philosophic challenges to adolescents (and young children) in the form of making a concrete choice.

In the first recorded discussion of moral education, Plato's Meno assumes the psychologist's fallacy and asks, "Can you tell me, Socrates, is virtue something that can be taught? Or does it come by practice? Or is it neither teaching or practice but natural aptitude or instinct?" Socrates' reply starts by rejecting Meno's psychologist's fallacy, that moral education practice can derive from a psychology theory of habit or instinct, saying,

> You must think I am singularly fortunate to know whether virtue can be taught or how it is acquired. The fact is that far from knowing whether it can be taught, I have no idea what virtue itself is.

Once the psychologist recognizes that he cannot talk about the psychology of moral development and learning without addressing the philosophic question "What is virtue?" or "What is justice?" he will start on a path that can only end, as the paths of Plato and Dewey ended, in writing a treatise that describes moral education in a school and a society that to the philosopher seems just. In my early work in moral education I did not commit the psychologist's fallacy of ignoring the teacher's or the philosopher's view in proposing moral-stage advance as the aim of moral education. This aim was justified by philosophers from Plato to Dewey who viewed development as the aim of education. I did commit the psychologist's fallacy of ignoring Plato and Dewey's "political" concern with the group and the community as a concern not embraced by a psychology of individual-stage advance. This book's chapter 7, on the "just community," partly remedies this neglect.

My colleagues and I committed another form of the psychologist's fallacy in our early educational work. We designed an educational program around a psychologist's theory. Our first venture into moral education was Moshe Blatt's dissertation experiment to stimulate moral-stage advance through classroom discussion of hypothetical dilemmas similar to those used in our research. The experiment was designed to test the cognitive-developmental theory of moral judgment change through cognitive conflict and exposure to the next higher stage. Blatt found that more than one-third of the students exposed to such discussions would advance during an academic year in which control students remained stationary, and that advance was always only to the next higher stage. While successful as a psychological experiment, the study left much to be desired as an approach to sound moral education.

One of many criticisms of the Blatt approach was that it was "teaching to the test," was raising scores on verbal interviews about hypothetical dilemmas. A partial answer for the psychologist is that stage change generalized to new dilemmas. Another partial answer is that the kind of change found was always developmental change to the next higher stage, not simply verbal learning of clichés. In the light of this, I argued that the Blatt approach to moral education had sound roots in the Socratic view of moral education.

Continuing work in the schools led me to a view closer to that of most of my critics, however, that moral education must deal directly with action and not just with reasoning, with "real-life" situations and not just with hypothetical ones. This obviously led the focus away from the formal curriculum to the "hidden curriculum" of the school. It led to the formation of a participatory democracy or "just community" as the context for moral discussion and moral education.

Our theory of moral education, then, is changing and, one hopes, growing; it is a theory developing through an interchange between psychological theorists and practitioners. It started with an emphasis in psychology, led to thinking through philosophic issues, and proceeded to expansion and revision in the light of continuing experience in classrooms and community meetings in a "just-community" school. The theory has changed as it has tried to organize and inform educational practices and decisions and not just research data. As teachers and theorists interacted, the theory changed or expanded to incorporate good educational practices, and teachers changed to incorporate the dictums of theorists as these dictums became meaningful in practice.

Fundamentally, then, we have abandoned the psychologist's fallacy that the relation between psychology theory and teacher practice is a one-way street. The movement to a two-way street is embodied in the history of the six-year grant from the Danforth Foundation to Edwin Fenton, Ralph Mosher, and myself, to help create programs of moral education viable in the eyes of teachers, students, administrators, and parents in the cities of Cambridge, Brookline, and Pittsburgh.

The first emphasis of the Danforth project has been on developing curriculum. We have assumed that moral development should not be "a course" but a dimension of the curriculum in any course, since any course raises issues of values as well as issues of fact in its studies. For practical purposes, this has led to a focus on integrating discussion on moral dilemmas with regular curricular objectives in history, social studies, and English. Rejecting teacher-proof assumptions, the project assumes that teachers need to integrate moral discussion with other curricular goals and content rather than simply use "canned" curricula. This Danforth assumption is embodied in chapter 6 of the present book, which deals with constructing curricula.

The second emphasis of the Danforth project deals with one of the practical problems inherent in discussing "real" as opposed to hypothetical moral decisions. Discussion of real moral dilemmas involves serious issues of confidentiality and trust and requires teachers to establish conditions of trust in their classrooms. This involves integrating Rogerian counseling psychology practices with Socratic cognitive-developmental questioning in teacher leading of the classroom. This emphasis on teacher as counselor as well as Socratic questioner is elaborated in chapter 5 in this book.

A third emphasis of the Danforth project has been the governance of the classroom and the school as a just community or participatory democracy. Such practices move us furthest away from the psychologist's fallacy of defining good educational practice in terms of deductions from a psychological theory. In the present book chapter 7 on the just community is based on the assumptions of the Danforth project.

Does this book fill a need? The book has been published at this time because of a renewed and growing interest in moral education over the last five years. Cognitive-developmental education is not new; it has a 2000-year history. Why has there been renewed interest in moral education, dead since the 1930s, in the 1970s? The answer can be either conservative or liberal-progressive. The conservative answer is that this interest is a reaction to crime, Watergate, and the decline of traditional sexual morality; it is a conservative return to the social basics of moral order and discipline, like the return to traditional academic basics in curricula. The liberal answer is that the current interest in moral education arises primarily from the rediscovery by liberals of the moral principles behind the liberal faith and the realization that these principles need to enter into education. Like the liberal reaction to Watergate, the liberal interest in moral education is a rediscovery of the principles of justice behind the founding of our nation. The liberals of the 1960s lost their awareness of the principles underlying liberalism, the principles of the Declaration of Independence and the Constitution. Instead of a faith in the principles of justice, the 1960s liberals put their faith in technology, in the social and physical sciences, and in rational political manipulation as tools of social progress. As the faith in rational instrumental *means* has disappointed liberals, an awareness of the need to have rational or moral social *ends* and principles of action, and to embody these ends in education, has been growing.

A principled or moral concern by teachers for the goals of moral education, however, will achieve little unless respect is paid to the complexity of the theoretical and practical dimensions of moral education. This book evidences that respect. The authors respect the lessons of our theoretical work. They respect the complexity and difficulty of the teacher's role. They express appreciation for my help in their learning of the theory. Let me express my appreciation for their help in learning to get past the psychologist's fallacy to a better understanding of the relation of theory to educational practice.

Lawrence Kohlberg

Preface

This book is the culmination of our efforts, begun separately, to understand moral education and apply the research of Lawrence Kohlberg to school settings. During the summer of 1976 we began to work as a team, teaching an intensive four-week course at Harvard University entitled Moral Development Theory in Practice. In that course we provided a set of readings dealing with the psychological, philosophical, and educational principles underlying Kohlberg's cognitive-developmental approach to moral education. When the readings proved insufficient for the task, the idea of writing this book unfolded.

Our experimental course and our work with teachers throughout North America have led us to recognize the need for a coherent explanation of Kohlberg's work from a practical and teaching perspective. Practicing professionals have questioned us extensively, hoping for a more adequate exposition of theoretical concepts and research data. This book is our answer.

We bring different interests and experiences to this work. Richard Hersh has written on curriculum and has worked for years in teacher training. Diana Paolitto's field is counseling; she has worked on both a theoretical and a practical plane to integrate counseling and teaching skills with a developmental approach to moral education. Joseph Reimer's primary interest is cognitive-developmental theory; he has conducted cross-cultural research and a number of research projects in developmental moral education. We have collaborated extensively in writing this book and see it as a common effort.

We wish to alert our readers to a usage in this book that

reflects our awareness of reality and the limitations of English grammar. Throughout the examples in this book we alternate male and female pronouns and adjectives in order to include all our readers yet not resort to awkward constructions.

Lawrence Kohlberg's patience, generosity, and encouragement have supported us during the writing. While we thank him, we wish also to acknowledge that any injustice to his work reflected in this book is our responsibility. We hope we have conveyed the worth of his contributions adequately.

The support, teaching, patience, and sacrifice of numerous other people have sustained our efforts. We particularly wish to acknowledge Ralph Mosher's contributions in integrating theory and curriculum development. We feel indebted to the teachers and counselors of the Brookline and Cambridge public schools of Massachusetts who are involved in the Danforth Moral Education Project; they helped us learn with them, in new and creative ways, about the practice of moral education. We are grateful to the many teachers and researchers who contributed their original work to the pedagogy and curriculum chapters of this book. We wish also to thank students in our 1976 course and the teachers in our workshops, who raised the important questions.

Finally, we could not have completed this manuscript without the loving support and patience of Gail Reimer, Frank Paolitto, and Carol Witherell. Special thanks are due Irene Glynn.

Part I
THEORY

I

Introduction to Moral Development

VALUES, MORALITY, AND SCHOOLS

A moral dimension is inherent in both the process and the content of schooling. Teachers and students encounter values and moral issues constantly, yet the issues are often hidden and thus are not perceived as important concerns. Even when teachers are aware of these issues, they may feel they lack the necessary skills to help students develop more adequate value positions and moral perspectives. Lawrence Kohlberg's work in moral development addresses such concerns and provides a conceptual framework through which teachers are better able to integrate moral issues with the process and content of teaching.

Kohlberg's theory works in practice. Teachers who use the theory increase their awareness of, and their skills in confronting, the moral dimension of schooling. This is illustrated in the two episodes that follow. In Episode 1, Mrs. Warren attends to a moral issue inherent in the interpersonal relations of her classroom. Mr. Hake, in Episode 2, focuses on a moral issue embedded in the content of his lesson.

Episode 1

Helping learning-disabled children become integrated into regular classrooms is a major educational priority in the United States. In one elementary classroom Brian, age nine, a boy with a mild case of cerebral palsy, has become the target of abuse by others in the class. He is teased about such things as his inability to unbutton his jacket and his lack of coordination on the playground during recess. As the ridicule continues, Brian is often seen crying during class.

One day, Brian is absent from school. Mrs. Warren takes this opportunity to ask her pupils to discuss what she believes is a serious problem in the class. The students seem surprised to hear that a "problem" exists, but they form a discussion circle.

Mrs. Warren explains, "Some people are born with a disease that prevents them from using their muscles in a normal way. It must be difficult to want to be like others and not be able to do so. I wonder what it would be like not to be able to do certain things *and* be made fun of by other children?"

There is silence. The tone of Mrs. Warren's voice has not been one of anger but one of concern and sensitivity.

One girl says, "I feel bad when Tim and Jack tease Brian."

Jack answers, "I didn't mean to hurt him."

The discussion continues. Nearly every child has something to contribute. Some students see the problem from Brian's point of view. Jeff says, "I would feel angry and hurt if kids teased me like that." Janet raises the issue of fairness: "It's not fair—it's like we are cheating when we play kickball and run fast but Brian can't."

This is an emotional discussion without formal resolution. The next day, Brian returns. Several students volunteer to help him unbutton his jacket. During recess, Brian reaches base safely three times in the kickball game. As the days pass, the ridicule stops.

Mrs. Warren recognized a problem involving the rights and responsibilities of students in her classroom. Was it fair to tease Brian? Kohlberg considers issues of fairness, rights, and responsibilities as moral issues, whether they exist in classrooms or in the society at large. When they arise in school, suggests Kohlberg, these concerns need to be addressed because attention to them helps students develop a more adequate moral perspective. Understanding this, and aware of how moral issues are part of classroom life, Mrs. Warren initiated discussion concerning the problem. By asking her students how they might feel if they were in Brian's shoes, she was effectively helping them engage in what Kohlberg calls "social role-taking," taking the point of view of the other person as a way of reflecting critically upon one's own perspective. This activity, which requires students to confront their own moral reasoning, is an important aspect of moral development.

Mrs. Warren demonstrated an awareness of, and an ability to use, a classroom-process moral issue to encourage moral reasoning. In the episode that follows, a teacher recognized and responded to a moral problem within the content of his history lesson.

Episode 2

Mark, an eleventh grader, has been reading *A Man Called Intrepid*, a book by William Stevenson that chronicles the secret intelligence operations of World War II. Mark has chosen this book for a nonfiction book report in English class. During an American history lesson he listens with more than usual interest as Mr. Hake discusses the irony of Churchill's losing the support of the British people once the war had ended.

Mark raises his hand and says, "It doesn't seem fair that Churchill was rejected by his people. He made tough decisions during the war that the people didn't even know about."

Mr. Hake replies, "What kind of decisions?"

Mark answers, "Well, one time, after the British had just figured out the secret German codes, Churchill found out that Hitler was going to bomb the city of Coventry. He had to decide if he should warn the people in Coventry that the raid was coming, which would tell the Germans their codes had been broken, or to keep quiet and use the knowledge of the secret codes to end the war sooner. He kept quiet, and later the secret code translation helped make the Allied invasion of Europe successful."

Jason, one of Mark's friends, asks, "But what about the innocent people in Coventry who died because Churchill didn't warn them?"

Joan says, "That's no different from Truman bombing Hiroshima."

"But Churchill and Truman believed they were saving more lives by what they did," Mark answers.

Mr. Hake asks, "Is it right to kill some people in order to save other lives?" After a full minute of silence, Mr. Hake rephrases his question: "Mark said that Churchill and Truman were concerned with saving lives. Yet both men knowingly allowed some to die in order to save others. Is it right to kill some people in order to save other lives?"

The silence continues, although several students nod their heads affirmatively. Taking these nonverbal clues, Mr. Hake asks, "Why?"

Susan speaks first: "I guess if you can save more lives in the long run then it may be all right."

Phil says, "In war anything goes anyway."

"As long as the lives you save are those of your own citizens, it's O.K." Elston adds.

Mr. Hake responds first to Elston's response. "Elston, do your own citizens have more of a right to life than others?"

Mr. Hake recognized the moral issue raised by Mark as relevant to the content of the lesson. Because of previous practice with Kohlberg's theory in this class, Mr. Hake and his students felt comfortable with the discussion that followed. Mr. Hake's question concerning the rightness of killing some to save others was purposeful. Kohlberg's theory explains how the development of moral reasoning requires that one's thinking be challenged. Mr. Hake purposely promoted a variety of viewpoints and actively probed the reasons for alternative points of view. Such teacher behavior, suggests Kohlberg, is an important means of promoting moral development.

Each of the preceding episodes illustrates examples of Kohlberg's theory in practice. The remainder of this book aims at helping educators understand these and other aspects of the theory and applying them in the classroom.

INCREASED DEMAND FOR MORAL EDUCATION

The public wants schools to pay attention to values and moral education. In 1976, the eighth annual Gallup poll of the public's attitudes toward the public schools showed that moral education was a major concern. In response to the question "Which of these ways do you think would do most to *improve* the quality of public schools overall?" 45 percent of the parents of public school children noted the need to emphasize moral development. To the questions "Which one do you think is most neglected by parents today?" and "Which one do you think is most neglected by schools?" parents answered, "High moral standards." Congruent with these concerns are responses to this query: "Parents now have the responsibility for the moral behavior of their children. Do you think that schools should take on a share of the responsibility or not?" Parents responded that schools *should* take on a share of the responsibility in 79 percent of the answers. Yet the school's role in such an endeavor is unclear, and public debate about the nature of that role remains confused.

Why the revived interest in moral education? Perhaps public discussion of, and media attention paid to, such issues as racism, the Vietnam war, Watergate, illegal corporate payoffs, crime, and drugs has sensitized people to the moral dimensions in society. Moreover, Kohlberg points to a lessening of belief in conventional morality, a weakening of faith that leads Americans and educators to seek guidance from scholars rather than from tradition. He further argues that the liberals of the 1960s replaced a belief in the principles of justice with faith in technology, science, and rational political manipulation as tools of social progress. As that faith has disappointed them, there has been a growing recognition that we need to articulate moral principles and promote moral education. The role of the school in this venture remains unclear, however.

SCHOOLS, DEMOCRACY, AND MORAL EDUCATION

Any discussion of the role of the school in values and moral education must begin with the assumption that the education is to take place within a social and political milieu called "democracy." In a totalitarian regime, for example, the determination of purpose and method of such education would be quite different. Once the "party line" was established, all that would be required are materials developed to teach it. Implementation of instruction in the "right" values and moral system would be centrally and tightly controlled. In a democratic setting such control is incompatible with the values of pluralism and individual freedom of belief.

Schools play a vital socialization role in the pursuit of democratic goals. This role requires that schools help persons acquire the appropriate knowledge and skills needed for citizen participation in a democratic society. In essence this is the conservation or societal maintenance function of schooling. In performing this function we rightfully expect schools to help students learn to respect our pluralistic heritage and to value individual and group differences. In addition to the conserving and transmitting function, schools also help students learn how to cope constructively with change. For change, too, is part of our heritage and future. Schools, then, are value-laden institutions by their very function; they must transmit the knowledge, skills, and values necessary for survival in an ever-changing society.

Teachers are instrumental in the transmission of values. As human beings they cannot be value neutral. Indeed, arguing for value neutrality is itself a value position. Teachers, by their pedagogical choices and their modeling behavior, are of necessity moral educators, regardless of the subject matter they teach. Thus, when the question is raised, "Should schools engage in values and moral education?" we have no choice but to answer that schools are necessarily institutions of significant moral enterprise.

To demonstrate that schools are involved in moral education does not solve the problem. What should teachers do as moral educators? Values inculcation has been one response to this question. Teachers in this mode "give" students the right values and moral answers, through telling students what they ought to believe. This method, often viewed as preaching or moralizing, has been criticized as a form of indoctrination and contrary to the kind of education needed for democratic citizenship. An alternative model, abhoring the indoctrination possibilities of inculcation and more in keeping with democratic beliefs, is *values clarification*.[1] Based on the use of reason and inquiry, values clarification provides teachers with a variety of classroom strategies and experiences, encouraging students to explore such questions as: Is it good or bad to have values different from others? What should we do when our values seem unclear? How do we engage in the valuing process? This model has become the most popular means of explicit values education in the United States. Nevertheless, values clarification also raises important questions in the moral domain, questions for which it provides few answers.

THE LIMITS OF VALUES CLARIFICATION [2]

Recognizing that the complexity of modern life confronts each of us with many value choices, the proponents of values clarification advocate a process for arriving at personal values in a rational and justifiable way. They suggest that attempts to teach values to students through moralizing have not been successful, in large part because no agreement exists about what the "correct" values are. Students, they say, are confused about values as they are exposed to conflicting value positions given by parents, teachers, clergy, media, and peers.

The values-clarification approach acknowledges that values are not absolute. Accordingly, teachers should not attempt to teach particular value positions. Rather, they should teach a form of value inquiry that involves the following processes:

Prizing one's beliefs and behaviors:
1. prizing and cherishing
2. publicly affirming, when appropriate
Choosing one's beliefs and behaviors:
3. choosing from alternatives
4. choosing after consideration of consequences
5. choosing freely

Acting on one's beliefs:

    6. acting

    7. acting with a pattern, consistency, and repetition.[3]

Each of the seven value indicators helps a person determine how strongly he or she holds to a particular value position. Values clarification focuses on the philosophical question "What is good?" by providing teachers and students with strategies for becoming more aware of their own values, the values of others, and what is to be valued. The strategies suggested by proponents of values clarification are quite useful for this purpose. We must recognize, however, that raising students' consciousness of values creates additional values and moral questions because students quickly recognize that values often conflict. To resolve conflicting notions of "good" requires that one ask the question, "What is right?" For example, both the Israelis and Palestinians could utilize the seven indicators of the values-clarification approach to arrive at different positions concerning the value of an independent Palestinian state. How should one decide? What principles of basic human rights might serve as moral criteria to help resolve such a conflict?

What the values-clarification model lacks, then, is the ability to help students cope with value conflicts. These dilemmas require the question that philosopher William Frankena refers to as "basic principles, criteria, or standards by which we are to determine what we morally ought to do, what is morally right or wrong, and what our moral rights are." [4] In failing to consider critical questions, proponents of values clarification imply that all values are relative and of equal value, leaving only situational ethics. This solution avoids or reduces the complexity of moral education and often results in the use of arbitrary authority by the teacher to resolve values conflicts. Consider the following episode:

Teacher: So some of you think it is best to be honest on tests, is that right? (*Some heads nod affirmatively.*) And some of you think dishonesty is all right? (*A few hesitant and slight nods.*) Well, are there any other choices or is it just a matter of dishonesty versus honesty?

Sam: You could be honest some of the time and dishonest some of the time.

Teacher: Does that sound like a possible choice, class? (*Heads nod.*) Any other alternatives to choose from?

Tracy: You could be honest in some situations and not in others. For example, I am not honest when a friend asks about an ugly dress, at least sometimes. (*Laughter.*)

Teacher: Is that a possible choice, class? (*Heads nod again.*) Any other alternatives?

Sam: It seems to me that you have to be all one way or all the other.

Teacher: Just a minute, Sam. As usual we are first looking for the alternatives that there are in the issue. Later we'll try to look at any choice that you may have selected. Any other alternatives, class? (*No response.*) Well, then, let's list the four possibilities that we have on the board and I'm going to ask that each of you do two things for yourself: one, see if you can identify any other choices in this issue of honesty and dishonesty; and two, consider the consequences of each alternative and see which ones you prefer. Later, we will have buzz groups in which you can discuss this and see if you are able to make a choice and if you want to make your choice part of your actual behavior. That is something you must do for yourself.

Ginger: Does that mean that we can decide for ourselves whether we should be honest on tests here?

Teacher: No, that means that you can decide on the value. I personally value honesty; and although you may choose to be dishonest, I shall insist that you be honest on your tests here. In other areas of your life, you may have more freedom to be dishonest, but one can't do *anything any time,* and in this class I shall expect honesty on tests.

Ginger: But then how can we decide for ourselves? Aren't you telling us what to value?

Sam: Sure, you're telling us what we should do and believe in.

Teacher: Not exactly. I don't mean to tell you what you should value. That's up to you. But I do mean that in this class, not elsewhere necessarily, you have to be honest on tests or suffer certain consequences. I merely mean that I cannot give tests without the rule of honesty. All of you who choose dishonesty as a value may not practice it here, that's all I'm saying. Further questions, anyone? [5]

The teacher's use of power is the solution, but the moral perspective underlying the teacher's explanation is lacking. Kohlberg's theory explains why there is a need to provide students with a more adequate moral solution to value conflict and how such a resolution might better be achieved.

KOHLBERG—BEYOND VALUES CLARIFICATION

Kohlberg, through his work in moral philosophy, developmental psychology, and educational research, provides educators with an extension of values education to the moral domain. In doing so, his work offers an alternative to, and an extension of, values clarification. Values clarification is concerned with defining values; Kohlberg wishes to define the moral perspective supporting those values. Values clarification attempts to make students aware of their own and other's values; Kohlberg attempts to increase the awareness of moral reasoning in self and others. Values clarification promotes student-teacher interaction as a way of analyzing values; Kohlberg stresses such interaction for its development of moral reasoning.

Kohlberg combines philosophy and psychology to explain (1) what is meant by morality and (2) how one develops more adequate modes of moral reasoning. The results of his philosophical analysis and psychological research provide teachers with a powerful rationale for, and explanation of, how to promote moral growth.

Kohlberg confronts the issue of the relativity of values, left unanswered by values clarification, by using moral philosophy to define the essential structure of morality as centering on the principle of justice. In a democracy, he claims, this moral concern is of utmost importance. Educating people for democratic citizenship requires making certain value choices based on moral standards. Kohlberg points out that in the absence of a clear understanding of moral principles, people in positions of authority, including teachers, all too often resort to the capricious and expedient use of their authority as the means of resolving moral conflict. Watergate was a powerful national experience in this kind of moral choice making.

Kohlberg's research in psychology has demonstrated that our conception of justice (What is right?) changes and develops over time as we interact with our environment. Building on the work of Piaget, Kohlberg described a series of six stages of moral development, with each subsequent stage providing a more complex system of moral reasoning and hence a more adequate conception of what is just and right. His research has shown that the stages of development and the sequence of growth through those stages exists in other cultures as well as our own. Nevertheless, while the sequence of the moral reasoning stages is cross-cultural, environmental factors as they come into contact with more complex moral reasoning influence the *rate* of growth and the *level* (stage) of development attained.

Teachers also can facilitate the development of moral reasoning. When students' values conflict with school rules, for example, the teacher has a responsibility to help students clarify and resolve the moral dimension of the issues. Should fighting on the playground be treated only as a violation of institutional authority, or should students be asked to consider the broader issue of treating one another fairly? (This concern was exemplified by Mrs. Warren's behavior in Episode 1.) Schools also have an obligation to prepare students for citizenship. Teachers have a responsibility to help students understand and uphold their own and others' rights as guaranteed by the U.S. Constitution, a document that exemplifies moral reasoning at the highest level. Kohlberg believes that teachers should help develop in students the capacity to understand and act in accordance with the principles embodied in the Constitution.

PURPOSE AND FORMAT

This book's purpose is to help teachers translate Kohlberg's theory into practice. Specifically, learning about Kohlberg's work should help the teacher to achieve (1) a recognition that an essential role of the teacher is the role of moral educator, (2) an increased sensitivity to the moral dimensions of the content and process of instruction, and (3) the explanatory power to plan and implement a moral education curriculum. This book is divided into two parts: theory and practice.

Theory

An explanation of Kohlberg's theory of developmental moral education is outlined in chapters 2, 3, and 4. The purpose of these three chapters is to provide teachers with a rationale for, and an explanation of, developmental moral education. Kohlberg's work provides a new conceptual lens through which teachers may view their students' thinking and development and reconstruct their own role of teacher as moral educator. Kohlberg's explanation of the stages of moral development is based on the work of the Swiss psychologist Jean Piaget. Chapter 2 explains the basic Piagetian concepts. These concepts are utilized in chapters 3 and 4, which are devoted to an explanation of Kohlberg's research results and theory of moral education. Concrete examples and answers to the most frequently asked questions about the theory are provided.

Practice

A demonstration of moral education in practice can be seen in chapters 5, 6, and 7. The Piagetian concepts provided in the previous chapters are here illustrated in teaching practice. These three chapters provide examples of the full range of teaching strategies prescribed by research results and actual teaching experiences. Each chapter utilizes illustrations from elementary and secondary teachers using the theory in their classrooms.

Chapter 5 explains appropriate teaching strategies. Emphasis is placed on how to use many practices to promote moral development. Chapter 6 extends the strategies chapter by focusing on the creation of curriculum materials. Emphasis is placed on how to create a moral-development curriculum out of existing content and school life. Chapter 7 explains Kohlberg's concept of the "just community" and its application as an organizing structure and process for schooling.

A NOTE OF CAUTION

Our main task has been not to oversimplify a body of knowledge that is inherently complex. This statement notwithstanding, we have endeavored to make the complex clear. We hope that teachers will not assume that moral education is something to be added on to the curriculum nor that moral education exists as a separate component of schooling. We do not advocate a "Thursday is moral education day" approach. We believe, as Kohlberg does, that schooling is moral education and that teachers are moral educators.

Although Kohlberg's work is a rich resource, we recognize that his work is insufficient to encompass all of moral education. We try to address the limitations of the theory throughout the book, but we wish to point out here that it is not our intention to provide *the* model of moral education. We do not wish to encourage a "bandwagon effect" created by educators who continue to believe in single, complete models. Such educators, once they have seized upon such a model, create a bandwagon onto which others may quickly jump. But the bandwagon effect, the usual fate of educational theory made popular by a demand for short-term results, causes a premature rush to practice and results in the simplification of theory so that it (1) is reduced to the point of nonrecognition, (2) is packaged as if a mechanistic approach will produce a desired change, (3) results in expectations for the practitioner and consumer that no operational definition could fulfill, and therefore (4) is ultimately rejected.

The polemical representation of any model or theory contributes to bandwagon effects. We have tried in this book to avoid the polemical, but we wish to alert the reader to the inherent limitations of our enterprise.

First, we wish to acknowledge that there is more to the field of values and moral education than is encompassed by Kohlberg's theory. Second, as later chapters explain, Kohlberg's work, while embedded in a rich research and practical base, is still evolving and constantly expanding through further research and criticism. Third, we have worked closely with Kohlberg, as his prefatory remarks indicate. We admire and respect his contributions. We are biased. But we have tried to be fair. Despite our bias we hope we have been successful in providing a context for understanding both the extensive nature *and* the limitations of Kohlberg's work.

2
Piaget: A Conceptual Introduction to Kohlberg

Chapters 2, 3, and 4 of this book are devoted to introducing Kohlberg's theory of moral development. Our aim is to provide the reader with an overview of Kohlberg's work. There are several distinct parts to his work, each of which has to be grasped if we are to understand the scope of his theory. The distinct aspects of Kohlberg's theory may be stated as (1) the cognitive-developmental approach to human development, (2) the delineation of the stages of moral judgment, (3) the attempt to explain the development of moral judgment in terms of a consistent theory of moralization, and (4) the application of the research on moral development to the theory and practice of moral education. This chapter deals only with the first part, leaving the remaining aspects to chapters 3 and 4.

To understand Kohlberg's view of the nature of human development, we begin by turning to the work of Jean Piaget, the Swiss psychologist who has had the greatest influence on Kohlberg's thinking. The conceptual foundations of Kohlberg's theory are built on Piaget's work in the field of cognitive development.

JEAN PIAGET

Jean Piaget is a Geneva-born octogenarian scholar who has, over the past fifty years, revolutionized the field of child psychology. His influence has been compared with that of Freud; but, unlike Freud, Piaget writes in a cumbersome, technical style that is hard to read in the original French or when translated into English. His influence in America dates from the late 1950s, the post-Sputnik era when our national interest turned to improving the intellectual quality of school curricula, and American educators realized that Piaget had evolved a theory of intellectual development that was more complete and more convincing that any comparable one.[1] Since the 1950s, his major works have been made available to American readers, and commentaries on his theory and research have been written to help clarify their meaning and implications.[2]

The primary focus of Piaget's research has been the development of human intelligence. Piaget presents a *developmental* conception of intelligence, describing how the *cognitive processes* that underlie intelligence in the individual develop from one chronological period to the next. To get a sense of Piaget's approach, let us begin with a story from his autobiography.[3]

Piaget was originally trained as a biologist. After finishing his doctorate, he became interested in psychology. One of his first jobs was in the Binet Laboratory in Paris. (Binet is well known for having constructed the first successful intelligence test.) Piaget's task was to develop a standardized French version of certain reasoning tests. He began his work enthusiastically, but soon found recording correct answers on standardized tests rather dull. To liven up the work, he began looking at the wrong answers children gave and found them intriguing. Why were most children of a given age unable to solve certain problems in reasoning? More important, why were the "wrong" answers they offered so similar to one another and so different from the "correct" answers offered by older children? These questions provided a clue that Piaget was to follow systematically and on which he was to base his theory of cognitive development.

Intelligence tests could not provide answers to Piaget's questions. They are designed to test *how much* children know and *how well* they can reason in relation to other children of their age. They are *not* designed to explain *why* children reason as they do or offer the answers they do. Intelligence tests attempt to assign to children a relatively constant "quotient" of intelligence; such tests do not explain how children's thinking changes over time. Piaget set for himself the task of describing in *qualitative* terms how patterns of thinking employed by children as they reason *develop* over time so that problems that at one age seem insurmountable can be solved easily several years later.

PIAGET'S METHODOLOGY

To get at the *process of reasoning* that children employ, Piaget abandoned the standardized test and developed in its place a format that would allow the experimenter a wider view of how children arrive at their solutions to given problems in reasoning. Piaget selected the clinical method developed by Freud and other clinical psychologists. While clinicians use this method to allow clients a maximum of freedom in following the spontaneous course of their thoughts, Piaget adapted the clinical method to pose specific problems to children and allow them the freedom to solve the problems as best they could. Piaget would observe a child's approach to a problem, watch the child try to solve it, and ask questions of clarification so that he could understand the kind of reasoning that guided the child's efforts.

It soon became clear to Piaget that the fundamental differences in the way children reason are age-related; they reflect the different *forms* of reasoning that children of different ages use in solving problems. For example, if you ask a group of four-year-olds which is larger, the sun or the earth, most will say that the earth is larger. If you then ask how they know the earth is larger, they will probably say because the sun looks so small. That is, they "logically" conclude that what looks smaller *is* smaller. Ask a group of seven-year-olds the same question, and most will answer that the sun is larger. Inquire how they know the sun is larger when it looks so small, and they will say that it looks small only because it is far away.

If we simply compared the children's answers, we would conclude that seven-year-olds know more than four-year-olds because they have learned more about the relative size of the earth and the sun. If we go beyond the answers and look at the reasoning children use, a second difference appears. The younger children do not guess at answers. They use a consistent *logic* in arriving at the wrong answer. They consistently identify the perceived size of the sun with its actual size. The seven-year-olds, in contrast, do not identify the two. They understand and use the logical principle of perspective to differentiate between perceived and actual size. Thus, the two groups offer different answers because they use a different logic (form of reasoning) to arrive at their conclusions.

Piaget insists that the different uses of logic cannot be attributed simply to older children knowing more because they were taught more. Rather, the difference is *developmental*. As children mature and gain greater experience of the object world, they grow in their capacity to understand relations between such objects as the sun and the earth. They grow more adept at seeing the world "as it is." In other words, they become more intelligent.

The average seven-year-old looks at the sun and understands more about it than does the average four-year-old. At seven, the child not only knows *about* the sun's relative size and distance from the earth, but he also logically relates these discrete data in order to judge that the sun is larger than the earth. Even if the average four-year-old were taught this information, he would not be able to apply it, for he has not yet developed the cognitive capacity to understand why the logical principle of perspective makes sense. To understand a logical principle properly, we must have developed it as part of our capacity to make sense of the world in which we live.

INTELLIGENCE AS ADAPTATION TO ONE'S ENVIRONMENT [4]

Although Piaget's research has been primarily devoted to studying how human intelligence develops throughout childhood, his work cannot be fully appreciated without considering the biological perspective that forms the basis of his theory.

Piaget believes that human organisms share with all other organisms two "invariant functions": organization and adaptation. *Organization* refers to the organism's tendency to systematize its processes into coherent systems. Thus, mammals do not simply operate by random biological activities; rather, they organize these activities into systems (e.g., the respiratory and digestive systems) that regulate entire biological functions, such as breathing and eating. These organized systems could not function properly, however, unless they were *adapted* to the environmental conditions in which the mammal lives. For example, digestive systems differ depending on what foods are primarily available to the animal in question.

The human mind, according to Piaget, also operates in terms of these two invariant functions. The psychological processes of the mind are highly organized into coherent systems, and these systems are carefully attuned to adapt to changing environmental stimuli. The function of adaptation in psychological and physiological systems operates through two complementary processes: assimilation and accommodation. *Assimilation* refers to the way an organism deals with an environmental stimulus in terms of its current organization, while *accommodation* involves a modification of the current organization in response to environmental demands. Let us illustrate these processes, which usually operate in conjunction with one another, by presenting one sociological and one psychological example of adaptation.

Consider a primitive tribe in a remote corner of the earth. The tribe's activities are highly organized to ensure that necessary survival functions are carried out; they are designed to establish and maintain an *equilibrium* (a harmonious relationship) between the organism (the tribe) and its environment. If this equilibrium is broken, for example, by an unexpected change in climate that rudely disrupts the tribe's customary agricultural or hunting practices, the tribespeople will be highly motivated to find a way of restoring the disrupted equilibrium. They will have to adapt to the new situation.

In Piaget's model of adaptation, the first tendency of an organism (the tribe) is to assimilate the new problem to old practices. The tribe may call on its elders to remember if this situation had arisen before, and if so, how it was dealt with. If the tribe has a traditional way of dealing with sudden climatic change, the new incident may be *assimilated* to old patterns, and equilibrium can be restored. If old patterns do not work effectively, they will have to be *accommodated* to meet the new situation. This may require much effort; someone has to figure out how the new situation differs from previous ones and how the old ways are to be modified to meet the new situation. If the task is accomplished, equilibrium will be restored. In addition, the organization of the tribe's activities must be modified to include this new kind of response. The modification may be slight (the inclusion of a new ritual or a new technique for hunting) or it may be so major (the need to migrate to a new environment) that it requires a reorganization of many old activities.

In this model the functions of organization and adaptation are closely interrelated. Without an organized system of activities, the tribe would have no base of experience on which to draw in meeting the new crisis. A system not sufficiently flexible to adapt to the new condition would prove dysfunctional, and the organism (the tribe) would suffer greatly. That which ties the two functions together is the organism's tendency to establish and reestablish equilibrium (balance or harmony) with the environment. That which allows for the reestablishment of equilibrium is the organism's intelligence, in this case the tribespeople's discovering how to modify old practices to meet new conditions.

As a second example, consider a college freshman who has come to college from a conservative background. At home he was acquainted with people of similar background and similar views. At school he is exposed to a wider range of people, some of whose ideas challenge his accustomed way of thinking and acting. Yet he values the newness of this encounter and wants to integrate the college experience with his previous experiences. How will he do so?

This freshman is surprised to learn that many people on campus have more liberal political views than he has. Being a curious person, he engages others in political discussions and discovers that on some issues he is persuaded by the cogency of their reasoning. He finds this disturbing because he has always considered himself a political conservative, but is able to reconcile this discrepancy by conceding some points to his liberal friends while retaining a general allegiance to the conservative persuasion. He has *assimilated* some liberal views into his existing conservative philosophy, but he has not fundamentally altered that philosophy.

This solution becomes harder to maintain in the following spring. The campus comes alive with controversy over a bill being considered by the state legislature. Petitions are circulating in support of both the liberal and conservative positions. Unsure of his position on this issue, the freshman engages others in discussion and finds himself once again persuaded by the logic of the liberal position. He feels a particular conflict when his conservative friends ask him to sign their petition. He has to refuse, and in their anger they accuse him of having become a liberal. Although uncomfortable with this designation, upon reflection the freshman realizes that his political views have changed considerably. Not only does he agree with the liberals on specific issues, but his general approach to political issues has changed. He has *accommodated* his political philosophy to new considerations, and in this process, that philosophy itself has been reorganized.

It may seem strange to compare a college freshman to a primitive tribe. But one of the great strengths of Piaget's theory has been to show how intelligence, as part of the biological function of adaptation, operates in almost all human activities. Intelligence operates in an adolescent's political decisions, in a primitive's hunt, and in a child's games. By uniting these diverse uses of intelligence into one system of development, Piaget has supplied us with a unique understanding of how human intelligence operates and develops.

THE DEVELOPMENT OF PSYCHOLOGICAL STRUCTURES

In Piaget's theory, development is clearly related to—is actually a product of—the human mind's tendency to systematize its processes into coherent systems and adapt those systems to changing environmental stimuli. The mind does not simply absorb discrete data that it happens to encounter as the human organism interacts with the environment. Rather, the mind "seeks" to organize itself. It seeks from the environment specifically relevant information that it can "use" to "construct" a system of order that makes sense of, and thereby enhances, interaction with the world.

To illustrate the mind's "activity," consider these two children "working" at making sense of their environment.

Visiting one evening with some friends, one of the authors was introduced to the friends' seventeen-month-old son, Tony. The boy seemed to remember the visitor and place him in a familiar context. Tony then pointed outdoors and asked his father if the car parked at the curb was "Joe's car?" The boy had not seen Joe drive up, and he had never seen Joe's car. Why then did he ask about the car?

Tony's father helped solve the riddle. The boy and his father had been driving together that day in their car, and the boy had been fascinated by the car. He assumed, correctly, that any visitor to their house would come in a car. Cars were "on his mind." So, without any prompting from his parents, he sought out the information about Joe's coming that interested him. His mind was tending to its own order.

Or consider Talya, a four-year-old Israeli girl. Talya's mother kept a journal of her activities during the 1973 Yom Kippur war. One entry reads:

> "Talya made up a song tonight before going to bed: 'Let everyone come home and live together and let the Arabs and the Russians not hit the Jews and let Yossi not hit me.' " [5]

This four-year-old was trying to make sense out of a complex set of stimuli called war. She imagined that soldiers in the field hit one another as Yossi (her friend) hit her. In her song she brought together the two images and prayed that the hitting would end on both fronts.

Although we cannot predict the precise questions, comments, or songs that children at a given age will construct, we can be reasonably sure of the kind of information they will find relevant. For relevant information is *stage*-related. If, as Piaget assumes, the mind operates in an orderly fashion regulated by given mental structures that have developed to a certain point in a child's life, then those structures will determine the information that will be relevant to a child's interests. Telling Tony that Joe's car was made in Japan would be irrelevant. Telling Talya that Israelis and Arabs fight with tanks and jets and not with their hands (as Yossi does) would not help her make sense of war and would hence make little difference, given her psychological operations.

Piaget refers to the given psychological structures—the methods of organizing information—that have developed in a child's life as the child's *stage of development*. Tony, at seventeen months, is at a stage of development different from that of four-year-old Talya. Tony is actively organizing the relation between driving a car and arriving at his house. Talya is organizing the more complex relation between aggression and danger at home and on the battlefield. At his age, Tony could not attempt Talya's mental integration. Talya, at her age, would no longer be interested in relationships that fascinate Tony. An older child would not find Talya's integration helpful or accurate in dealing with thoughts and feelings about war. Thus, a *stage* describes the organized cognitive possibilities and limits that characterize a child's thinking and feeling processes at a given point in the child's development.

CHILDHOOD STAGES OF COGNITIVE DEVELOPMENT

Piaget's theory describes stages of cognitive development from infancy through adolescence: how psychological structures develop out of inborn reflexes, are organized during infancy into behavioral schemes, become internalized during the second year of life as thought patterns, and develop through childhood and adolescence into the complex intellectual structures that characterize adult life. Piaget divides cognitive development into four major periods: *sensorimotor* (birth to two years); *preoperational* (two to seven years); *concrete operations* (seven to eleven years); and *formal operations* (eleven and older).[6]

Piaget spent a number of years observing and analyzing in detail his own children's activities during infancy and early childhood. He calls this early, preverbal period the sensorimotor level of development, because the child is limited to the exercise of his sensory and motor capacities.[7] Although this is a fascinating period, we do not have the space to deal with it in this book and will begin with the next period of development, preoperational thought.

PREOPERATIONAL THOUGHT

Infants are limited in their interaction with their environment to the exercise of sensorimotor capacities; the turning point to the next level of development is the emergence of thought. *Thought,* which Piaget defines as the "internal representation of external actions," develops only toward the middle of the second year.

How does thought develop? Imagine an eighteen-month-old child playing with objects in his house. He opens and closes boxes, picks things up, pulls things apart, and tries to put things back together. His attention is focused solely on the objects he sees. But there comes a point when the child begins looking for objects he cannot find. He may remember some toy that he has not seen in a while. This act of memory is possible, Piaget assumes, because the child has developed an internal representation of the object. Piaget has devised experiments to test the persistence of children's interest in disappearing objects and their ability to trace an object from one to another hiding place. If the child not only remembers that the object exists when it is out of sight but also realizes where to look for it when it is out of sight, Piaget says he has developed the ability to represent the object internally. That is, he can think about an object without its being visually present.

Piaget insists that thought is the basis for the development of language and not the result of language development. Yet it is clear, as other psychologists have shown, that thought and language develop as complementary systems during the early years.[8] By the age of three or four, most children are able to use language freely and have developed mental symbols to internally represent increasingly larger portions of the world. They interact freely and verbally with both peers and adults. At this point, Piaget observes, their interaction is curiously *egocentric;* they seem cognitively centered on themselves and fail to take into account others' points of view.

You can notice the egocentrism of young children when you speak to them on the phone. For example, in speaking to a four-year-old girl, one of the authors was treated to a description of a long list of objects. It was hard to tell why these objects were being described or what relation existed among them. As it turned out, the little girl was describing gifts she had received for Christmas and was pointing to each one as she described it. She did not think to mention the context (that they were gifts) or to consider that the listener could not see the things to which she pointed. The little girl was not being inconsiderate; she was being egocentric. She had not yet developed an awareness that the listener's perspective was different from her own.

Similarly, children of this age often fail to distinguish between what is objectively and subjectively real. They simply consider both to be real. Characters in books and on television, dolls and imaginary friends, ghosts and monsters, humans, animals, and plants—they all can hear what one is saying, see what one is doing, and threaten one with possible retaliation. No wonder ghosts, monsters, and bad dreams frighten children as they do. What is experienced in an adult world as fantasy, superstition, or magical thinking, is experienced in a child's world as reality.

Piaget's contribution to understanding this period of development has been twofold: he has documented fascinating examples of egocentric and realistic thinking among children,[9] and he has shown that the imaginative or intuitive quality of their thinking is the result of its being *preoperational* or prelogical.

Let us return to our example of the sun and the earth. We said that most four-year-olds think the sun is smaller than the earth because the sun looks smaller; they follow the logic that what looks smaller *is* smaller. This tendency is consistent with

Piaget's description of egocentric thought. The only possible perspective that children of this age consider is their own perspective; the way things appear to them *is* how they are.

By referring to this way of thinking as "following a logic," we have used "logic" to mean a consistent way of thinking. But this logic is not logical, for the basis of logic involves stepping out of one's own position to check whether what one sees, feels, or believes is both internally consistent and consistent with the objective facts of the situation. This is precisely what young children cannot do. Therefore, Piaget refers to their thinking as *pre*logical. Logic enters only with the next stage of development.

CONCRETE OPERATIONS

The seven-year-olds, looking up at the same sun as the four-year-olds, know that the sun is larger than the earth because they have developed the ability to step back from their immediate perceptions and adjust what they see to what they know to be true: the sun is far away. They interject between their perceptions and their judgments the logical principle of perspective. They therefore can be said to be thinking logically about this problem.

As we have noted, Piaget does not believe that such learning sequences are isolated instances; instead, they are part of a larger transformation in the way children think. In the terms of his theory children in this age range (seven to eleven years) develop from the stage of preoperational thought to the stage of concrete operational thinking.

The term *concrete operational* refers to the logical operations that children perform on concrete objects. "Operations" are mental actions that are reversible. Addition and subtraction are examples of reversible mental actions. Let us say we have two equal piles of marbles, each with eight marbles. We take three marbles from the first pile and add them to the second pile. We ask a child, "Can we again make the piles equal?" By seeing that he can restore the original equality by subtracting three marbles from the pile on which we added three marbles, the child is performing a reversible mental action. He reverses (or undoes) the addition with the subtraction: $3 + (-3) = 0$.

This stage of thinking is called *concrete* operational because children of this age generally think things through in terms of concrete objects. We see this in noting what interests them most. They want to know how *much* it costs to buy candy, how *tall* is the tallest building, how *large* is the biggest whale, how *many* home runs has a ballplayer hit. They carefully watch the distribution of goods to see that everyone gets an *equal* share. In the world they construct there are few, if any, abstractions, but there are a multitude of concrete distinctions that make all the difference.

Testing for Concrete Operations

The stage of concrete operations includes the ability to perform concrete operations on a number of different tasks. Piaget has devised ways of testing whether children use concrete operations or preoperational thought in reasoning about each task. Children are not always consistent in usage, but the general pattern is that a child who has mastered one task will be able to master other tasks of comparable difficulty. Children who are not able to solve *any* of the problems posed by the tasks are defined as being at the preoperational stage. Children who solve *all* or *most* of the problems are defined as being at the stage of concrete operations. Children who solve *some* problems but fail to solve others are seen as being transitional between the two stages. Since stages are abstract descriptions of change over time, there is no reason to expect children to be at one or another stage under all circumstances. The theory does predict that once children have mastered concrete operations, they will prefer solving tasks by using this higher stage and will not regress to preoperational reasoning.

Two of the best-known Piagetian tests for concrete operations are for the tasks of classification and conservation. They are reported in the examples that follow.

In testing for classification skills, we place before a child a number of small objects. We are interested in knowing how the child groups the objects together to form different classes. What goes with what? In the child's mind, what are the lines of connection and division that join and separate different objects?

Let us imagine that eight triangles and eight circles are placed before a child. Of the sixteen forms, some are large and some are small, some are blue and some are red. Thus it is possible to class the objects according to geometric form, size, or color. It is also possible to form subclasses within classes: there are small red triangles, large blue circles, and so forth. Now we ask the child to put together the things that are alike.

What Piaget observes is that children use different strategies for performing this task. Younger children usually display the least well defined criteria for classification. They may begin by separating triangles from circles and then switch midway to separating blues from reds. They know that triangles are different from circles and that blues are different from reds, but they do not consistently stick to one defining pattern of classification. Piaget would say that these children are preoperational in relation to this task.

A second group of children, perhaps a year or two older, will be more consistent in their classification efforts. They will begin with triangles and circles, or with reds and blues, and continue along these lines until they complete the task. In addition, they will be able to form subclasses, separating large triangles from small triangles, for example. Thus they would seem to have mastered the task of classification of concrete objects.

Piaget, however, believes one further step is involved. Once a child has formed classes and subclasses, does he comprehend the relation between them? For example, if we place before a child eight wooden beads, three of which are red and five of which are blue, he will probably see at a glance that there are two more blue beads than red beads. But does he think there are more *blue* beads or more *wooden* beads? Does he understand that the whole (represented by the wooden beads) is greater than any of the parts (e.g., blue beads)? Usually there is a gap in time between when a child can group objects into classes and when he masters the logical relationship between class and subclass.

Why is Piaget concerned with this third step? The answer returns us to the concept of *equilibrium*. Piaget is concerned that the concept of a stage define the point at which a level of thinking reaches an equilibrium. In relation to the task of classification, we have seen that the stage of preoperational thinking ends at the point where children can separate objects along the lines of a single dimension. They can distinguish circles from triangles, reds from blues, and so on, but they cannot consistently group these objects into classes when the objects are defined by two or more dimensions. They cannot look at one dimension (form) while consistently ignoring (holding constant) the other dimension (size and color). The next stage of development represents a full step forward. That full (third) step is achieved only when the child has mastered the logical relationship between class and subclass—between the whole and its parts. The child at the second step cannot look at the difference between the parts (red beads and blue beads) and still remember their relation to the whole (all the wooden beads). Even at the third step, this ability is limited to the consideration of concrete objects with concrete characteristics such as form, color, and size. Nevertheless, this achievement does represent an equilibrium—a resting point—in the development of concrete operations. It therefore defines the stage of concrete operations for the task of classification.

The second task we will consider as a test for concrete operations is the conservation of continuous quantity. The child is presented with two identical beakers, each filled with equal amounts of liquid. When the child agrees that the two same-shape beakers contain the same amount of liquid, the contents of the second beaker are poured into a third beaker of a different shape. This beaker is low and wide, and in it the liquid rises to a lower level. The child is now asked if the first and third beakers contain the same amount of liquid.

Children at the preoperational stage, who define amount by their immediate perceptions, see that the liquid rises to a lower level in the third beaker and conclude that it has less liquid than the first beaker. They do not change their minds even after they see the liquid poured back to the second beaker and resume its equal status. Once the amount of liquid appears to be less, they forget what it looked like originally.

Children in transition oscillate back and forth in their judgment. They can see more than one perspective, but they cannot consistently determine which beaker has more liquid in it. The children judged to have reached concrete operations are those who can consistently conserve the quantity of liquid. They understand that no matter what the level of the liquid is, the level is only a function of the shape of the beaker and does not affect the amount of liquid. The amount of liquid is the same whatever the shape of the beaker.

How are they able to determine this? Piaget stresses the role of reversibility. Concrete operational children can mentally reverse the operation of the pouring of the liquid. They can, so to speak, mentally pour the liquid back into the second beaker and see that it would come up to the same point as before. Since no liquid was lost in pouring, the amount in the third beaker is the same as the amount in the first beaker. This means that it is also the same amount as in the second beaker.

Décalage

An important characteristic of children's cognitive development is that they do not suddenly become capable of concrete operations in all their activities. The opposite is usually the case. They become concrete operational in certain areas but not in others. Gradually, over several years (which in our society generally corresponds to the elementary school years), their capacity for this stage of reasoning increases and spreads out to include a greater number of activities. This spreading out is called *décalage* by Piaget.

FORMAL OPERATIONS

Although the development of concrete operations represents a major advance over preoperational thought, concrete operations are still a limited basis for knowing one's world. A person at this stage perceives the world in terms of its concrete characteristics and is not yet able to organize those perceptions in terms of more abstract logical categories. Since almost all Western systems of knowledge—science, mathematics, the humanities—are organized by formal logical categories, to be limited in our society to concrete operations represents a considerable cognitive deprivation.

To illustrate the difference between concrete operations and *formal operations*, the next level of cognitive development, consider this exercise in classification. Let us imagine two children, one ten and the other twelve years old, before whom are placed the following pictures of animals: a duck, a dog, an ostrich, an elephant, an eagle, and a bat. The children are asked to separate the pictures into two groups of animals that go together. Both children perceive that the animals can be divided into birds and mammals and proceed to do so.

The ten-year-old has little trouble. She divides the animals into those who have wings and fly and those who walk on all fours. Thus the duck, the ostrich, the eagle, and the bat are grouped together, while the dog and the elephant form the other group.

The twelve-year-old has more trouble than the younger child. He begins by replicating the ten-year-old's classification, but feels uneasy about the bat. It certainly looks like a bird, but he remembers that mammals are animals that nurture their young by the mothers' feeding them milk. He thinks that this is true of the bat, and so he finally decides to place it with the dog and the elephant.

The difference between the children's performance may not be due solely to learning and memory. Even if the ten-year-old has learned that the bat is "an exception to the rule," she may not understand why and hence may not remember what she learned. For if, as we assume, the ten-year-old constructs her classification by concrete operations, her mind's eye is likely to be drawn to, and bound by, the more obvious and concrete ways the bat resembles the birds. Means of nurturing is a far less obvious criterion for classifying animals. When it is concretely weighed against the bat's having wings, it seems to pale in significance.

If the twelve-year-old, as we assume, has begun to construct his classifications by formal operations, he will haltingly be able to transcend the logic of concrete operations and place in perspective the more obvious similarities between the bat and the birds. He will understand that the less visible and more abstract property of mammary glands logically overrules visible similarities. Thus, although a bat has wings and flies as birds do, it belongs to the class of mammals who nurture their young in a particular way.

Formal operations, then, mark the ability to reason in terms of formal abstractions, to perform "operations on operations." Once a child understands that objects can be classified by logically formal criteria—that nations can be understood in terms of their form of government and molecules by their chemical formulas—the child can begin systematically to compare and contrast various objects by these criteria. In addition, the given can be seen in relation to other hypothetical possibilities. Thus the author's ending a short story in a certain way can be seen against the possibility of his having chosen other plausible endings.

Piaget, together with his colleague Barbel Inhelder, has researched the development of formal operations primarily in mathematical and scientific thinking.[10] This reflects Piaget's belief that these areas represent the clearest examples of formal logical operations. Yet, as we shall see, the development of formal operations also marks a turning point in the child's social, emotional, and moral development.

The stage of formal operations covers varying degrees of ability to think abstractly. Research shows that, in our society, the earliest signs of this stage appear by the age of eleven or twelve. Nevertheless, there is a marked difference in the kinds of abstractions the average eleven-year-old and the average seventeen-year-old can handle. It has therefore made sense to speak of substages within formal operations that correspond to different degrees of ability to think abstractly. In the discussion that follows, we use the terminology of a recent American study, and delineate two substages: beginning formal operations and basic formal operations.[11]

Beginning Formal Operations

The main characteristic of this first step in the development of formal operations is the formation of the *inverse of the reciprocal.* To understand this development, let us backstep to the formation of *simultaneous reciprocity* during the stage of concrete operations.

We tell a nine-year-old that Eliot is Mark's older brother. We then ask, "Who is Eliot's younger brother?" To answer correctly, the child has to understand that "younger" and "older" are simultaneously reciprocal terms. For Eliot to be Mark's older brother, Mark has to be Eliot's younger brother.

The inverse of the reciprocal, however, is more complex. As an example, we tell a child to imagine that all tall men are handsome. Thus,

If a man is tall, he is handsome.

We ask:

If a man named John is not handsome, is he tall?

The child thinks, in this case *tall* equals *handsome.* If someone is not handsome, then he cannot be tall. We then ask a second, more difficult question:

If John is not tall, is he handsome?

Children at the concrete operational stage tend to treat this relation as if it were simultaneously reciprocal, and so they answer: "No, he is not handsome." This is of course not correct. All people who are handsome are not tall, and a person can be *not* tall and yet handsome. We said all tall men are handsome, but we did not say that all handsome men are tall.

Two difficulties are involved in solving this problem. The first is that it is hypothetical. In the child's experience it is not true that all tall men are handsome. To deal with the problem, the child must consciously suspend his actual experience and accept the hypothetical condition. This involves the ability to distance himself from concrete experience, which is difficult for children at the stage of concrete operations. The second difficulty involves thinking in the category "not tall" or "not handsome." While "tall" and "handsome" are concrete categories, their inverse, "not tall" and "not handsome," are abstract categories. They are derived from the concrete, but are not themselves concrete. Thus, while children know that "Canadians" refer to people who live in (or are citizens of) Canada, if we ask them who are "not Canadians," it is hard to think of everyone who does not live in Canada.

You might ask why anyone should be concerned with whether children can think in the inverse of the reciprocal. One answer can come from a consideration of the Golden Rule: "Do unto others as you would have them do unto you." Children at the concrete operational level think this means: what he does to you equals what you should do to him. Thus, if he hits you, you hit him back. But children who have reached beginning formal operations realize that this interpretation is not what is meant. Rather, you should treat him *not* as he treats you but as you would want him to treat you.

Basic Formal Operations

The formation of the inverse of the reciprocal is only the first step toward reasoning in formal logic. Most readers will be familiar with the next important step from their study of science: the ability to look at a problem, think of several possible solutions, formulate a hypothesis by selecting the solution most likely to be correct, and test the hypothesis by systematically experimenting with several possibilities.

One way Piaget has tested for basic formal operations is to present subjects with a pendulum. The subject is shown that this pendulum comes with an adjustable string, which may be shortened or lengthened. A number of different weights also may be attached to the pendulum. Of course the pendulum may be swung with either greater or lesser force. The subject is then handed the pendulum and weights and told to discover what determines the speed of movement of the pendulum. What makes it swing faster or slower? The experimenter watches the subject solve this problem.

A crucial difference between subjects at the concrete and formal levels is how they approach the problem. Does the subject simply rush in and begin manipulating the pendulum, or does he seem to plan the experiment by considering several alternative possibilities for what might cause the pendulum to swing at a given speed? The second approach is characteristic of basic formal operations. The person at this stage is capable of mentally envisioning the alternative possibilities and planning how to determine which one is correct.

Typically, a subject at the concrete operational or the beginning formal level will try out several possible "variables" (e.g., the length and the weights) and will measure under which conditions (e.g., long string with a lot of weight, short string with light weight) the pendulum swings fastest. He will then arrive at his answer.

In contrast, a subject at basic formal operations will have thought about the alternative possibilities and will begin to hold variables constant so that he can isolate which one or ones cause the speed to vary. He is careful not to mix the variables together. First he tries the variable of weight. At each weight level, he holds the other variable (length of string and force of push) constant so as to be sure he does not confound the variables. When he discovers that weight has no effect, he tries length, holding weight and force constant. By this process he discovers that only the length of the string causes the pendulum to swing faster or slower. A shorter string—with either a lot or a little weight and with or without a push—will cause the pendulum to swing faster than a longer string.

In our society, basic formal operations, which itself develops in two steps, typically begins to develop during middle adolescence. Not all adolescents or adults reach this stage. A recent study in California of a large sample of adolescents and adults showed that only about half had reached basic (or consolidated) formal operations.[12]

The principle of *décalage* applies to formal operations. People reach formal operations at different points not only in relation to such tasks as the pendulum exercise, but also, and this is more important, in their thinking about social and interpersonal issues. For the value of Piaget's stages is not limited to describing the structure of scientific reasoning, but extends to reasoning in the social and moral domains as well.

THE RELATION OF COGNITION TO AFFECT

A natural reaction to reading about Piaget's work is to assume that it deals only with cognition (thought) and not with affect (feeling). This is not true. Piaget's special interest has been intellectual development, but he has clearly stated that intelligence operates in both areas of life. In fact, he believes that any separation of the two areas is artificial. There can be no cognition without affect and no affect without cognition.[13]

What, then, is the relation between the two? Put simply, affect motivates the operations of cognition, and cognition structures the operations of affect.

Piaget's theory is based on the principle of interaction. No development of structures could take place if the organism were not in constant interaction with its environment. Human interaction or adaptation, as we noted, is characterized by our actively seeking out parts of our environment with which to interact. In this process, interest plays a central role. Something in the environment catches our attention and stimulates our interest. Interest is experienced as feeling. We feel moved to find out about something out there. It may be a new toy, an attractive person, or a constellation we have not seen before. Or we may feel moved to explore something within ourselves: a new idea, a conflict between ideas, or a conflict between our ideas and our feelings. In all these cases, if we did not feel the attraction of the new stimuli, we would not direct our attentional and cognitive processes to that aspect of the environment. A person who is emotionally cut off cannot function cognitively.

Affect, however, could not be experienced as feeling or emotion unless it were given meaning by a cognitive structure. When a woman says she feels happy or sad, she is not simply reporting a somatic sensation. Rather, she is interpreting that sensation in terms of a cognitive category called "being happy" or "being sad." A man who says "I don't know whether to laugh or cry" means that he is not sure how to (cognitively) interpret a given event and hence experience the appropriate emotional reaction. Our emotional reactions often can go either way, depending on the interpretation we apply to a given situation.

Affect develops parallel to cognition; the emotions we experience change as we develop new abilities to interpret our social situations. Consider the difference in emotional states in middle childhood and adolescence. Children at the concrete operational level get angry at concrete events. Take away a little girl's toy, deprive her of a privilege, treat her unfairly, and she is likely to get angry. She will tell you she is angry at you for doing that to her. But children at this stage do not feel depressed or "high" or ambivalent. These latter emotions, which characterize adolescents and are structured by formal operations, refer not to concrete events but to one's sense of self. One's "self," however, is an abstract category; it cannot be seen or touched. It must be cognitively imagined, and only then can it be felt.[14]

Moral judgment is the area in which Piaget has dealt most explicitly with the relationship between cognition and affect. For what is moral judgment if not a cognitive structuring of how we feel we ought to treat others and how others ought to treat us?

THE MORAL JUDGMENT OF THE CHILD

Piaget began studying children's moral judgment early in his career as part of an effort to understand how children orient themselves to the social world.[15] Influenced by the French sociologist Emile Durkheim, who argued that the essence of moral education is teaching children to limit themselves in obedience to society's moral rules and to dedicate themselves to the good of the society,[16] Piaget focused his study on how children develop a respect for rules and a sense of solidarity with their society. With characteristic ingenuity, Piaget began not with explicitly moral rules but with the rules of street games that children play among themselves.

We have noted earlier in this chapter that children aged three to five tend to be egocentric when communicating with others. Similarly, as Piaget observed, they play games egocentrically. In playing baseball,[17] for example, they don caps, swing bats, throw and catch balls. But they often swing without looking at the ball, throw without aiming the ball in the right direction, and close their eyes just when the ball they are supposed to catch is approaching them. Each of their actions is isolated. They seem unable to coordinate one set of actions with another, with the result that they rarely play in unison or cooperate with others to win the game they are playing.

Seven- or eight-year-olds play the same game quite differently. They swing the bat or throw the ball on cue, watching carefully what other players are doing so that they can coordinate their actions with those of the others. They play by the rules and expect everyone else to do the same. In addition, they play together as a team, cooperating with their teammates to beat the other team and win the game. Their sticking to the rules is quite literal, however. One rarely sees them consciously adapting rules to meet the requirements of a specific situation.

In contrast, eleven- and twelve-year-olds begin playing with the rules. They know why there are rules and how to abide by them, but they also realize that there are occasions when rules can and should be altered. If, for example, there are not enough players on each team to cover the whole field, the teams may agree to limit where the batter can fairly hit the ball. They may modify the rules to say that no one can hit to right field because they do not have enough players to cover that field.

These distinct ways of organizing the playing of games— egocentric imitation of others, literal playing by the rules, and cooperative adaptation of the rules—can loosely be seen as stages in children's practice of rules. There is a progression from one stage to the next in both the degree of social cooperation (how well children coordinate their actions with one another) and respect for rules.

When Piaget interviewed children of these ages to elicit their articulated understanding (consciousness) of these rules, he found a similar stagelike progression. The first understanding of rules emerges at around age six when children believe that rules are "laws"—they have always been there and cannot be changed, for they are fixed and immutable. This view continues to predominate until about age eleven, when a new understanding emerges. Rules are now seen as emanating from the agreement of those involved in playing the game, who, if they wish, can change the rules to meet changing situations.

Taken together, these two stagelike progressions present a paradoxical picture. Six-year-olds, who are often still imitating actions and are weak on coordinating actions with others, articulate a view of rules as immutable. They seem to have the highest respect for rules. But eleven-year-olds, who can coordinate their actions and cooperate extensively with others, say that rules can be changed rather freely. Is it possible that they respect the rules to a lesser degree than do six-year-olds?

Piaget's response takes us to the core of what is meant in this theory by moral development. The six-year-old's respect for law is based on a very partial, egocentric understanding of rules. As a child who is first consciously entering the world of social interaction, the six-year-old is most aware of the presence of authorities (usually adults), who insist on his following the rules. He does not know why they so insist, but only that he had better listen or else. He imagines that the authorities' rules are fixed, for he cannot put himself in their place and understand the process by which they made their decisions. Nor can he step outside his own role and view his actions from the perspective of others. Thus he believes he is faithfully following the rules even when he is not, and imagines terrible consequences were he to deviate from their rulings. Understandably, Piaget calls this the stage of unilateral (one-sided) respect.

As the child gains greater experience in interacting with others, particularly with his peers, his understanding of rules changes. Involved in joint pursuits, peers more easily communicate their intentions to one another and can see one another as people who make decisions. They develop a feeling of equality and an understanding that the other person acts and thinks very much as they do. This sense of sharedness, based on the ability to coordinate thoughts and actions, matures into a moral concept of cooperation. Rules emerge as agreements made to ensure that everyone will act in similar ways. Respect for rules is mutual rather than unilateral: one respects rules because others do and because one wants to participate equally in the joint activities of the group.

The move from the first to the second stage is not a purely cognitive process. Children do not simply think up a new definition of rules and respect. Rather, the cognitive redefinition (the new understanding or consciousness) emerges as children work out a new set of social relationships. As they become peers—one of several players on a team or members of a class—they slowly develop moral concepts to guide their behavior. In this process respect for rules becomes more adaptive. Children's behavior becomes more rationally guided by rules as they better understand the social contexts in which rules operate.

This social development involves both cognition and affect. Obviously, if children were not emotionally drawn to playing with their peers, there would be no motivation for working out a new set of relationships. But, in the working out, emotions are also cognitively restructured. Respect in the first stage is based almost entirely on fear. By the second stage, although children still fear other people, they have learned to distinguish respect from fear. Respect is now based on a feeling of common involvement, on a sense that it is only fair for everyone playing the game to play by the same rules. Children no longer need to fear an authority to abide by jointly agreed-upon rules.

Piaget's work on children's moral judgment extended beyond the rules of games to cover their understanding of law, responsibility, and justice. Nevertheless, it did not extend to children beyond the age of twelve. Nor did Piaget ever work out in detail the stages of moral judgment. After these initial studies, he returned to his work on the development of logic and the delineation of the cognitive stages we have reviewed in this chapter. Further work on delineating the stages of moral judgment was continued, as we shall see in the next chapter, by Lawrence Kohlberg.

3

Kohlberg: The Development of Moral Judgment

Kohlberg's theory of moral development, formally called *the cognitive-developmental theory of moralization*,[1] is deeply rooted in Piaget's work. In particular it is based on ideas in Piaget's *The Moral Judgment of the Child* (New York: Free Press, 1965).

In retrospect, it seems that the field of psychology was not ready for *The Moral Judgment* when it was originally published in 1932. Piaget's main assumption, as we noted, was that cognition (thought) and affect (feeling) develop on parallel tracks and that moral judgment represents a naturally developing cognitive process.[2] In contrast, the assumption of most psychologists at that time was that moral thinking is a function of other, more basic social and psychological processes. Freud, for example, was very concerned with issues of morality, but in his studies of the formation of conscience, he viewed conscience as under the control of the unconscious and irrational superego. Moral thinking, in his view, is *not* an autonomous, rational process; it is most often the product of unconscious forces, over which the individual has little or no awareness. Psychologists who did not accept Freud's theory of the superego usually shared his assumption that morality is primarily the result of feelings learned early in life and has little to do with rational thought processes. They believed that to understand morality, a person has to study the socialization process by which children learn (through conditioning and reinforcement) to abide by the rules and norms of their society.

This approach to moral development still prevails in many circles, but there is a growing receptivity to the Piagetian view of moral development. This trend is in part the result of Piaget's generally increasing influence, but it also may be related to larger historical trends. The assumption that morality is simply the result of unconscious processes or early social learning leads to a relativist position: morality is relative to one's social upbringing. Relativism is increasingly difficult to accept: Were Nazi war criminals correct when they claimed that they were only following the orders of their superiors and were therefore acting in accordance with their society's morality? Is it morally acceptable for politicians to wiretap their political enemies' offices because that is the American way of succeeding in politics? A person who rejects these claims must explain on what basis he is criticizing other people's morality. He must assume the existence of some moral principles whose validity is not limited to any given society. Such principles are not learned in early childhood; they are the product of mature rational judgment.

Several prominent American social scientists—among them, David Riesman,[3] Erik Erikson,[4] and Erich Fromm,[5]—have attempted to analyze the psychological differences between more mature and less mature ("autonomous" versus "conformist") forms of moral commitment. The first to return to Piaget and systematically develop the conceptions of moral growth that he suggested was Lawrence Kohlberg.

Kohlberg, born in 1927 and educated at the University of Chicago, is one of a number of American psychologists attracted to Piaget's work in the 1950s. The unique contribution of Kohlberg has been to apply to the study of moral judgment the *concept* of stage development that Piaget worked out in relation to cognitive development. In a sense, Kohlberg has helped finish Piaget's unfinished work; but in the process, he has greatly expanded and revised Piaget's original findings.

THE CONCEPT OF MORAL JUDGMENT

Although we refer to Kohlberg's theory as a "theory of moral development," it is more properly a description of the development of moral judgment. Thus we must first understand how, in Kohlberg's view, moral judgment operates in people's lives.

Many people think of morality in terms of the values they have acquired from their social environment. Thus a person is thought of as *having* values, and a moral person is supposed to act on these values. While this common-sense view accords well with much of everyday experience, it does not consider what happens when a person's values come into conflict with one another. How does one decide which value to follow?

Let us take as an example a woman in our society who has been brought up to believe that abortion is wrong, but who finds herself with an unwanted pregnancy. The law in her state allows for abortion; her feminist friends counsel her on her right to control her own destiny and have the abortion. Her lover is in favor of the abortion for practical reasons, but her parents and church believe abortion for nonmedical reasons is wrong. The woman is faced with contradictory views based on very different values. How does she decide what to do?

Undoubtedly many factors influence her decision. Emotional issues, social issues, and the practical issues of the costs involved for her in either aborting or having the child must be considered. There is also a moral issue involved: which value does she believe takes precedence in this situation?

Kohlberg is interested in this last issue, for it involves the woman's exercising her moral judgment. The woman could base her decision on purely practical considerations, but because abortion is a value-laden issue in our society, she will probably consider the moral aspects of the problem. In so doing, Kohlberg would say that she is facing a moral dilemma in which she has to choose between two rights: (1) the right to pursue her own happiness and welfare and (2) the right of the fetus to life. It complicates matters that her friends give precedence to one right, whereas her family and church give precedence to the other; but it does not change the essential dilemma. The woman has to weigh the competing claims of these two rights and decide which right takes precedence.

How is this done? It is a logical process even though it may be experienced as a grueling emotional crisis. The process is similar to the one described in Piaget's theory. The unwanted pregnancy has introduced *disequilibrium* into the woman's life; it has brought to a head whatever conflict existed in her value system. If she is to restore *equilibrium,* she must decide what she believes in and justify that decision to herself and perhaps to others. She may try to *assimilate* her problem to her accustomed way of thinking, or she may find her accustomed way inadequate. In the latter case, she must *accommodate* her thinking to deal with the new crisis and figure out how to resolve the conflicts in her value system. In the process, she may reorder that which she values.

To concretize this example further, let us imagine that the woman we have been discussing is a twenty-year-old college undergraduate named Jane, who has been living for the past year with her lover, Bob, who is also a student at the college. Jane decides to go home and tell her parents about Bob and the pregnancy. Her parents urge her to get married and have the baby. They argue that she can finish college when the child is a little older, and that if she and Bob love each other, the marriage will legitimate and even sanctify the conception. They feel strongly that what she and Bob did was wrong, but they think that it is now the responsibility of the young couple to live with the consequences and not take the easy way out by having an abortion.

Jane understands why her parents think marriage would be right in this situation. She returns to college to talk over the possibility with Bob and discovers that he is willing to marry her. But she is uneasy; she is not sure that she is ready for marriage, or that Bob is the right person for her to marry. She had chosen to live with Bob as a college boy friend, but she had not considered marriage or parenthood. Jane was not irresponsible; she had been using a method of birth control and had been honest with Bob about her feelings. She can understand why her family and church think this abortion unwarranted, but she is not sure that she agrees with them. Jane had always planned on graduate school and a career; now she is discovering how important her professional aspirations are to her. Why give them up, rush into marriage, and become an unwilling mother? Is that really in the child's best interest? Must she give in to social pressures to be a good daughter and a responsible person? Perhaps, in her case, having the abortion would be the responsible thing to do. She could live with Bob's disappointment and her parents' disapproval. Jane decides to have the abortion.

Whether we agree with Jane's reasoning or not, we can see that she is seriously grappling with the many sides of the dilemma: her own value conflict, her parents' opinion, her relationship with Bob, her career aspirations, and her responsibility to the fetus. If in the end she gives preference to her right to pursue her own life, it is not because she has failed to consider the right of the fetus to life but because she interprets "life" to mean the ongoing care that the child deserves and that she is not sure she is capable of providing at this time. Her decision is based, rightly or wrongly, on her estimate of what would serve everyone's best interest, including her own. She does not deny responsibility, but she believes that a woman can be responsible without bowing to conventional expectations of how she ought to behave.[6]

The exercise of moral judgment is a cognitive process that allows us to reflect on our values and order them in a logical hierarchy. In facing this dilemma, Jane discovered that she valued pursuing her career aspirations more than pleasing her parents and lover. She redefined for herself what she meant by "responsibility" and "the value of life." She did so by defining what her rights were in this situation and balancing those rights against the rights of the other persons involved. One might feel that she did not sufficiently consider why pursuing a career is so inherently valuable or whether abortion itself is right or wrong. But Jane's case illustrates a central point in Kolhberg's work: the exercise of moral judgment is not confined to a few rare moments in life; it is integral to the thinking process we use to make sense out of the moral conflicts that arise in everyday life.

ROLE TAKING: THE ROOTS OF MORAL JUDGMENT

What is the source of moral judgment? When does it begin in human life and how does it develop in relation to social experiences?

No one would claim that a young child exercises moral judgment. We do not hold a two-year-old responsible for his actions in the same way as we do an older child. We implicitly recognize that many of a two-year-old's actions are not done with the intent to harm, and although we shape his behavior through praise and blame, we do not judge it as "right" or "wrong." We teach him specific rules about proper and improper behavior and hope that, with time, he will come to understand *why* some actions are right or wrong and be able to guide his behavior accordingly.

From a developmental perspective, then, children learn about rules of proper behavior before they are capable of understanding their meaning. For example, consider the rule about being considerate to your parents. A mother of a three-year-old comes home from work tired and with a headache. She explains to her son that because of her headache, she cannot play with him now; she expects that he will understand. But he does not understand; he grows angry and upset. A fight ensues, with the mother wondering why her son cannot be more considerate.

Piaget would explain that the young boy cannot be more considerate because he does not fully understand his mother's message. Children's thinking and social interaction at this age are characteristically *egocentric*. They are not yet capable of distinguishing between their own perspective (what they want) and the perspective of others (what others want of them). The little boy senses that his mother is upset, but he does not understand what it means for someone else to have a headache. He cannot put himself in his mother's place and feel her headache. He is not being inconsiderate; rather, he is genuinely limited to seeing only his own perspective.

It is one of the wonders of development that children grow beyond egocentrism. If this boy had been an eight-year-old, he probably would have reacted differently. He still would have felt disappointed, but he would have been able to get beyond that single perspective. He could have put himself in his mother's position and seen what it would be like for someone else to be tired after a day's work. Having a headache might then seem to be a legitimate reason for not being able to play with him.

Kohlberg would attribute the difference between the three-year-old's and the eight-year-old's reaction to the development of *role-taking* ability: the capacity "to react to the other as someone like the self and to react to the self's behavior in the role of the other." [7] The ability to take the role of another person is a social skill that develops gradually from about the age of six and proves to be a turning point in the development of moral judgment. [8]

If we accept Kohlberg's definition of moral judgment as the weighing of claims of others against one's own, it stands to reason that only when the child can take the role of the other, and perceive what the other's claim is, can he weigh his own claim against the other's. The three-year-old does not even perceive that his mother has an independent claim; the eight-year-old perceives her claim and proceeds to weigh its legitimacy against his wanting her attention. In deciding to respect his mother's claim to being tired, the eight-year-old is exercising his moral judgment.

LOGIC, ROLE TAKING, AND MORAL JUDGMENT

Although we devoted the last chapter to describing cognitive development, and this chapter to describing moral judgment, the division is essentially analytic and of our own making. Children go through both developmental sequences at once. They do not divide their experience into the "physical" and the "social" world; they play with, and think about, physical objects as they are interacting with other people.

Thus a developmental phase such as egocentrism has both cognitive and social dimensions. The four-year-old who is cognitively incapable of imagining that the sun could be any larger than the size he perceives it to be is equally incapable of imagining that his mother may have a legitimate reason for not wanting to play with him. In both cases his immediate perceptions or desires define reality for him. To develop beyond egocentrism, the child has to develop new cognitive structures that allow for a new understanding of both the physical and social worlds.

A new understanding of the physical world is occasioned by the child's developing concrete operational thinking. A new understanding of the social world is occasioned by the development of role taking and moral judgment capacities. These two developmental sequences are related to, and influence, each other.

We said that seven-year-olds who are cognitively capable of differentiating between the perceived and the actual size of the sun interject between their perceptions and their judgment the logical principle of perspective. We attributed this ability to the development of a concrete logic that adjusts their immediate perception (the sun as a ball in the sky) to what they know to be true about the relation between the two objects in question (the sun looks smaller because it is far away from the earth).

We can similarly perceive role taking as operating as a "principle of perspective" in social relations. For example, two eight-year-old girls both want to play with the same doll. By exercising her role-taking abilities, each of the girls can interject between her immediate desire for the doll and her decision to grab the doll for herself an awareness that her friend also wants to grab the doll for herself. That awareness puts her desires into a new perspective; her desires do not exist by themselves, but in relation to someone else's desires. From the perspective of two people wanting the same object, a new course of action—

sharing—emerges as a logical possibility that would allow both people at least partially to fulfill their desires. Once this option is understood as a possibility, it gradually makes more and more sense, and eventually the children come to feel that in such situations one *ought* to share with others because that is most fair. When this happens, a new stage of role taking has led to an equally new stage of moral judgment.

Empirical research on the relationship between the development of the cognitive and the socio-moral stages has shown that children tend to be concrete operational before they develop to the parallel stages of role taking and moral judgment.[9] This suggests two possible relations between these developmental sequences. First, the development of cognitive stages is a necessary condition for the development of the parallel socio-moral stages. An eight-year-old, for example, cannot develop the perspective on social relations provided by that stage of role taking unless he already has worked out "the logic of perspective" in relation to physical objects such as the sun and the earth. Second, the cognitive stage, although a necessary condition, is not a sufficient condition. Working out "perspective" in relation to the physical world is an easier task than developing a "perspective" on social relations. A child can achieve the physical perspective and yet not be ready to take the parallel step in relation to socio-moral development. The reason for this may be that, for example, to accept sharing as a logical way of dividing property requires a restructuring of one's emotional reactions in a manner that is not involved in figuring out the size of the sun in relation to the earth. We would expect the former to require greater maturity, and hence more time to develop.

We cannot forget that a developmental unity exists in the child's life. There is a parallel in the development of cognition and affect, but children seem to progress slightly more quickly in their understanding of the physical world than in their understanding of how to structure relations in their social world.

AN ELABORATION ON THE CONCEPT OF STAGES

In chapter 2 we defined a "stage" as a consistent way of thinking about one aspect of reality. Kohlberg's main contribution has been to apply this concept of stage to the development of moral judgment. He has shown that, from middle childhood to adulthood, there are *six stages* in the development of moral judgment.

Before we describe Kohlberg's methodology and the six stages he has delineated, we need to elaborate further the characteristics of a stage system. Since neither Piaget nor Kohlberg claims that all human growth or change in behavior can be described in terms of a stage sequence, it is important to note the characteristics of those areas of human development that lend themselves to being described in terms of stages.

The following are the necessary characteristics of cognitive stages of development: [10]

1. *Stages imply qualitative differences in modes of thinking.* Two people at different stages may both share a similar value, but their way of thinking about the value will be qualitatively different. One adolescent, for example, may value friendship because friends watch out for your interests and help you in a pinch. Another adolescent may value friendship because friends care for you as a person and empathize with your problems. The value is similar, but the meaning of the value has changed.

2. *Each stage forms a structured whole.* As we saw in Piaget's work, when a child develops to concrete operations, he does not simply modify selective responses. He restructures his whole way of thinking about such issues as causality, perspective, and conservation. Similarly, in the moral realm, a stage change implies a restructuring of how one thinks about a whole series of moral issues.

3. *Stages form an invariant sequence.* A child cannot reach the stage of concrete operations without passing through the stage of preoperational thinking. Similarly, in the moral realm, children must understand that a person's life is more valuable than property before they can develop an understanding of why human life is sacred and ought to be preserved at all costs. The sequence is defined by the logical complexity of each successive stage. A later stage

must develop after an earlier stage because achieving the later stage involves mastering cognitive operations that are logically more complex than the operations characterizing the earlier stage. Thought develops only in an upward direction, toward greater equilibrium.

4. *Stages are hierarchical integrations.* When a person's thinking develops from one stage to the next, the higher stage reintegrates the structures found at lower stages. When an adolescent girl develops formal operations, she does not forget how to use concrete operations. Presented with a simple problem, such as grouping coins by their monetary value (pennies, nickels, etc.), she will use her concrete operations. Presented with a more complex problem, she will tend to use her more advanced powers of reasoning. Similarly, once she understands a friend to be someone who empathizes with her feelings, she will not stop expecting her friends to do her concrete favors. Nevertheless, friends who only do concrete favors for her will not be as valued (preferred) as friends who also empathize with her feelings.

The stage concept stands at the center of the cognitive-developmental approach. In attempting to establish the existence of six stages of moral judgment empirically, Kohlberg has had to demonstrate that the development of people's thinking about moral issues is characterized by these criteria. Were he not able to show this, he could not claim to have delineated cognitively based stages of moral judgment.

KOHLBERG'S METHODOLOGY

To ascertain someone's stage of moral judgment, Kohlberg has devised a research instrument to tap the process of reasoning that the person uses to resolve moral dilemmas. Kohlberg's assumption has been that indirect methods are not needed to "trick" people into revealing their thinking about moral issues. One has only to pose to them moral dilemmas that will arouse their interests and to ask them directly what the best solution to the dilemma would be, and why.

Kohlberg has followed Piaget's example and adapted a modified clinical method of interviewing subjects. The interview format he uses, the Moral Judgment Interview, is made up of three hypothetical dilemmas. Each dilemma involves a character who finds himself in a difficult situation and has to choose between two conflicting values. Each dilemma is read to the subject, and several standardized questions are posed. The subject is asked how the character *ought* to resolve the problem and why that would be the right way to act in this situation. The three dilemmas are chosen to cover a number of different moral issues. To determine a subject's stage of moral development, the researcher must see how consistently the subject reasons across a range of moral issues.

Two of the moral dilemmas used by Kohlberg, dilemmas 3 and 1, are reprinted below. Note that the dilemmas can be used with both children and adults. They have to be comprehensible to both and pose a situation that both would find morally problematic. These dilemmas achieve these goals insofar as they are written clearly and the conflict of values they raise is interesting to people at six different stages of moral development. Were a dilemma too hard or too easy for any given population, it would fail to produce their best thinking about moral issues.[11]

Dilemma 3

In Europe, a woman is near death from a special kind of cancer. There is one drug that the doctors think might save her. It is a form of radium that a druggist in the same town has recently discovered. The drug is expensive to make, but the druggist is charging ten times what the drug cost him to make. He paid $200 for the radium and is charging $2000 for a small dose of the drug. The sick woman's husband, Heinz, goes to everyone he knows to borrow the money, but he can get together only about $1000, which is half of what it costs. He tells the druggist that his wife is dying and asks him to sell the drug cheaper or let him pay later. The druggist says, "No, I discovered the drug and I'm going to make money from it." Heinz is desperate and considers breaking into the man's store to steal the drug for his wife.

1. Should Heinz steal the drug? Why or why not?
2. If Heinz doesn't love his wife, should he steal the drug for her? Why or why not?
3. Suppose the person dying is not his wife but a stranger. Should Heinz steal the drug for a stranger? Why or why not?
4. [If you favor stealing the drug for a stranger]: Suppose it's a pet animal he loves. Should Heinz steal to save the pet animal? Why or why not?
5. Why should people do everything they can to save another's life, anyhow?
6. It is against the law for Heinz to steal. Does that make it morally wrong? Why or why not?
7. Why should people generally do everything they can to avoid breaking the law, anyhow?
7a. How does this relate to Heinz's case?

Dilemma 1

Joe is a fourteen-year-old boy who wants to go to camp very much. His father has promised him he can go if he saves up the money for it himself. Joe has worked hard at his paper route and has saved the $40 it costs to go to camp and a little more besides. But just before camp is going to start, his father changes his mind. Some of the father's friends have decided to go on a special fishing trip, and he is short of the money it would cost. He tells Joe to give him the money he has saved from the paper route. Joe doesn't want to give up going to camp, so he thinks of refusing to give his father the money.

1. Should Joe refuse to give his father the money? Why or why not?
2. In what way is the fact that Joe earned the money himself something very important for the father to consider?
3. The father promised Joe he could go to camp if he earned the money. Is that promise something very important for the father or Joe to consider? Why or why not?
4. Why in general should a promise be kept?
5. Is it important to keep a promise to someone you don't know well and probably won't see again? Why or why not?

6. What do you think is the most important thing for a good son to be concerned about in his relationship with his father in this or other situations?

6a. Why is that important?

7. What do you think is the most important thing for a good father to be concerned about in his relationship with his son in this or other situations?

7a. Why is that important?

In responding to dilemma 3 the subject is asked to choose between the values of life and law. In this situation, does the value of the wife's life take precedence over the value of observing the law, or vice versa? In responding to dilemma 1 the subject is asked to choose between the value of authority and the values of property and contract. Should Joe give up the money and respect his father's authority, or do Joe's earning the money himself and his father's promising he could go to camp outweigh the value of listening to his father?

The first question in each dilemma is designed to elicit the subject's initial thoughts on the conflict. Subsequent questions are used to *probe* his thinking further. Since what will interest the researcher are the subject's *reasons* for choosing one value over the other, probing the subject's reasoning process is a particularly important part of the interview. For example, if someone says Heinz should steal to save his wife's life because he loves her, the interviewer will want to know (1) if the subject thinks the value of the wife's life is contingent upon Heinz's loving her or (2) if the wife's life is valuable in and of itself. The subsequent question, "Should Heinz steal the drug even if he does not love his wife?" helps clarify that distinction. Such distinctions are crucial, for they define the qualitative differences in judgment that distinguish one stage of moral development from another.

After the interview is completed, the researcher begins to analyze it for structures of moral judgment. He is not, as we said, much interested in whether the subject thinks Heinz should or should not steal the drug. His main interest lies in the reasoning used. The answer or conclusion would represent the *content* of the subject's thinking, while the reasoning would represent the *form* or structure of thought. The researcher looks for consistent use of form across several dilemmas. By identifying a consistent use of form, he establishes the stage or stages of moral judgment that characterize the subject's reasoning.

The distinction between form and content is important to bear in mind. Because this methodology relies on the subject's verbal response, the question arises: "To what extent does the subject's answer represent his thinking about what he would do if faced with a similar situation in real life?"

Kohlberg readily concedes that the *content* of the subject's responses is not a reliable basis for concluding anything about that person's "real" thinking. A subject who says, for example, that Heinz should steal the drug to save his wife's life does not necessarily imply that he himself would steal if he were in a similar position. But Kohlberg believes that by focusing on the *form* or structure of the subject's reasoning, one does get a sample of his "real" thinking. Kohlberg assumes that once a person has developed a structure of reasoning, it is as available to him in thinking about real-life situations as it is in solving hypothetical dilemmas. Whether other constraints in a real-life situation would or would not influence the use of the available structures of reasoning is an empirical question that, as we shall see, is being investigated in several current studies.

SIX STAGES OF MORAL JUDGMENT

Kohlberg's theory of moral development and moral education grows out of, and depends on, his empirical delineation of the stages of moral judgment. Since he defines moral development in terms of movement through the stages, and moral education in terms of stimulating such movement, it is clear that to understand his theory, one must be thoroughly familiar with the definition of these stages.

The six stages of moral judgment are outlined in table 1. We devote the remainder of this chapter to reviewing the table and explaining the stages. It is best, though, to begin with specific words of caution:

TABLE I
THE SIX STAGES OF MORAL JUDGMENT

Level and Stage	Content of Stage		Social Perspective of Stage
	What Is Right	Reasons for Doing Right	
Level I: Preconventional Stage 1: Heteronomous morality	Sticking to rules backed by punishment; obedience for its own sake; avoiding physical damage to persons and property.	Avoidance of punishment, superior power of authorities.	*Egocentric point of view.* Doesn't consider the interests of others or recognize that they differ from the actor's; doesn't relate two points of view. Actions considered physically rather than in terms of psychological interests of others. Confusion of authority's perspective with one's own.
Stage 2: Individualism, Instrumental purpose, and Exchange	Following rules only when in one's immediate interest; acting to meet one's own interests and needs and letting others do the same. Right is also what is fair or what is an equal exchange, deal, agreement.	To serve one's own needs or interests in a world where one has to recognize that other people also have interests.	*Concrete individualistic perspective.* Aware that everybody has interests to pursue and that these can conflict; right is relative (in the concrete individualistic sense).

Level II: Conventional Stage 3: Mutual interpersonal expectations, Relationships, and Interpersonal conformity	Living up to what is expected by people close to you or what people generally expect of a good son, brother, friend, etc. "Being good" is important and means having good motives, showing concern for others. It also means keeping mutual relationships such as trust, loyalty, respect, and gratitude.	The need to be a good person in your own eyes and those of others; caring for others; belief in the Golden Rule; desire to maintain rules and authority that support stereotypical good behavior.	*Perspective of the individual in relationships with other individuals.* Aware of shared feelings, agreements, and expectations which take primacy over individual interests. Relates points of view through the concrete Golden Rule, putting oneself in the other guy's shoes. Does not yet consider generalized system perspective.
Level II: Conventional (continued) Stage 4: Social system and conscience	Fulfilling duties to which you have agreed; laws to be upheld except in extreme cases where they conflict with other fixed social duties. Right is also contributing to the society, group, or institution.	To keep the institution going as a whole and avoid a breakdown in the system "if everyone did it"; imperative of conscience to meet one's defined obligations. (Easily confused with stage 3 belief in rules and authority.)	*Differentiates societal point of view from interpersonal agreement or motives.* Takes the point of view of the system that defines roles and rules; considers individual relations in terms of place in the system.

TABLE I (concluded)

Level and Stage	Content of Stage		Social Perspective of Stage
	What Is Right	Reasons for Doing Right	
Level III: Postconventional; or Principled Stage 5: Social contract or utility and individual rights	Being aware that people hold a variety of values and opinions and that most of their values and rules are relative to their group. Relative rules usually upheld in the interest of impartiality and because they are the social contract. Some nonrelative values and rights (e.g., *life* and *liberty*) must be upheld in any society and regardless of majority opinion.	A sense of obligation to law because of one's social contract to make and abide by laws for the welfare of all and for the protection of all people's rights. A feeling of contractual commitment, freely entered upon, to family, friendship, trust, and work obligations. Concern that laws and duties be based on rational calculation of overall utility, "the greatest good for the greatest number."	*Prior-to-society perspective.* Rational individual aware of values and rights prior to social attachments and contracts. Integrates perspectives by formal mechanisms of agreement, contract, objective impartiality, and due process. Considers moral and legal points of view; recognizes that they sometimes conflict and finds it difficult to integrate them.

| Level III: Postconventional; or Principled (continued) Stage 6: Universal ethical principles | Following self-chosen ethical principles. Particular laws or social agreements usually valid because they rest on such principles; when laws violate these principles, one acts in accordance with principle. Principles are universal principles of justice: equality of human rights and respect for the dignity of human beings as individuals. | The belief as a rational person in the validity of universal moral principles and a sense of personal commitment to them. | *Perspective of a moral point of view from which social arrangements derive.* Perspective is that of a rational individual recognizing the nature of morality or the fact that persons are ends in themselves and must be treated as such. |

Source: Lawrence Kohlberg, "Moral Stages and Moralization: The Cognitive-Developmental Approach," in *Moral Development and Behavior: Theory, Research and Social Issues*, ed. Thomas Lickona (New York: Holt, Rinehart and Winston, 1976), pp. 34–35.

1. *It takes a long time and a lot of effort to grasp the stages in their particularity.* Be patient and expect some difficulties along the way.
2. *Be careful to distinguish form from content.* Our experience in teaching the stages has shown that many initial misunderstandings result from students' focusing on content descriptions rather than on the more basic formal or structural differentiations between stages.
3. *People are not stages.* Stages are descriptions of ideal stopping points (equilibriums) along the paths of development. People, especially young people, are likely to be transitional between stages and to use more than one stage of reasoning. When we say a subject is "at" a given stage, we mean only that the stage mentioned describes his most common (not exclusive) way of reasoning about moral issues. Therefore, do not try to stage people of your acquaintance prematurely.

How to Begin

Having raised the flags of caution, we can proceed with the table of moral stages. We suggest that table 1 be read in the following order:

1. Note that horizontal lines divide the table into three *levels* of moral reasoning. These are the roughest, yet most basic, developmental distinctions to be learned. They represent three possible perspectives that a person can adopt in relation to a society's moral norms: level I, preconventional; level II, conventional; and level III, postconventional, or principled.
2. Note that each of the three levels is divided into two *stages*. Each moral stage operates within the bounds of a broader level of perspective but has more distinct structural characteristics. The levels define approaches to moral problems; the stages define the criteria by which people exercise their moral judgment. Each stage is defined by:
3. A *social perspective* (right-hand column).
4. A *set of reasons* (middle column) why given actions are to be judged as right or wrong.

5. A preferred set of values (left-hand column) that indicates *what is right* for oneself and one's society.

Levels of Moral Reasoning

To gain a broad overview of the system, we begin with the three levels of moral reasoning. A person at the *preconventional level* approaches a moral issue from the perspective of the concrete interests of the individuals involved. He is concerned not with what society defines as the right way to behave in a given situation but only with the concrete consequences individuals would face in deciding upon a particular action. In considering the Heinz dilemma, for example, a person adopting this perspective would focus on such questions as:

Will Heinz be punished for stealing?
Can Heinz live without his wife?
Wouldn't any man steal to save his wife's life if he needed her?

The perspective focuses on Heinz's (or any person's) pursuing his concrete interests while avoiding untenable risks.

A person at the *conventional level* approaches a moral problem from a member-of-society perspective. He realizes and takes into consideration that the group or society expects an individual to act in accordance with its moral norms. The person strives not only to avoid punishment or censure, but also to live up, in a positive way, to accepted definitions of a good member or role-occupant. In facing the Heinz dilemma, a person who adopts this perspective would focus on such questions as:

Wouldn't a good husband be expected to do all he could to save his wife?
Won't the authorities help Heinz solve the problem without his having to steal?
Can a society survive if it allows its members to break the law in such situations?

The concern is to be a good role-occupant (husband) and yet protect society's as well as one's own interests.

A person at the *postconventional*, or *principled*, *level* approaches a moral problem from a prior-to-society perspective. That is, he can see beyond the given norms and laws of his own society and ask: what are the principles upon which any good society is based? People who have either envisioned or actually begun utopian or revolutionary societies have used this perspective (e.g., biblical prophets, the Founding Fathers of the United States, Karl Marx in his early writings). Less dramatically, people faced with difficult moral dilemmas, the solutions to which are not defined adequately by their society's norms and laws, may adopt this perspective. In relation to the Heinz dilemma, this perspective might suggest the following questions:

Is this an instance of breaking the law that might be morally justified by the need to save the life of an innocent victim?

Can the laws of this or any society be fashioned so as to prevent the loss of innocent lives and yet protect a druggist's legitimate exercise of his right to property?

The three levels broadly define the scope of moral development as described by Kohlberg. The first level most often characterizes children's moral reasoning; still, many adolescents and some adults persist in this reasoning. The second level usually arises during preadolescence, comes into fuller prominence during adolescence, and remains dominant in the thinking of most adults. The third level is the rarest. It arises, if at all, during adolescence or early adulthood and characterizes the reasoning of only a minority of adults.[12]

It may be helpful at this point to begin drawing parallels between moral development and cognitive development. People adopting a preconventional perspective are highly concrete in their approach. This suggests that their moral reasoning is based on either the preoperational or the concrete operational stage of cognitive development. People adopting a conventional perspective consider the more abstract issues of what their society would expect of them. They are using moral reasoning that is based at least on beginning formal operations. People adopting the postconventional perspective think in the purely formal categories of what would be the best solution given these moral principles. They are using reasoning based on advanced or consolidated formal operations.[13]

Defining Stages

Once you understand the three levels of moral reasoning, you are ready to consult table 1 for the six stages.

STAGE 1

Kohlberg's original research dealt with boys aged ten through sixteen.[14] The least developed stage he found among these subjects he called stage 1. Had Kohlberg begun by studying younger children, he may have defined this stage a bit differently. However, his work on stage 1 has been supplemented by Selman [15] and Damon,[16] and we recommend their works to readers particularly interested in moral development in children between the ages of four and ten.

Stage 1 represents the moral reasoning of the child who has taken his first step beyond egocentrism. If the egocentric child cannot take the role or perspective of any other person, the next step in development is the ability to take the perspective of one other person at a time. In the case we gave earlier of the child whose mother came home from work with a headache, the first developmental step beyond egocentrism would involve the realization that the mother had a reason for not wanting to play. What that reason means may elude the child, but its existence is recognized.

What follows from this recognition is the desire to do what the mother wants. The expressed wishes or orders of the authority figure become rules or commands that the child understands he must follow, for if he does not, he believes he will be punished.

The inevitability of physical punishment is central to this stage's conception of doing right. The child does not yet understand that punishment is one possible response to wrongdoing. He sees physical punishment as automatically following wrongdoing. (The child's ditty "Step on a crack, Break your mother's back" is reflective of this thinking.) He also (from our perspective) greatly exaggerates the punishment that is likely to follow.

To understand this reasoning, we must recall that we are speaking of a child whose cognitive understanding is limited to the preoperational or the early concrete operational level. His reasoning is still intuitive rather than logical. Thus, although the child associates disobedience with punishment, he does not match the punishment to the "crime," but imagines punishments that are all out of proportion to the "offense." He takes the role of the adult, but imagines that the "big" adult will react in a "big" way. A typical response to the moral dilemmas is that Heinz and Joe cannot disobey the authorities, for they will be severely punished if they do. Note the "cannot"; the child believes that they *are not able to,* for the punishment that would follow would be too great to bear.

Stage 1 is surprisingly primitive, so much so that it is often missed by adults. One of the authors was visiting a friend and telling him about a social planner who had incurred the wrath of the whole town he had helped plan and establish. The friend's seven-year-old daughter was listening and volunteered a solution: "They can all just beat him up." It was said in so matter-of-fact a tone that the father did not even hear it. But, for one familiar with this stage of reasoning, the response made sense. The child at this stage thinks only in terms of physical problems and physical solutions. If a lot of people do not like someone, he must be bad. If he is bad, they can punish him by beating him up. At this stage the problem is that simple; the child does not yet recognize other people's rights and feelings and does not consider why the man was wrong or what will happen to the townspeople if they beat him up. The problem ends when the punishment is given.

Piaget described this stage, which he called "heteronomous morality," at length. He was surprised that even children who came from homes where the parents did not use physical punishment went through this stage. This stage of reasoning is inevitable at a certain age—perhaps five to eight years—and is the necessary first step beyond egocentrism. It may parallel what Freudians call the formation of the superego.

Stage 1 does not usually continue in our society by children beyond the years of preadolescence. Selman reports from his clinical work a case of a very disturbed fourteen-year-old still using this reasoning with some regularity.[17] Nevertheless, the primitive nature of this stage makes its use dysfunctional even among preadolescents. Almost all children develop the capacity for at least stage 2 reasoning.

STAGE 2

Although still within the preconventional level of reasoning, stage 2 represents a major advance over stage 1. The advance is heralded by changes in the child's cognitive and role-taking abilities.

Most children, while still at stage 1, begin to develop concrete logical operations. They become able to distance themselves from their immediate perceptions and look at a problem from a more distanced, logical perspective. For example, in a problem of classification, they can hold the whole class (e.g., all the beads) in mind and compare it with its parts (red beads and blue beads). In the conservation of liquid, they are not fooled by the height of the liquid in the beaker, but look at the process of pouring the liquid from one beaker to the next and then reverse that process in their minds. By reversing it, they see that the amount of liquid has not changed in the pouring; thus the two beakers, although they look different, contain the same amount of liquid.

In the social realm, a similar development takes place in role taking.[18] After the initial breakthrough of being able to take the role of one other person at a time, the child begins to coordinate perspectives. That is, after discovering that other people have wills independent of his own, the child slowly discovers that another's will or perspective is not as static as he initially imagined. Rather, the other person can put himself in the child's place and see why the child is doing what he is. As a result, the other can change either his original position or his judgment of the child's actions.

To illustrate this development, imagine a first-grade student who comes home with a reading assignment. She asks her mother to listen to her read, and the mother does. The mother then suggests that they continue in the reading because she will not have time to read with her daughter the next night. But the little girl refuses; the teacher said to read only these pages.

The first-grader is at the first stage of role taking. She can take her teacher's role, but she does so literally and without coordinating it with her mother's role. With time, the child will begin to realize that the teacher would not necessarily object to her going on in the reading with her mother. If the teacher knew why the mother wanted to continue, the teacher might agree that the mother's reason made sense.

As children realize that other people change their views when they gain a new perspective on a situation, children change the basis for their own moral judgments. To follow our example, at stage 1 the girl will think it wrong not to do exactly what the teacher said, but once she realizes that the teacher's view can change, she no longer has any reason to believe this action would be considered wrong. As long as she has a good reason for doing something—that is, a reason she can explain to the teacher—she has every reason to believe it would be all right to do it.

Although seemingly different, this calculation is similar to the logical operation involved in conserving the amount of liquid. What the child did looks different from what the teacher said she should do. But if we follow the process (the mother asking her to continue) and reverse it (if the teacher could see my mother asking me), we see that what happened was not disobedience (a change in the given order), but obedience in a different form (which parallels the same amount of water in a different-shaped beaker).

It is remarkable how adept children in grade school get at taking the role of the teacher and second-guessing how he will react to their actions. They realize that their actions will take on a different meaning if they can be presented in a different light. Thus the great effort to make up the right excuse for the right occasion.

With regard to moral development, a new standard of judgment is arising: the standard of *fairness*. If someone has a good reason for doing something, it is only fair that he or she be judged by that reason and not by the arbitrary will of an authority figure. The central value of stage 1—authority—is relativized at stage 2. An authority is like everybody else insofar as he has to play by the rules of the game, which are the rules of fairness.

But what is considered fair? At stage 2, fairness primarily involves everyone's getting an equal share or chance. This takes both a positive and a negative form. The positive involves the proverbial cutting of the pie or distributing of goods and benefits. People of equal status ought to get equal shares. Everyone in a class ought to get the same amount of attention or homework unless there is a clearly understood reason why one person has special needs and hence a special status. In a family, age might qualify as a special status. It usually seems fair to children that an older sibling is entitled to some extra privileges. But watch how carefully the younger child calculates whether the proportional difference in privilege is equal to the proportional difference in age. Beware of the child who believes he has not gotten his fair share! Nothing seems more unjust at this stage.

The negative form operates in accordance with retributive justice. Children at stage 2 no longer believe that punishment follows automatically on the heels of disobedience or wrongdoing. They believe that wrongdoing involves concretely harming someone else without due cause, and they also believe that the punishment ought to match the crime. What constitutes "due cause" depends on the circumstances—on why you harmed the other person. Every grade school teacher knows that if one child hits another, the one who is hit believes that he has the right—if not the duty—to hit the other child back. Justice is not complete until the wrongdoing is returned—the act reversed. No matter how many times the teacher says, "Two wrongs don't make a right," the children believe that hitting back is not wrong; it is what the other deserves. But the other deserves what he gave and not more. If Billy hits Seth once, Seth does not have the right to hit Billy ten times, unless Billy hit him really hard. In that case, what Seth is returning is not an act of hitting, but an act of hurting. In either case, proportion defines retributive fairness.

For teachers, what is frustrating about children's thinking at this stage is that it remains preconventional. Fairness is certainly a moral category, but it need not have reference to societal rules or laws. At stage 2, the relevant moral action takes place among individuals, each of whom has the right to pursue his own interests. It is considered fair to get away with what you can. If a teacher gives a test and does not proctor it carefully, it is fair—from this preconventional perspective—for the students to cheat. "Who is it hurting," a student at this stage will ask, "if I take my answers from her sheet?" The answer that it is hurting oneself does not yet make sense. How is it hurting oneself if one student gains points and the other student loses nothing? Harm is understood only as a concrete reference; a vague sense of hurting oneself simply does not register. No wonder teachers have so much trouble convincing students that cheating is morally wrong.

With regard to Heinz and the druggist, however, most stage 2 subjects have no trouble seeing how the druggist is causing Heinz great harm. They see it as natural for Heinz to want to steal the drug—given that Heinz cares about his wife. If he did not, which is his business, then he probably would not take the risk. Why bother? Stage 2 respondents do not see a husband as having an obligation to his wife. Rather, husbands have the right to steal for their wives if they want to. In the opinion of reasoners at this stage, if Heinz does steal, it is most likely that he will not really be punished. What judge would not understand why Heinz stole? What better reason to steal than to save your wife's life? At a preconventional stage, the issue of law arises only insofar as one has to get around the law to fulfill one's legitimate needs. The action takes place entirely from the perspective of the individuals involved: Heinz, his wife, the druggist, and the judge.

Stage 2, as we have noted, begins to develop in our society among seven- and eight-year-olds and remains the dominant stage throughout the grade school years. Studies of adolescents show that among middle-class populations, stage 2 reasoning recedes considerably, but it remains a fairly dominant mode among working-class and lower-class youth. Among adults it continues to persist, but more as a minor stage.

STAGE 3

The development of stage 3 marks the preadolescent's or adolescent's entry into the conventional level of moral reasoning. As such, it involves shifting one's social perspective from the concrete interests of individuals to the interests or standards of one's group or society.

The change in social perspective is usually preceded by a change in both cognitive and role-taking abilities. On the cognitive side, preadolescence often marks the emergence of beginning formal operations. With regard to classification problems, we spoke of the child's coming to understand the inverse of the reciprocal as illustrated in the following problem:

If a person lives in London, he lives in England.

1. If a person does not live in England, does he live in London?
2. If a person does not live in London, does he live in England?

To solve this problem correctly, the subject must understand that as a class, London is included in the larger class of England, but that not all of England is included in London. Thus, while the answer to question 1 must be "no," the answer to question 2 is "we don't know." Since the class of "not London" includes other areas of England as well as all other countries, a person not living in London may or may not be living in some other part of England.

To understand a class of "not London" involves the ability to think in abstractions and hence represents the beginning of formal operations. Similarly, to understand a social norm also involves thinking abstractly. Thus, stage 3 moral reasoning usually reflects at least beginning formal operations.

In the social realm, role-taking abilities usually take an important step ahead between stage 2 and stage 3. At stage 2 the child becomes aware that other people can take his role as he can take theirs. Thus the child can anticipate how others will react to his actions and can plan his actions accordingly. But what awaits the next stage of role taking is the ability to step outside the two-person relationship and look at it from a third-person perspective.

To illustrate this development in role taking, imagine that two twelve-year-old girls are interested in the same boy and are invited to the same party, which he will be attending. If one of the girls is at the second stage of role taking, she will be able to take the role of her rival and anticipate that the other girl will be carefully watching her moves. If the second girl is at the third stage of role taking, she will be able not only to anticipate her rival's reaction but also to take the role of other people who will be watching the two girls compete. She may be concerned with how they will react to seeing her compete with the other girl. This realization may embarrass her or encourage her; in either case, she will be thinking about an extra dimension of the social situation, one that the stage 2 girl will not be considering.

Taking a third person's perspective proves crucial to the development of moral judgment, for it allows the person to perceive how the group will react to his dealings with other individuals. To pursue our example, if the second girl thinks that others at the party will perceive her as moving in on the first girl's attachment to the boy, and hence as being unkind, she is likely to take their perceptions into account. If her moral judgment (as opposed to her role-taking ability) were still at a stage 2 level, she would probably define the problem as the other girl's getting even with her for butting in on her friend's relationship. But were the perspective of the group to become morally important in its own right (aside from the threat of retaliation), her concern would move from possible retaliation to what others would think of her as a person for doing this to her friend.

To expand this point, people thinking in stage 2 terms are aware that others are watching their actions and reacting to them. But they usually anticipate only concrete behavioral reactions. If, as a result of your hurting someone, other people are going to dislike you and actually exclude you from their group, it is worth your while to think twice before taking that action. If you are at a stage 3 level, however, you watch not only for people's concrete behavioral reactions but also for their more subtle psychological reactions. What will they think of, or feel about, you? Will they be as accepting of you as before? Will they still think you are a good person or a good group member? At this stage you realize that other people have expectations of how you *should* (not only how you *would*) behave, and judge you as a person accordingly.

At stage 3, then, the motivation for moral action becomes living up to what significant others expect of you as a member of their group or society. As the reasons (motivation) for doing right change, so does the concept of what is right in relation to others. At stage 2, what is right is simply the pursuing of your own interests without unduly harming anybody else. At stage 3, more is expected of yourself and others. The awareness that others have positive expectations of you leads to a new view of interpersonal relations. When two people enter a relationship, they place their trust in one another and expect that the other will care for them and respect that trust. Relationship is more than an equal exchange of benefits (as it is viewed at stage 2); it involves mutual commitment. To break that commitment or to violate trust becomes for a stage 3 person what acting unfairly is for a stage 2 person: the cardinal wrongdoing.

The Heinz dilemma amply demonstrates this point. What are Heinz's obligations to his wife in this situation? From a stage 2 perspective, Heinz does not have any obligations per se. He certainly has the right to steal to save his wife if he wants to; if he does not want to steal, neither his wife nor anyone else has any legitimate gripe against him. From a stage 3 perspective, by being married to this woman, Heinz has definite commitments to her. He should care for her and try to save her life. (Whether this includes stealing for her is a point on which stage 3 respondents do not agree.) Even if he no longer loves his wife, the fact that he once loved her and committed himself to her means that he still should be concerned about her.

In relation to the druggist, stage 2 respondents believe that he was basically within his rights to pursue profit, and that although he may have been foolish not to give Heinz a break (and hence incur his retaliation), he had no obligation to do so. Stage 3 respondents, in contrast, often get angry just thinking about the druggist. What kind of man is he? Doesn't he have a heart? He may not have known Heinz personally, but as a druggist, a member of the medical profession, he committed himself to help cure people; now he is turning Heinz away for purely selfish reasons. Selfishness, from a stage 3 perspective, is another form of violating trust and commitment and is therefore almost always wrong.

Stage 3, as we noted, begins to develop during preadolescence; it is the dominant stage during adolescence, and along with stage 4 remains the major stage for most adults in our society. It is a mature (or equilibrated) structure insofar as it proves an adequate mode for dealing with most conflicts arising among people who know one another. Its inadequacy surfaces when one must deal with problems on a societal level. For such problems, stages 4 and above prove more adequate.

STAGE 4

Whereas stage 3 role taking is primarily characterized by the ability to take the third-person perspective of *significant* others, stage 4 role taking is primarily characterized by the ability to take the shared point of view of the *generalized* other. That is, a person takes the perspective of the social system in which he participates: his institution, society, belief system, and so on.

To illustrate this, imagine an incident at a summer camp. A group of adolescents approaches the camp director with the request that they be allowed to plan an overnight retreat. They say that they have discussed it among themselves and with their counselors and believe that a retreat in which they can make the plans and rules would best facilitate the unification of their group. The director asks whether they would be willing to abide by camp rules concerning curfew, the use of drugs and liquor, and the like. They answer that they will have to decide this for themselves as a group. The director replies that although he can see that their proposal might benefit the unification of their group, he does not think that from the perspective of the whole institution (the camp), he can allow them to set this precedent. They may have the best intentions in mind, but another group might use the precedent for less honorable purposes. Thus, for the sake of the camp, he must refuse their request.

The adolescents in this example base their appeal on the welfare of their own group. The camp director considers their request from the wider perspective of how it will affect the whole institution. The ability to take the perspective of the whole social system, in contrast to the perspective of the immediate group, characterizes stage 4 role taking. It involves a greater cognitive ability, for one must keep in mind the interests of each constitutive group and compare them to the interests of the whole. Many adolescents do not yet have this ability and hence interpret such decisions as mean and unfair. However people feel about such responses, it should be clear that they are based on a broader perspective than appeal to the interest of a single group within the system.

The ability to view social problems from the perspective of the whole system usually provides a new basis for moral judgment. In relation to the Heinz dilemma, people at stage 3 would be primarily concerned with Heinz's commitments as a husband and with the druggist's inhumanity and failure to live up to what is expected of a member of the medical profession; but they generally would not be concerned with how Heinz's decision affects the social system. From a stage 4 perspective, however, the latter becomes the primary concern. People at this stage agree that Heinz is obligated to help save his wife and that the druggist has acted inhumanely, but they also are concerned about Heinz's stealing, for he would be weakening the moral order of society. Law emerges for stage 4 reasoners as a central value. They are not necessarily advocates of what is called "a law and order" position; nevertheless, they appreciate that any society is bound together by certain social and moral agreements, many of which are codified into a system of law, and that any action that breaks those agreements threatens to a degree the solidarity and cohesion of that social system.[19]

Not all, or even most, stage 4 respondents decide that Heinz should not steal to save his wife's life. As they appreciate the centrality of the value of law, they often also appreciate the centrality of the value of life. In a sense, this dilemma is hardest to resolve at stage 4. Persons at this stage realize that human life is sacred and that law's purpose is often to guard the sacredness of life. Thus, when the values of law and life openly conflict, they have trouble choosing between them.

To understand stage 4 moral reasoning we must distinguish form from content. A person at this stage may not place the highest value on his society's laws. He may, for example, adopt a Marxist position and argue that law in a capitalist society is a sham, designed only to protect the interests of the ruling class. Or he may adopt a supernaturalist position and argue that only God's law is sacred; when the law of society conflicts with a higher law, the latter must take precedence. The preferred system is a matter of content. What characterizes these arguments as stage 4 is the structure of reasoning, which looks at a given social issue from the perspective of a fixed system of laws and beliefs. A Marxist at this stage may argue that Heinz should steal because a system that honors property and profit more than human life is morally bankrupt. Yet, faced with a conflict between promoting the revolution and saving human lives, he is as likely to argue for the primacy of the revolution as a capitalist is to argue for the primacy of law and property rights. The form of justification is the same; only the content (what is valued) changes.

Stage 4 reasoning begins to develop during mid-adolescence. It is a highly equilibrated stage and often proves to be the highest stage to which adults develop. It adequately handles societal as well as interpersonal issues. Kohlberg, however, believes that stage 4 is not adequate for dealing with situations in which a system of laws or beliefs comes into conflict with basic human rights. If a person lives in a society in which the legal system systematically denies to some people basic human rights, should he agree that to preserve the social and moral order, he ought not violate what he considers unjust laws? Stage 4 reasoning has no adequate response to this question. While people at this stage may argue for working within the system for change, if the system itself is unjust, they may be forced to choose between adherence and dissent. Kohlberg believes that within the structure of stage 4 reasoning, no persuasive criteria exist for when to choose dissent over adherence. He has therefore delineated postconventional stages that can deal more adequately with these moral conflicts.

STAGES 5 AND 6

Stages 5 and 6, the stages of principled moral reasoning, are the most controversial areas of Kohlberg's theory. Stages 5 and 6 are derived philosophically, but some moral philosophers, as we shall see in the next chapter, disagree with Kohlberg's formulation of the "highest" stages. Less empirical data are available on these than on the other stages, and they therefore have been questioned more seriously by psychologists.

Kohlberg defined stages 5 and 6 originally in his doctoral dissertation (1958). Using those definitions, he found that some adolescents use this kind of moral reasoning as minor stages.[20] After further reflection on his definitions of these stages, Kohlberg clarified his conception of them [21] and found that they are rarely attained before a person reaches his twenties.[22] The descriptions of stages 5 and 6 provided in table 1 reflect Kohlberg's later thinking, but they require elaboration.

Once an adolescent has reached stage 4, his moral reasoning is based on full formal operations and is consistent with the reasoning of most adults. What, then, can motivate his constructing a new stage of moral reasoning? In other words, what would an adolescent or young adult find unsatisfactory about stage 4 reasoning that would lead him to question its suppositions and seek a new basis for moral judgment? Kohlberg suggests that the "crisis of relativism" may provide such motivation.

The limits of stage 4 reasoning are most noticeable when a person at that stage must deal with diversity outside his own system. For example, what validity can a stage 4 adherent of a given religious system grant to people of very different traditions? If he believes that homosexuality is a sin, can he view homosexuals as anything other than sinners? If he is a devout communist, can he concede the validity of socialism? Insofar as stage 4 people conceive of morality as a fixed system of laws and beliefs, they can grant little validity to other views without threatening their own.

Adolescents, though, are often tolerant of, and even attracted to, views other than their own. In exploring alternative conceptions of morality, they may find they have no valid grounds for concluding that their way is more moral than the alternatives. As a result, they may adopt a relativist perspective: all values or morals are equally arbitrary, and the best you can do is what you think is right as long as you do not deprive others of doing what they think is right.[23]

Kohlberg's research suggests that relativism is not usually a stable moral position. Once young people enter a position of social responsibility within their society, they tend either to shelve these questions and return to their stage 4 moral reasoning or to construct a principled rationale for moral decision making. Stages 5 and 6 represent such principled rationales. Stage 5 is the more available and hence the more common stage. Stage 6 represents a philosophically more adequate position, but it is a rarity among nonphilosophers.

Stage 5 can be seen as a direct outgrowth of relativism. It incorporates the relativist's perspective that values are relative to one's group but seeks a principle that will bridge these differences. The principle of social contract is helpful. In a business deal between two men, each of whom has his own interests to protect, the partners come to an agreement and draw up and sign a mutually binding contract. The contract usually represents a compromise, but it allows each man to pursue his own interests without unduly interfering with the other's right to pursue his interests. There is nothing sacred about the contract itself; nevertheless, each part is obligated to abide by it, for it represents the best hope of legitimately satisfying their rights and needs.

The notion of seeing one's obligations to society in the form of a social contract is well known in political and social philosophy. The U.S. Constitution can be seen as a social contract among the states of the Union. Marriage or friendship involves an implicit or explicit social contract between mates or friends. The advantage of this concept is that it does not attempt to prescribe a fixed formula of obligation for each relationship, as is usually done at stage 4. Rather, legal or social commitments are viewed as something to which each partner to the contract freely obligates himself knowing that the others have equally and freely obligated themselves. Their mutual agreements define the nature of their obligations to one another. Contracts are not inherently good or bad unless they involve an abrogation of such basic human rights as life and liberty. Such contracts would be morally invalid. Thus, for example, even if one person voluntarily sells himself into slavery, the other does not have the moral right to hold him to that agreement.

Kohlberg gave the Heinz dilemma to two moral philosophers who held positions similar to those described by stage 5. He quotes selections from each of their responses:

Philosopher 1: What Heinz did was not wrong. The distribution of scarce drugs should be regulated by principles of fairness. In the absence of such regulations, the druggist was within his legal rights, but in the circumstances he has no moral complaint. He still was within his moral rights, however, unless it was within his society a strongly disapproved thing to do. While what Heinz did was not wrong, it was not his duty to do it. In this case it is not wrong for Heinz to steal the drug, but it goes beyond the call of duty; it is a deed of supererogation.

Philosopher 2: It is a husband's duty to steal the drug. The principle that husbands should look after their wives to the best of their ability is one whose general observance does more good than harm. He should also steal it for a friend, if he were a very close friend (close enough for it to be understood that they would do this sort of thing for each other). The reasons are similar to those in the case of wives. If the person with cancer were a less close friend, or even a stranger, Heinz would be doing a good act if he stole the drug, but he has no duty to.[24]

Philosopher 1 begins with what should ideally be agreed upon in any society: "The distribution of scarce drugs should be regulated by principles of fairness." This was not the agreed-upon principle in Heinz's society; thus the druggist "was within his moral rights." Heinz has no duty to steal, for that is not part of the usual contract between husband and wife. Yet if he does steal, it will be "a deed of supererogation"—a good deed beyond the call of duty.

Philosopher 2 believes that Heinz is obligated to steal to save a wife or a close friend, for if Heinz were to universalize the principle (ask what would happen if everyone in this situation were to steal to save a wife or a close friend), he would find its "general observance does more good than harm." This philosopher further applies the argument to stealing for a stranger that philosopher 1 applied to stealing for one's wife.

Kohlberg's dissatisfaction with these responses and with moral reasoning based on the concept of social contract has led him to formulate a "higher" stage 6. His thinking about this stage has been strongly influenced by the Harvard philosopher John Rawls.[25] Kohlberg cites a third philosopher's response to the Heinz dilemma as an example of stage 6 reasoning:

> *If the husband does not feel very close to or affectionate with his wife, should he steal the drug?*
> Yes. The value of her life is independent of any personal ties. The value of human life is based on the fact that it offers the only possible source of a categorical moral "ought" to a rational being acting in the role of a moral agent.
>
> *Suppose it were a friend or an acquaintance?*
> Yes, the value of a human life remains the same.

The difference here is that this philosopher does not make the act of stealing contingent upon any prior agreement between Heinz and the other person involved; rather, he sees it as "a categorical moral 'ought' " that any "rational being acting in the role of a moral agent" would accept as his duty to perform.

The argument for this position as a more adequate moral reasoning is complex, for it is based on the philosophic concepts of reversibility and universalizability. Rather than try to summarize the argument, we cite here a selection from Kohlberg's writings and suggest that the interested reader pursue the argument on his own.

> Since Kant, formalists have argued that rational moral judgments must be reversible, consistent, and universalizable, and that this implies the prescriptivity of such judgments. We claim that only the substantive moral judgments made at stage 6 fully meet these conditions, and that each higher stage meets these conditions better than each lower stage. In fully meeting these conditions, stage 6 moral structures are ultimately equilibrated . . . . Universalizability and consistency are fully attained by the reversibility of prescriptions of

actions. Reversibility of moral judgment is what is ultimately meant by the criterion of the fairness of a moral decision. Procedurally, fairness as impartiality means reversibility in the sense of a decision on which all interested parties could agree insofar as they can consider their own claims impartially, as the just decider would. If we have a reversible solution, we have one that could be reached as right starting from anyone's perspective in the situation, given each person's intent to put himself in the shoes of the other . . . .

At stage 6, reversibility is attained by a second-order conception of Golden Rule role-taking. In the Heinz dilemma, Heinz must imagine whether the druggist could put himself in the wife's position and still maintain his claim and whether the wife could put herself in the druggist's position and still maintain her claim. Intuitively we feel the wife could, the druggist could not. As a result, it is fair for the husband to act on the basis of the wife's claim. We call the process by which a reversible moral decision is reached, "ideal role-taking." Stage 6 moral judgment is based on role-taking the claim of each actor under the assumption that all other actors' claims are governed by the Golden Rule and accommodated accordingly. This is what is meant by calling stage 6 reversibility the second-order application of the Golden Rule. The steps for an actor involved in making such a decision based on ideal role-taking are:

1. To imagine oneself in each person's position in that situation (including the self) and to consider all the claims he could make (or which the self could make in his position).
2. Then to imagine that the individual does not know which person he is in the situation and to ask whether he would still uphold that claim.
3. Then to act in accordance with these reversible claims in the situation.[26]

Kohlberg has not found subjects (other than philosophers) who have naturally developed to a stage 6 conception of morality. But he cites a study showing that when stage 5 subjects are exposed to stage 6 arguments, they prefer them over their own arguments. As we shall see, this adds some psychological support to the philosophic contention that stage 6 represents a more adequate structure of moral reasoning than does stage 5.

SUMMARY

In this chapter we have introduced Kohlberg's concept of moral judgment, shown its relationship to Piaget's work on cognitive development, and presented in some detail the six stages of moral judgment.

It would be contrary to our teaching experience to expect that on first exposure a person could assimilate and accommodate all the information contained in the description of the stages. A way other than rereading that may prove helpful in this endeavor is to interview several children and adults using the two dilemmas provided earlier in the chapter (pp. 54–56). Gaining personal experience through hearing and examining people's use of moral reasoning will help readers see these stages as more of a reality. Our hope is that once readers learn to identify stage-related arguments, they can become better listeners and respondents in discussions involving moral issues. That, in turn, is an important step in becoming more effective moral educators.

4

Kohlberg's Theory of Moral Development and Moral Education

Although the six stages of moral judgment form the core of Kohlberg's work, much else in his theory of moral development and moral education remains for us to consider. In this chapter we review some of his main theoretical arguments by looking into some questions that have been raised by students in our courses on moral development.

Theoretical discussions often become technical and involved. To avoid unnecessary complication, we have tried as much as possible to use nontechnical language and answer questions plainly. Readers who are interested in pursuing Kohlberg's arguments in greater detail are referred to original sources.

Question 1:

How can Kohlberg claim that there is one sequence of stages that accurately describes the moral reasoning of all people? Doesn't he know that values differ from person to person and from society to society?

Kohlberg is certainly aware of cultural relativity. He knows that different societies have different values and socialize their children to follow their society's values. Yet he defends the claim for the existence of a single sequence of stages of moral judgment on both philosophic and psychological grounds.[1]

Kohlberg begins his argument by asking: What are the real differences in moral values from society to society? If we take as an example the value of human life and the concomitant prohibition from the taking of innocent life, how much cultural variation is evident? We see that some societies practice human sacrifice, patricide, or infanticide—all of which are outlawed as murder in Western societies. Within our own society, debates over abortion and euthanasia reflect serious differences of moral opinion on the value of life.

Despite these obvious cultural differences, Kohlberg argues that there is a common recognition of the value of life and a common concern for preserving human life. If a nomadic people set out for a new camp and leave behind some of their weaker members to die, it is not because they are indifferent to the value of life. Quite the opposite. They perceive that the lives of all tribal members might be in danger, and so they decide to leave behind the few. Faced with a similar choice, most Western people would also sacrifice the few to save the many. They might disagree on the criteria for choosing whom to sacrifice, but that disagreement would presuppose a common adherence to the basic value of human life.

The value of human life is one of ten basic moral values that Kohlberg believes are common to all human societies:

The Ten Universal Moral Issues
1. Laws and rules
2. Conscience
3. Personal roles of affection
4. Authority
5. Civil rights
6. Contract, trust, and justice in exchange
7. Punishment
8. The value of life
9. Property rights and values
10. Truth

One may disagree with the particular values Kohlberg has chosen as being universal, but it would seem hard to deny that some values or moral institutions are universally common, even though the practices associated with these values may vary radically in different societies.

Even if we accept the hypothesized existence of some universally accepted basic moral values, how would their existence substantiate the claim of one universal sequence of moral stages? Kohlberg's reasoning at this point is complex.[2] He does not believe that these universal values are directly taught to children. Rather, the basic values are embodied in common social institutions such as the family, the legal system, and the economy. All societies have family units in which personal roles of affection are embodied, economic systems in which rules of fair exchange are formalized, legal systems in which the value of law is upheld, and so forth. Children in every society are exposed to, and taught to participate in, these institutions. Yet children begin learning the basic values before participating in the institutions in which these values are embodied. A child does not, for example, have to go to court to begin thinking about the value of laws and rules; he does not have to enter the market to begin thinking about the value of fair exchange. The rudimentary experience of these values already has taken place within the house and the peer group. The values arise out of the child's experience of interacting with adults and peers, and operate as conceptual modes for regulating social interaction.

This last point is a crucial one for understanding Kohlberg's position. As long as you think of basic moral values as having to be taught to children, you will end up focusing on the particular culturally bound rules of behavior that children learn in each society. Once you consider that the function of value concepts is to regulate social behavior and that children develop moral concepts by having to get along with other people, you will see how the development of value concepts can be a universally common experience.

Children in our society play baseball; children in Europe and Latin America play soccer; children in other societies play other organized games. No matter what game is being played, to play the game, children have to agree on certain rules and follow them. Similarly, children in our society exchange baseball cards; children in Switzerland exchange marbles; children elsewhere exchange other objects of value. Regardless of what objects are being exchanged, if the exchange is to take place amicably, the children have to develop a concept of fair exchange and stick to it. In any of these cases, children develop the moral concept by engaging in activity and regulating their behavior according to the concept involved.

A stage of moral judgment represents prescribed modes of deciding how one ought to interact with others in conflict situations. Whether a society teaches children rules about crossing streets or swimming in lagoons, if a child is to distinguish between what he *may* do and what he *must* do, he has to develop a concept of rules as obligatory. Given children's common cognitive limitations (as detailed in Piaget's work) and their commonly limited social experience (involving role taking and participating in social institutions), Kohlberg assumes that they also have limited modes of judgment available to them for resolving moral conflict. Children aged six to seven develop a concept of rules as absolute and of punishment as inevitably following the breaking of rules. Usually by age ten children have also developed the mode of reciprocity and the concept of fair exchange. These commonly available modes of judgment are what universally constitute the first two stages of moral judgment. As children gain more experience within social institutions and learn to take the role of the community, they develop modes of judgment that universally characterize the conventional stages of moral judgment.

Question 2:

Even if one can see that the earlier stages may be universal, what about the later stages? They sound particularly influenced by Western society's moral concepts.[3]

As we mentioned in the last chapter, no doubt stages 5 and 6 are the most controversial that Kohlberg proposes. The influence of Western philosophy is clear in their formulation. Yet

Kohlberg would argue that they, too, are universal, although perhaps not in the same empirical sense as stages 1 through 4.

A study by Carolyn Edwards on the development of moral stages among different populations in Kenya sheds light on the question. Edwards found that adults who had never left their traditional villages displayed mostly stage 2 and stage 3 moral reasoning, whereas adults who had been educated in government-run high schools displayed some stage 4 moral reasoning. Adults who had received a university education displayed greater percentages of stage 4 and stage 5 moral reasoning.[4]

These results can be interpreted in two ways. Traditional village life, with its reliance on traditional institutions and face-to-face interaction among inhabitants, provides *role-taking opportunities* that stimulate the development of moral judgment to stage 3. By participating in the running of village institutions, adults learn to take the perspective of the whole community and to judge their own actions and those of their fellow tribespeople from that perspective. As we reported in the last chapter, stage 3 is a mature (or equilibrated) structure insofar as it proves an adequate mode for dealing with most conflicts arising among people who know one another.

Nevertheless, how do we account for the absence of stage 4 moral reasoning among villagers and for its development among Kenyans educated in high schools and universities? Edwards argues, following Kohlberg, that because villagers do not have much direct experience in participating in the national political and legal systems of Kenya, they do not have the role-taking opportunities necessary for developing to stage 4. The more formally educated Kenyans have these opportunities and are hence more likely to develop to the higher stage. Yet one could also argue that stages 4 and 5 are not indigenous to tribal culture, and that what Edwards has picked up are values and modes of reasoning that Western-educated Kenyans have learned and are teaching to upwardly mobile youth in the high schools and universities.

Kohlberg would claim that we cannot resolve this difference of interpretation on the basis of Edwards's study. To establish a developmental sequence, longitudinal data are needed. Edwards's data, however, are cross-sectional; that is, she did not follow the same village youth over a period of years to note differences among those who remained at home and those who went off to receive a higher education. Thus we cannot tell whether, given the same educational experience, village youth would develop, as urban youth do, to the higher stage of moral judgment.

The finding that no village adults have developed beyond stage 3 does not present a problem to Kohlberg's theory. The theory does not claim that every stage need be present in every society. Rather, Kohlberg says that insofar as every society provides certain institutionally based role-taking opportunities for its members, the members will develop modes of moral judgment that will reflect those role-taking opportunities. The modes of judgment will develop in a given sequence (from stage 1 to 2, etc.), but the sequence may end at stage 3 or stage 4, depending on the social experience available in the given society.

The theory does predict that it is more likely for individuals from economically developed societies to reach higher stages of moral judgment. This is true because, in those societies, individuals are faced with more complex social and moral issues. An examination of stages 4, 5, and 6 will show that they develop as modes for dealing with moral issues arising mainly in complex institutional settings. Two tribes may live alongside each other, and their members may be aware of differences in their social customs, but the problem of the relativity of values will not arise. That problem occurs only in more developed, modern societies, and hence the greater probability of the development of stage 5 in these societies.

Should, however, individuals from less developed societies move through the first four stages and find conventional moral reasoning to be inadequate for dealing with the moral problems they face, they would follow the same developmental progression as individuals from Western societies, developing principles of moral judgment. Kohlberg would cite individuals such as Gandhi as historical examples of this happening.

Critics might say that individuals such as Gandhi were Western-educated and applied what they learned from the West to the East. Kohlberg could respond by asking why the doctrines of human rights and nonviolence were so appealing to Gandhi. Was this only a clever political ploy to use Western "principles" against Western colonialists, or was there something inherent within these doctrines that made moral sense to Gandhi, given his particular political and moral sensitivities? Kohlberg would argue in favor of the latter. He does not believe that moral principles are inherently Western; he believes that they would make sense to any person who has developed through conventional moral reasoning and seen its limitations. Moral principles, as principles of logic, happened to have been articulated most fully in the Western philosophic tradition. Their validity, however, is independent of their original articulation.

Question 3:

By saying that some people develop to "higher" stages than others, isn't Kohlberg claiming that they are better than other people? By extension, isn't he claiming that some societies are more moral than others?

To understand why Kohlberg considers the stages that develop later in the sequence to be "higher" and hence "better," we have to return to his definition of morality: "The term 'moral' refers to decisions based on moral judgments." [5]

Although Kohlberg defines morality in terms of a person's moral judgment, he reminds his readers of two other possible definitions. One could say that to be "moral" is to act morally, or that to be "moral" is to adhere to the norms and laws of one's society. The problem with these definitions is that they do not adequately explain why a given action is considered moral and under what circumstances the action might not be moral. To give two obvious examples, most people would agree that telling the truth is "more moral" than lying and that honoring one's country is "better" than betraying it. Yet, if a bystander saw a gunman chasing a person, the bystander would be under no moral obligation to tell the gunman where his intended victim was hiding. The onlooker might even be morally obligated to lie, or at least to evade the truth. Similarly, if a person's country is involved in what he thinks is an unjust war, he is not necessarily wrong for refusing to serve in that war, even if the government considers such a refusal to be traitorous.

What these examples are meant to illustrate is that an action by itself is neither moral nor immoral. The moral element enters when a person explains *why* he is acting as he is: what in the given circumstances justifies his acting as he does. Not all justifications are equally valid. Quite the opposite. Some justifications, or moral judgments, are more adequate than others. Hence some stages of moral judgments are "better" than others.

A "higher" or "better" moral judgment, then, refers to one that is more "adequate." To follow our first example, a person who says he lied (or would lie) to save the life of an innocent person is offering an intuitively more "adequate" justification for his actions than a person who says he lied (or would lie) to help a friend get in free to the movies. For while it is clear to most of us that saving an innocent life should take precedence over telling the truth, it is not clear that helping a friend save the price of a movie ticket should take precedence over telling the truth.

In referring to "life" taking precedence over "truth," we are returning to our initial definition of moral judgment as the cognitive operation by which a person decides which of his values should take precedence over other values when values conflict. Such value conflicts usually occur when someone is trying to decide how to act and whose claim to honor in a conflict of interest between two or more persons (one of whom may be the actor himself). By saying that some moral judgments are more "adequate," Kohlberg is arguing that (1) some values ought to take precedence over others, and (2) some ways of weighing rights or claims in a moral conflict situation are better than others.[6]

To clarify Kohlberg's first claim, the reader should ask himself or herself what value (see the list on p. 90) should take precedence over the saving of human life. Should property take precedence? Should you sacrifice your property to save someone's life? Should roles of affection take precedence? Should you sacrifice a close relationship with a person to save a life? Should law take precedence? Should you break a law to save a life? Should conscience take precedence? Should you sacrifice a point of conscience (breaking a confidence, engaging in violence, profaning a holy object) to save a life? Should contract take precedence? Should you save the life of a person with whom you have no implicit contract of mutual responsibility? Kohlberg claims that as a person's moral judgment grows more adequate, he will be able to differentiate the value of life from all other values and see that it should take precedence over them. He will also see that saving a person's life is what *ought* to be done, independent of whether he feels like it or whether other people would be likely to do the same.

The second claim is related to the social perspective a person takes on a moral conflict. In a conflict situation, whose interests does one take into consideration and what does one consider to be a legitimate moral claim? We have seen in the last chapter that while people at the preconventional level of reasoning take into consideration only the concrete interests of the individuals involved in the situation, people at the conventional level also take into account the interests of the group or society and the feelings and expectations of the individuals involved. Conventional moral reasoning is more adequate than preconventional because it handles more moral problems, conflicts, or points of view in a more stable or self-consistent way. In the Heinz dilemma, for example, while a subject at stage 2 would not even consider the wife's feelings and expectations or Heinz's obligation as a husband, a subject at stage 3 would focus on these (or similar) considerations. Hence, at the higher stage, the person can handle aspects of the dilemma not yet relevant to the lower-stage definition of the problem.

In turn, moral reasoning at a principled level handles more points of view in a more self-consistent way than does conventional reasoning. Kohlberg understands a moral principle to be "a universal mode of choosing . . . which we want all people to adopt in all [similar] situations." [7] It is more adequate on several counts. First, since a moral principle is a guide to action rather than a rule of action, it allows for greater flexibility. Let us return to our example of abortion. From a conventional perspective, abortion is one of many moral issues about which a person turns to her system of laws and beliefs for a decision on how to act. If her religious system, for example, forbids abortion in most cases, then she is supposed to abide by that ruling. If her political or feminist system supports abortions, she believes they are permissible. But no moral principle prescribes or prohibits abortion. Rather, a principled approach looks at the interests and rights of the parties involved (the mother and the fetus) and asks whose claim in this situation ought to take precedence. Is it more consistent with our understanding of the quality of life to allow the woman to make this decision, or would we be neglecting the fetus's right to physical life if we left the decision entirely to the personal interest of the woman? There would be no one correct answer. In each case the persons involved would have to weigh the issue in relation to their particular situation.[8]

Second, a principled approach is more adequate because it attempts to view the conflict from the perspective of any human being rather than a member of a particular society or religion. From the perspective of one's own society it might make sense to say people ought to be loyal to their country. But would a conventional American also want dissidents in the Soviet Union to be loyal to their country and thereby cease undermining its (self-defined) moral order? Apparently not, given the popular response in this country to Soviet dissidents. How, though, can a person consistently maintain a rule of loyalty to his own country and at the same time encourage disloyalty in other countries? He can do so only if he maintains a principle of being primarily loyal to the preserving of human rights and secondarily loyal to his own country insofar as it preserves human rights. Then he could apply consistent, universalizable criteria to a person in any country who has to decide when to protest and when to support his country's actions.

Kohlberg's claim that principled morality is "better" or "more adequate" than conventional morality is based on a particular philosophic conception of morality. Kohlberg follows the formalist tradition in philosophy, maintaining that moral language is sui generis and has to be understood in its own right. More adequate moral judgments are not "better" because they are truer in a scientific sense or more efficacious in a pragmatic sense. Rather, within the domain of moral language itself are formal criteria, such as differentiation and universalizability, by which one set of moral judgments can be judged as being more or less adequate than another set.

By following a particular philosophic definition of morality, Kohlberg has been able to join philosophy to psychology. He has been able to delineate what a highest stage of moral judgment would have to be like to qualify, by those philosophic criteria, as "truly moral." Given that definition, he has been able to trace the logical steps through which moral judgment develops from its point of emergence in childhood until it reaches that highest stage. In achieving that degree of clarity, Kohlberg has had to accept two important limitations. The first is the criticism by other philosophers that his definition of the highest stages is too narrow. Perhaps more versions of principled morality exist than the ones Kohlberg delineates.[9] The second is that by concentrating on the cognitive-judgmental side of moral development, he has not been able to do full justice to the emotional and behavioral sides of moral development. Moral judgment may be an essential ingredient of moral development, but it is not the whole picture.

This last distinction helps us answer the question at hand. We have to distinguish between a person's having "more adequate moral judgment" and his being "a more moral person." The theory explains how people's judgment develops and implies that the more adequate one's judgment, the greater potential one has to act morally in certain difficult moral conflict situations. Nevertheless, it remains an open empirical question to what extent principled moral agents act on their principles. Even if it can be proven (e.g., in experimental situations) that they are likely to act on principle, it does not necessarily mean that they accomplish more social "good" than people acting on lower stages. A person may be principled and still limit her action to relatively narrow spheres of life. A person may understand what is right and decide to act, but be limited in her effectiveness by an inability to judge correctly how and when her action would prove most helpful to those about whom she is morally concerned. The relation between knowing and doing the good is a complex one.

These empirical questions aside, Kohlberg argues that in another sense it is improper to extend moral-stage theory to a value judgment of who is a better person.

> We need to make clear that our claim that Stage 6 is a more moral mode of thought than lower stages is not the claim that we can or should grade individuals as more or less moral . . . . From a moral point of view, the moral worth of all people is ultimately the same; it is equal . . . . The claim that Stage 6 is a more moral way of thinking is not an assignment of higher moral worth to the Stage 6 individual.[10]

Thus, the better one understands the theory, the clearer one sees that it speaks of the adequacy of structures of moral reasoning and does not classify people as being "more" or "less" moral. People are not stages.

Question 4:

> If Kohlberg's theory concentrates on the development of moral judgment, then what, if anything, does it tell us about the way people act on their judgment? Aren't people more likely to talk about moral values than to act on them?

Yes, people are more likely to talk about moral values than to act on them. Kohlberg cites studies showing that people's moral actions are influenced more by situational factors than by the values they espouse. For example, many people who say cheating is wrong will nevertheless cheat in experimental situations if they perceive a low risk of detection. If they perceive a high risk of detection, they are less likely to cheat. Perceived risk, then, rather than espoused values, seems to inform their actions.[11]

Kohlberg, however, makes a fundamental distinction between people's espoused values and the way they structure their judgments about moral issues. (This is the distinction between content and form elaborated in chapter 3.) Kohlberg asks whether the inconsistency between values and action is equally true of all people in all situations. For example, a minority of subjects in most experimental studies resist cheating even when the risk of detection is low. Kohlberg considers it likely that this minority is made up primarily of people who reason at the higher stages of moral judgment, because people who reason at the higher stages are less likely to be influenced by situational factors and more likely to act consistently on their values.

Richard Krebs, a student of Kohlberg's, tested this hypothesis with sixth-graders.[12] Over 120 students from both working- and middle-class backgrounds were given several experimental cheating tests and were interviewed on Kohlberg's Moral Judgment Interview. The students were almost evenly divided among those who scored primarily stage 1, stage 2, stage 3, and stage 4. The following were the percentages of students at each stage who resisted cheating on all the experimental tests:

Stage	Percent
1	19
2	36
3	22
4	45

The data support Krebs's main hypothesis that the students at stage 4 were less likely to cheat than those at the lower stages. The difference in resistance to cheating between students at stage 4 and all other students proved to be statistically significant. Nevertheless, the data leave us with two major reservations:

1. There is not an even progression from stage to stage, for students at stage 2 were more likely to resist cheating than students at stage 3.
2. Even though students at stage 4 were most likely to resist cheating, a majority (55 percent) at that stage still cheated. Thus it cannot be claimed that each movement up a stage

is likely to decrease cheating or that even at stage 4, which seems to be a turning point, most students resist cheating.

Kohlberg cites (although without reference) another cheating study, this one of college students. It was found that while over 40 percent of the students at the conventional level (stages 3 and 4) cheated, only 11 percent of the students at the postconventional level (stages 5 and 6) cheated. Kohlberg concludes that "the principled subjects are considerably less likely to cheat" and that perhaps by stage 5 we should find a greater consistency on the cheating issue between judgment and action.[13]

The scoring system used now would probably not show stage 6, but because we are referring here to research done previously, we are using the scoring system on which that study was based.

Experimental cheating tests, however, are one step removed from real-life decisions. Subjects may not know that they are being observed for their cheating behavior, but they do know they are involved in an experiment and may not attribute much importance to their actions. Will the same correlations between stage of moral judgment and action hold true in real-life situations?

The one major study that addresses this issues was done in the 1960s as part of a larger study of student activism. Haan, Smith, and Block, three psychologists at the University of California at Berkeley, were studying student activists in the aftermath to the Free Speech Movement of 1964–65. One of their interests was to test the relation between the students' stage of moral reasoning and their decision to join the FSM's protest against the administration's policy.[14]

The background to the protest was a decision by the university's administration to rescind its earlier permission, given to civil rights workers, to solicit funds and organize drives on campus. The civil rights workers decided to contravene this ruling and continue their activities, but the administration called in the police to stop them. In reaction, the Free Speech Movement was formed. It organized a sit-in (the first of the 1960s) at a college hall to protest the administration's actions.

The police were again called, and the protesters were arrested for their disturbance.

A year after the protest, Haan and her colleagues sent out Moral Judgment Interviews to Berkeley students. A total of 214 interviews were returned and reliably scored; of these, 53 were from students who had participated in the sit-in. The respondents' moral stages were spread from stage 2 through stage 6. The following percentage of students at each stage chose to participate in the sit-in:

	Stage 2	Stage 3	Stage 4	Stage 5	Stage 6
Men	60%	18%	6%	41%	75%
Women	33%	9%	12%	57%	86%

By far the highest percentage of those who sat-in were among the stage 6 students.[15] Stage 5 students were far more likely to have sat-in than stage 3 or stage 4 students. Surprisingly, stage 2 male students were almost as likely to have sat-in as stage 6 males. Elliot Turiel has since suggested that in the transition between stages 4 and 5, adolescents stake out a relativistic stance that, while similar in structure to stage 2, is better understood as a substage between stages 4 and 5. This suggestion may apply to these students. They may be acting on perceptions shaped by this transitional stage.[16]

To make sense of the data, we must first consider what kind of moral action a sit-in in protest of an administration's policy is. Clearly, it is different from deciding whether to cheat on a test. Most people (at all moral stages) would say that cheating is wrong, but most people would not agree that a sit-in is morally right. Thus, while the interesting question with cheating is whether people will live up to their espoused values, the Berkeley protest produced two interesting questions: (1) What are people's judgment of the situation? (2) Do people act on their judgment? Fortunately, Haan and her colleagues gathered information about students' perceptions of the situation, so that both questions can be answered.

Only a small percentage of students at the conventional stages joined the protest. Is the action of this majority in accord with their judgment of the situation? Probably; for the logic of conventional reasoning would generally lead to the conclusion that in this situation one ought to abide by the law. Protesting the administration's ruling is not like Heinz's stealing the drug to save his wife's life. Saving a wife's life may justify breaking the law; protesting does not.

For the principled students, however, protesting the administration's ruling did justify breaking the law. Why? They perceived the administration as unjustly infringing on the students' freedom of expression. As a basic human right, comparable to the right to life, the right to free expression takes precedence over one's obligation to abide by the law. When the law infringes on a basic right, one has the right, even the obligation—as long as one is willing to take the consequences of one's actions—to protest the injustice by an act of civil disobedience. The majority of principled students acted on this perception and paid the consequences (their arrests).

The stage 2 students who joined the sit-in perceived the issues differently. They were critical of American society in general and angry in particular at the administration for what they saw as a power play against the students. For them, the issue was not protecting human rights but fighting back against an oppressive figure of authority. They acted on the perception by sitting-in against the administration.

We may conclude, then, that the students' stage of moral judgment did have a direct influence in shaping their perception of the issues involved in the Berkeley protest. Once students formed their judgments, they tended to act on the logic of their stage of moral reasoning.

But how to explain that while acting on their judgment, both stage 2 and stage 6 students decided to join the protest? Was this a truly moral act if it appealed to people at both the highest and lowest stages?

This seeming paradox helps clarify the distinction between a "moral action" and a "behavioral choice." The behavioral choice of sitting-in was neither moral nor immoral. What invests the choice with a moral element is the rational motivation for having sat-in. A moral action by definition involves judgment, feeling, and behavior. Although both sets of students sat in, the students at stage 2 acted to express their anger and get back at the administration. The students at stage 6 acted to protest an infringement of basic rights. Although different motivations led to the same behavioral choice, the two groups of students were involved in two different moral actions. Kohlberg would argue that getting back at an authority is not a principled ethical decision, but protesting an infringement of rights is.

Taken together, the two studies in judgment and action allow us to draw some tentative conclusions about the role of moral judgment in influencing moral action.

1. The hypothesis that people at principled stages will tend to act with greater consistency on their moral judgment draws support from both studies. The data encourage the belief that helping students reach these stages is a worthwhile educational goal insofar as it will influence both judgment and action.

2. We should be cautious about generalizing from these studies to all other possible moral conflict situations. While the cheating study suggests that people at the principled stage are better able to resist temptation, and the Berkeley study suggests that they are more willing to protest injustice, both situations involve relatively straightforward choices. One either cheats or does not cheat; one either joins the protest or watches from the sidelines. In other situations, though, the choices are less clear and the ability to act less straightforward. Sartre's famous example of the Frenchman during World War II who has to choose between joining the Resistance or staying home to care for his aged mother poses a more complex choice. A medical student at Berkeley who would have had to choose between staying on duty at the hospital or joining the protest would have been faced with a similarly complex choice. How principled judgment helps shape such moral choices is an as yet unexplained question.[17]

3. The contrast between the way the students at the conventional stages acted in the two studies suggests that the particular setting plays an important role in promoting consistency between judgment and action.

At Berkeley the conventional students tended to act consistently with their judgment in choosing to uphold law and social order rather than engage in the protest. In the cheating tests, though, most students at stage 3 and half the students at stage 4 did not act consistently with their belief that cheating is wrong. The difference may simply reflect the fact that at Berkeley all one had to do to uphold the law was to refrain from acting (sit-in); in the cheating test one had to actively resist temptation.

There is another possible explanation. At Berkeley the setting seemed to provide a clear conflict between the moral claims of the administration and those of the protesters. The setting had the properties of a real-life moral dilemma, which elicited the moral judgment of all those involved. In contrast, if most people's decision to cheat (on either an experimental or an actual classroom test) hinges primarily on the perceived risk of detection, it is possible that they do not perceive the decision to cheat as involving a moral issue. The classroom setting calls forth a pragmatic, achievement-oriented choice rather than a moral choice. Thus, rather than ask themselves, "Should I cheat?" they ask, "Can I get away with cheating?"

If this suggestion is plausible, it redefines the difference between the higher-stage people who resist cheating and the people who cheat. The former define the situation as involving a moral issue, whereas the latter do not. Hence, while the higher-stage people both exercise their moral judgment and act on it, the other people do not perceive their moral judgment as being relevant and therefore have no opportunity to act on it.

This suggestion implies that one possible way classroom teachers can reduce the likelihood of conventional students' cheating is to help them define cheating as a moral issue. We discuss this in further detail in chapter 7.

Question 5:

Isn't Kohlberg basing a great deal of theory on little data? How much of his theory can really be proven?

This is perhaps the hardest question to answer, because the empirical basis of Kohlberg's theory is shrouded in controversy. It may be best to begin by reviewing how Kohlberg has attempted to validate empirically the existence of stages of moral judgment.

Kohlberg began his empirical study by interviewing seventy-two American boys from the ages of ten to sixteen. On the basis of their responses to his dilemma, he initially worked out the six stages of moral judgment. This study was cross-sectional, however, meaning that each boy was interviewed only once; age trends were established by comparing boys of different ages. Kohlberg realized, though, that to establish his claim of an invariant (nonreversible) sequence of stages, he would have to follow the same children over time to see if each child went through the stages in a set order.[18]

Kohlberg followed fifty of the boys—half of them middle class, half lower class—from his original study. After twelve years, he and Kramer issued a preliminary report in which they found "a picture of autogenetic change as directed and sequential, or stepwise." [19] There were two cases of regression, or backward movement. Some college youth seemed to regress temporarily to a lower stage only to return to their original sequence after college. Some delinquents who went to reform school or jail also regressed as a result of that experience.

Unfortunately, the full findings from that longitudinal study have never been published. Kohlberg has been criticized by some for this failure, but he has insisted that he will publish the study only when his system for scoring Moral Judgment Interviews is worked out in more complete detail. At this time that task is well under way, and the full results should be published in a year or two.

While this longitudinal study has been in progress, a number of other studies have been undertaken. Kohlberg reports studies of boys between the ages of ten and sixteen in cities of Taiwan and Mexico and in isolated villages in Turkey and the Yucatán (Mexico).[20] Other studies have been done in India, Kenya, the Bahamas,[21] and Israel.[22] Of these, only the studies in Turkey, the Bahamas, and Israel were longitudinal. The largest cross-sectional study done to date in the United States was of 237 Americans aged ten to fifty.[23] Many smaller-scale studies have been done in the United States, especially of school-age children.

Two friendly critics have recently reviewed the studies to date. Both have concluded that although we must wait for the publication of Kohlberg's longitudinal study to pass any conclusive judgment, the currently available data generally support the claims of Kohlberg's theory.[24] Less friendly critics have reviewed some of the studies and found them faulty and less convincing.[25] In the field of psychology one has to expect that when the data are incomplete (as they almost always are), psychologists of different theoretical persuasions will view them with varying degrees of acceptance.

We will in a limited space try to review some of the available data so that the reader can get a sense of what can be said with some certainty about the development of moral judgment and what has not yet been proven.[26]

1. Among American middle-class children and adolescents, the following age-related trends have been found:

   a The usage of preconventional stages drops in percentage from age ten to age thirteen. While ten-year-olds use a mixture of stages 1, 2, and 3 in their moral reasoning, thirteen-year-olds use primarily stage 3 reasoning.

   b From ages thirteen to sixteen adolescents' usage of stage 3 remains stable, and a rise occurs in usage of stage 4 reasoning. There is some emergent usage of stage 5 as well.

   c From ages sixteen to twenty there is a consolidation of usage of stage 3 and stage 4; there is some further usage of stage 5 as a minor stage.

2. Among American middle-class adults (aged twenty-one–fifty) we find a predominant usage of stage 3 and stage 4 moral reasoning, with stage 5 reasoning accounting for 15 percent of total stage usage. Thus the conventional stages, which emerge during early adolescence, remain the core structures for adult usage. Stage 5 postconventional reasoning increases in usage, but only among a minority of American adults.

3. A study of lower-middle-class white and lower-class black students from Chicago shows that at age eleven, although both populations use a predominance of preconventional reasoning, the white population uses slightly more stage 3 reasoning than the black population. At age fifteen both groups use a predominance of conventional reasoning.[27] Thus the trend is the same as among middle-class children except that at each age the middle-class children are somewhat more advanced than the lower-middle-class and lower-class children.

4. Trends among middle-class boys from cities in Taiwan and Mexico are similar to those of American middle-class boys from ages ten to sixteen. Among the Taiwanese and Mexicans there is a greater usage of stage 1 at age ten, but by age sixteen they, too, use conventional stages of reasoning predominantly.

5. Among boys of the same age from isolated villages in Turkey and Mexico, we find the same sequence of stages, but the rate of development is much slower. Stage 1 accounts for 70 percent of their reasoning at age ten and for 40 percent at age thirteen. Stages 2 and 3 begin emerging by age thirteen, but only by age sixteen do they equal stage 1 in percentage. Thus there is a developmental sequence, but it is far slower than among the urban youth in the same countries.

These findings show that in the United States and in some other cultures, the development of stages of moral judgment is clearly age-related. The extent of usage of preconventional stages decreases with age, and the extent of usage of conventional stages increases with age. For children between the ages of ten and sixteen, the rate of development is greatest among middle-class Americans, with lower-class American and middle-class Mexican and Taiwanese following somewhat behind. The rate among village children is dramatically slower. There is evidence of some development of stage 5 reasoning among middle-class American adults, but no evidence of the development of stage 6 (using recent scoring standards).

While cross-sectional data cannot establish an invariant sequence of stages, several experimental studies have lent empirical support to this claim. These studies began with the hypothesis that if development through the stages is always in an upward direction, moving sequentially from one stage to the next, then children at a given stage should be most attracted to reasoning that is one stage above their own. This would be so because reasoning at stages lower than their own would be rejected as inadequate. Reasoning at their own stage would seem adequate, but if they are moving upward, reasoning above their own stage would seem more adequate. Reasoning that is too far above their own stage (defined as two stages higher) would be too difficult for them even to comprehend.

Turiel presented a group of seventh-grade American children with stage-related advice on how to resolve a moral dilemma. One third of this group received advice that was one stage below their own level of reasoning, a second third received advice one stage above their own level, and the last group received advice two stages above their own level. In posttesting the children, Turiel found that the children who were presented with advice one stage above their own level were more changed by the advice (they moved closer to the stage of the advice) than were the children presented with the other kinds of advice. Having the least effect was advice two stages above the subject's own level.[28]

Rest presented a group of American adolescents with a list of responses to the Heinz dilemma. The list included one reason at each of the six stages why Heinz should and should not steal the drug to save his wife. The subjects were asked to restate each response in their own words and rank the statements in order of how good they were. Rest found that the subjects tended to rank low all responses at stages below their own, to restate responses at two or more stages above their own in terms of their own stage, and to prefer the response at one stage above their own to the response at their own stage.[29] Thus Rest, like Turiel, was able to show that reasoning one stage above the subject's own level is what has most appeal for him.

Having reviewed the most widely cited studies on the development of moral judgment, we can respond to question 5 by admitting that a lot of empirical work remains to be done in substantiating the claims of Kohlberg's theory. Even after the results from the essential longitudinal study are published, many unanswered questions will remain. Some of these questions have already been raised and are the subject of recent research. Here are a few of the more interesting questions and studies:

1. Kohlberg's longitudinal data begin with children at age ten. Yet, Piaget's original work on moral judgment showed that four-year-old children were beginning to exercise social and moral reasoning. As we noted in chapter 3, William Damon has been studying development from the ages of four to ten.[30] Work remains to be done in integrating Damon's findings with Kohlberg's.

2. Curiously, Kohlberg began his work by studying only American boys. Although most other studies (including Piaget's) have included both sexes in their samples, Carol Gilligan has wondered whether Kohlberg's formulation of the conventional and postconventional stages has not been biased by the original all-male sample (which continues to be the sample for the longitudinal study).[31] Gilligan cites a number of studies showing that men are more likely than women to develop to stage 4 and stage 5; women tend to use stage 3 as their dominant mode of reasoning. Gilligan suggests that this apparent sex difference may reflect the current formulation of the higher stages more than women's failure to develop to these stages. The current formulation places great stress on the development of abstract principles of justice and welfare, but ignores such personal and interpersonal issues as the conflict between caring for others and taking responsibility for one's own actions. Women's development might become more visible were the research to give equal weight to both abstract and personal issues.

3. The lack of data on adult development beyond stage 5 has led John Gibbs to question whether stage 6 is to be con-

sidered a stage of natural development or an ideal equilibrium point in Kohlberg's system.[32] Until more work is done on adult development, neither Gibbs's nor Gilligan's questions can be answered.

4. Kohlberg has frequently claimed that his moral stages are universal. Nevertheless, although he and others have published (as cited above) results of some cross-sectional studies of development in other cultures, the claim to universality remains unsupported by sufficient data. The necessary data would have to come from longitudinal studies. Fortunately, the first of such studies will soon appear in print.[33]

5. The hypothesized relation between moral judgment and actions depends, as we noted, on the assumption that in conflict situations people use the same stages of reasoning that they use in solving hypothetical dilemmas in a Moral Judgment Interview. Two recent studies have sought to discover whether children use the same state of reasoning in facing real-life choices as they do in reasoning about hypothetical dilemmas. Susan DeMersseman found, using Damon's justice stages, that children aged four to nine did use the same stages of reasoning in both domains.[34] Robert Selman and Dan Jaquette have begun studying the social interaction of ten- to fourteen-year-old children who have special emotional and learning disabilities. The initial findings of Selman and Jaquette show interesting consistencies between hypothetical and real-life social and moral reasoning.[35] This is another area that needs, and is likely to receive, further study.

Question 6:

What does Kohlberg see as the implications of his theory of moral development for moral education?

Since the rest of this book is devoted to answering this question, we can conclude this chapter by briefly describing Kohlberg's involvement in the field of moral education.

There have been two strands in Kohlberg's educational work:

(1) incorporating within the classroom curriculum a concern for the discussion of moral issues and the stimulation of moral growth, and (2) restructuring the school environment to allow for greater democratic participation by students in the school's governing process. Underlying these efforts are two assumptions central to Kohlberg's philosophy of education: (1) schooling inevitably involves the transmission of values; [36] and (2) the aim of education ought to be the development of students' inherent capacities. [37] These two assumptions will be made more explicit as we review Kohlberg's educational endeavors.

The stimulus to get involved with classroom curriculum came from one of Kohlberg's students, Moshe Blatt. Blatt hypothesized that if Turiel (see above) could experimentally induce a small degree of change in children's moral judgment simply by exposing them to moral arguments one stage above their own, then a curriculum based on a consistent exposure to such arguments should have an even greater effect on children's development. With Kohlberg's agreement, Blatt ran a pilot project for twelve weeks in a Jewish Sunday school; once a week he discussed moral dilemmas with sixth-grade students. (The students were tested for stage of moral judgment before the project began.) After a dilemma was presented, the students were asked to propose solutions to the dilemma and explain why their resolution was best.

> As these arguments developed, the experimenter would take the "solution" proposed by a child who was one stage above the majority of the children . . . and clarify and support that child's argument. The experimenter elaborated this solution until he felt that the children understood its logic and seemed convinced that its logic was reasonable or fair. The experimenter made it a point to leave as much of the argument to the children as possible; he stepped in to summarize the discussion, to clarify, add to the argument and occasionally present a point of view himself. [38]

At the conclusion of this project Blatt retested the students and found that 63 percent of the class had gone up one full stage in their moral reasoning. With that discovery, developmental moral education began in earnest.

Blatt attempted to replicate these findings in very different educational settings. He set up a moral discussion program in four public school classrooms. Two were sixth grades and two were tenth grades. One sixth- and one tenth-grade class were made up of lower-class black students. All the students were pretested. Half the students participated in teacher-led moral discussions, while the other half participated in peer-led moral discussions. Overall, eighteen sessions were held; they were conducted twice a week for forty-five minutes each. At the conclusion of the program the students were retested. Students in the teacher-led groups showed an average increase of one third of a stage, while students in the peer-led groups showed less of an increase.

Although Blatt's second study was not as encouraging as his first, his work opened the way for others to set up discussion programs similar to his in other educational settings. Some of these programs met with success by stimulating development, but others were less successful.[39] On the basis of his experience with such programs, Kohlberg has concluded that moral change is most likely to occur when discussions succeed in arousing *cognitive conflict* among participants. When a participant is exposed to other views based on moral reasoning higher than his own, he may become unsure of the adequacy of his original position and begin to consider the merits of the other positions. He does not then simply switch positions; rather, he begins the process of restructuring his own way of reasoning about moral issues. The change that the posttest picks up (which is usually one third to one half a stage change) reflects the process of reconsideration and reorganization.

Although moral discussion programs have succeeded in stimulating moral growth, by themselves they do not constitute a curriculum for moral education. They are generally not integrated into the larger curriculum, nor do they aim to affect the student's educational experience in more than a limited way. From the time of the Blatt study Kohlberg has clearly stated that his goal is to develop a more encompassing program of moral education:

If brief periods of classroom discussion can have a substantial effect on moral development, a pervasive, enduring and psychologically sound concern for the school's influence upon moral development should have much deeper effects. Such a concern would pervade the curriculum areas of social studies, law education, philosophy and sex education, rather than representing a new curriculum area. More deeply, it would affect the social atmosphere and justice structure of the school.[40]

Over the past years Kohlberg, his colleagues, and his students have been working on extending the principles of developmental moral education to existing and new curricula.[41] Some of these attempts are reviewed in the chapters that follow, and we leave further discussion for them.

Parallel to this curriculum strand has been an effort to "affect the social atmosphere and justice structure of the school." Much goes on in schools besides formal learning. Schools are places in which students and teachers spend a good part of their time five days a week, ten months a year. As a social institution, schools are characterized by what Philip Jackson has called the crowds, the praise, and the power. Students have to learn to live as a member of a crowd of peers; they have to work hard to gain praise and avoid the censure of their peers and teachers; and they have to learn to either abide by or dodge the rule and authority structure set up by the administration and the teachers. Some observers have argued that students learn more, especially in social behavior and moral values, from the "hidden curriculum" than from the explicit, formal curriculum.[42]

Kohlberg believes that the hidden curriculum offers a rich opportunity for educators to involve students in moral learning. Although students can learn much from reading about and discussing social and moral issues, there is no substitute for participating in the deliberation on real-life social and moral issues. Since such issues arise naturally within the context of school life, why not, Kohlberg asks, use these opportunities for involving students in this deliberation? Why only teach about democracy when one can also practice democracy within the context of the school?

Kohlberg has embarked on two experiments in educational democracy. The first was within the context of a prison.[43] The second was with an alternative school within an urban high school.[44] The initial sense of those who have participated in the programs is that if they can maintain their viability, their potential influence on the lives of their students is probably greater than even the best formal classroom curriculum.

There is a long road from Blatt's experimental program to a democratic, alternative high school. Along the way there are many options in developmental moral education from which educators can profitably choose. The rest of this book is devoted to guiding the interested educator in how to choose and put into effect one or more of these options.

Part II
PRACTICE

5

The Art of Moral Education: The Teacher's Role

The first half of this book was devoted to a detailed discussion of Kohlberg's theory of moral development and related basic research. The separation of moral development theory from the practice of moral education in the chapters that follow is intentional. Organizing the book in this way parallels our approach to teacher training in moral education.

At the beginning of teacher in-service workshops we explore the question raised in chapter 1, "Why moral education?" Next we present the psychological and philosophical foundation of Kohlberg's theory to answer another question, "Why *this* particular approach to moral education?" Only then do we take the leap from theory into practice.

Our experience convinces us that a careful approach to theory helps teachers generate more effective and more creative learning experiences for their students. As we stated at the beginning of the book, we are skeptical of a "bandwagon" approach

113

to moral education. In leading in-service teacher-training workshops, we commonly find a premature rush to practice. It is natural for teachers, overwhelmed by the demands of daily life in the classroom, to seek a "quick-and-easy recipe" for becoming moral educators.

We are aware, however, that being an effective moral educator is no easy task. As a result, we are committed to the idea that a fundamental understanding of moral development theory and research, and a thoughtful, critical attitude toward the strengths and limitations of Kohlberg's theory, is necessary for sound practice. Theory as no more than an afterword to various teaching "techniques" does injustice to the complexity of both theory and practice.

We are vitally interested in the possibilities that a *variety* of experimental strategies may hold for furthering our knowledge of theory and better educational practice. At the same time, we feel that a basic understanding of the psychological principles underlying the theory gives teachers the awareness of what it means to become a moral educator and the ability and confidence to apply these notions on their own. On the basis of their research in classrooms, moral educators have identified a pedagogy that relates specifically to fostering students' moral development. Often, what is *not* said about these teaching strategies is that they assume a prior knowledge of the teacher's role and of prerequisite teaching skills.

In moving from theory to practice teachers must do two things. First, in their thinking they must reexamine their teaching role. That role is (1) to create cognitive conflict and (2) to stimulate social perspective taking in students. These two principles derive directly from the theories of Piaget and Kohlberg. Second, in their behavior teachers need to set in motion certain patterns of social interaction. We therefore present pedagogical steps, based on theory and research in classrooms, known to foster students' moral reasoning. These steps include the development of moral awareness, the art of asking questions, and the creation of a positive classroom atmosphere conducive to moral development.

The teaching skills suggested in this chapter are intended to link a cognitive-developmental conception of teaching to the major task of curriculum development, presented in the next chapter. In both chapters we have selected, as often as possible, unedited excerpts of classroom dialogue, teachers' daily journals, and curriculum materials. These examples include a variety of age levels. They range from lesson plans and self-evaluations of teachers beginning to implement moral education to transcripts of tape-recorded class sessions conducted by teachers with extensive experience in moral education. It is important, we feel, to present the unedited words of real teachers and students to illuminate the process of linking theory and practice.

A CONCEPTION OF TEACHING

In our work we have found that teachers are not able to begin curriculum practice until they reexamine their assumptions about their teaching role in the classroom. Three themes highlighted in the beginning of this book are fundamental to this paradigm shift: (1) the necessity of increasing our own awareness of moral issues before we can expect students to do so, (2) the recognition that many teacher and student interactions have a moral dimension, and (3) the realization that certain kinds of social interaction are more conducive than others to moral development.

This may seem quite an undertaking. Not only do teachers have to continue teaching under the usual pressures and constraints to which they are subject; in addition, we are asking them to step back a moment from the day-to-day rhythm of classroom life and question their assumptions and teaching philosophy. This is not easy. Further, for most of us, a personal reassessment of this dimension poses a significant risk. The experience of Phyllis Hophan, a third-grade teacher who had been taught Kolhberg's moral development theory and pedagogy, may provide insight into the kind of rethinking necessary to fill the moral educator role of teachers:

"It seemed simple enough at first," wrote Phyllis . . . of her feelings as she prepared to embark on a program of moral discussion in her classroom. "I had gained a general understanding of Kohlberg's stages. I was using a purchased kit. As long as I followed the questions in the manual, it seemed as if I could work with 24 children at once and surely 'goodness and mercy would follow them all the days of their lives.' Well, it didn't happen. The discussions were awkward, flat."

What went wrong? "I spent a great deal of time analyzing my questioning technique," teacher Hophan says, "and I found these problems : (1) I have fixed values, and my style of questioning made clear my feelings that I had the right answer and we were just playing a game to see who could guess what it was; I became aware of voice tones and facial expressions that slanted even the ready-made questions in the manual. (2) Because I perpetuated the unspoken belief that I was the sole source of wisdom, the children spoke only to me in response to my questions. (3) Not being able to see the dilemma from many points of view, I could not grasp all the possible implications—my questions consequently dealt with only the most obvious problems and therefore I could not carry discussions for any length of time. (4) I gave subtle approval to those children who responded in ways that showed higher stages of reasoning—even calling on them when no one else volunteered. (5) Since I truly felt that there was a 'right solution,' I dragged the discussion along, and prompted the 'leaders' in the group to give me that solution. At that point we concluded the discussion, leaving the children with no conflict at all."

Undaunted, this teacher took the following steps to try to solve her problem: "I spent many hours," she says, "practicing writing my own questions and then comparing them to those written for the same dilemma in the manual." She reduced the size of the discussion group to twelve, then six, then three—finding that the most animated discussions came in groups of six. She encouraged interaction among the children by directing responses away from herself with questions such as, "How do you feel about what _____ said?" To get at the reasoning behind opinions, she listed the "because's" offered for each proposed solution to a dilemma, and focused the discussions on those. To prevent children from looking to her for the "right answer," she took "devil's advocate" stands opposing fairness and advocating points of view unacceptable to the group.

Teacher Hophan also began to view her classroom through a different lens: "Suddenly I saw that the hours of the day were filled with real, immediate moral dilemmas." She decided that at the end of each week the children would discuss a slice of moral life from their classroom. During the week, they were invited to complete a sentence written on a chart at the front of the room: "This was the week when _____." On Friday, the class eagerly dicussed the chart's various entries: e.g., "there were fights on the morning bus," "someone had money taken," "Mrs. _____ kept the projector too long and we couldn't see that movie because you had to send it back." Having the problems posted ahead of time, teacher Hophan says, "gave me time to contemplate all aspects of the problem. I became less inclined to favor my first solution." Moreover, talking about in-school problems led children to raise dilemmas from their lives outside school and "many very rewarding discussions resulted."

In these exploratory efforts to develop children's moral reasoning, Phyllis Hophan hit upon . . . insights that we have come to regard as fundamental to the enterprise of being a moral educator. One is that morality begins at home. Any of us setting out to raise the moral development of someone else would do well to take stock personally, and to make a conscious attempt to live out the same moral values, such as empathy, tolerance, and respect for others, that we hope to foster in our students.

"I became very aware," teacher Hophan says, "that my personality and my own moral development were the cause of my inability to construct the environment I was seeking in my room." One of the things that greatly helped her, she says, was the chance to share problems and trade ideas each week with other teachers who were also trying their hand at moral discussions. "I practiced listening to others—to their points of view. If I've learned anything at all in the last three months, it's that no one can ask an open-ended question without first having an open mind. I had to clean house before I invited the children in." [1]

Let us reexamine Phyllis Hophan's self-reflections in detail to see what we may learn from her first attempts to become a moral educator. She describes six problems she encounters.

One: She realizes that she has not confronted her own moral beliefs and values system adequately. Thus, the first time she gives her students the opportunity to express their opinions about moral problems she is unprepared to cope with her own impulse to give them the "right answer," her own belief. The first step of the moral educator is to examine her own moral judgments, to open her mind to the divergent beliefs of others concerning what constitutes fair solutions to moral problems.

Two: This teacher avoids confronting the moral dimensions of the institution of which she is a part. Yet moral issues are inherent in the process and content of schooling. Questions of what is right and fair, what teachers' obligations are to their students, and what students' responsibilities are to one another are at the core of every classroom. Nevertheless, as Phyllis Hophan discovers, unless these moral components are recognized and examined, open-ended discussion of moral dilemmas becomes merely an "event," isolated from student learning. Teachers need to ask themselves how moral issues affect the fabric of daily classroom living.

Three: Phyllis Hophan's struggle reflects a previously unexamined belief in the centrality of her own authority in the classroom. Neglecting to take into account the impact on her students of her role as the "sole source of wisdom," Hophan becomes baffled when her students show little inclination to take risks in open-ended moral discussions. Moral educators need to ask themselves, "What is the effect of my authority role on what my students say and do?" As discussed in chapter 1, authority can *prevent* students from making certain statements. Moral educators need to be willing to see that students benefit from learning how to express their moral judgments openly and take personal stands on important moral questions. Educating students to think for themselves means that teachers cannot direct all the questions and answers.

Four: Phyllis Hophan realizes that her ability to understand her students' many perspectives on the same moral problem is limited. Trying to anticipate what students may say about a moral dilemma means that teachers first have to try to walk in their students' shoes. The adult needs to see the problem as young students conceive it: What is the conflict *for them?* This important social role-taking capacity is what lights the spark of open-ended moral discussion. Again, the teacher needs to broaden the way she sees others; to begin to understand that children and adolescents have the capacity to make their own moral judgments with a logic unique to their developmental level.

Five: Phyllis Hophan sees the limitations in her ability to ask good questions that stimulate interesting and challenging discussion. It takes time to learn to pose questions that expand people's notions of what is right, open their minds to new perspectives, generate new questions, and stimulate continued self-reflection long after discussion with others ends.

Six: This teacher recognizes her difficulty with group-management skills. We often mistakenly assume that the ability to listen and communicate effectively "automatically" occurs in certain groupings of people, but not in others. As Phyllis Hophan painfully learned, adults have the responsibility to help children with this basic process of group socialization. Unless children can listen to one another, learning through discussion will not take place.

Phyllis Hophan's experiences are not unique. In being honest with herself and in sharing those self-revelations with us, she helps us to see more clearly the problems and tasks that face all beginning moral educators. The rest of this chapter seeks to detail and clarify these tasks.

The model described here is designed to take the educator step by step through the process of becoming a moral educator, with developmental theory as an overriding rationale. Our concern in this chapter is with teacher tasks rather than student outcomes. Our intention is to take the perspective of the teacher who has never implemented Kohlberg's theory in practice. Each portion of the model defines the teacher's task, explains the reason behind each step, and offers specific examples of how to implement each idea.

Model for Implementing Developmental Moral Education

General task:
1. Understanding the nature of moral conflict from a developmental perspective

Specific task:
a) Recognizing different moral conflict for different age groups

General task:
2. Understanding the elements that promote moral growth

Specific task:
a) Creating cognitive conflict

b) Taking the perspective of students and stimulating their perspective-taking ability

General 3. Developing the awareness of moral issues
task:

Specific   *a*) Using a variety of moral dilemmas: hypothet-
tasks: ical and real dilemmas
       b) Using daily opportunities in the classroom to
       heighten moral awareness

General 4. Developing questioning strategies
task:

Specific   *a*) Beginning strategies to introduce open-
tasks: ended discussions
         (1) Highlighting the moral issue
         (2) Asking "why?" questions
         (3) Complicating the circumstances
         (4) Using personal and naturalistic examples
         (5) Alternating real/hypothetical problems
       b) In-depth strategies to facilitate moral growth
         (1) Refining the questions
         (2) Highlighting contiguous stage arguments
         (3) Clarifying and summarizing
         (4) Role-taking strategies

General 5. Creating a facilitative classroom atmosphere
task:

Specific   *a*) Planning the physical arrangement
tasks: *b*) Organizing effective groupings
       c) Modeling acceptance
       d) Fostering listening and communication
       e) Encouraging student-to-student interaction

General 6. Anticipating difficulties of practice
task:

Specific   *a*) Anticipating the effects of peer pressure
tasks: *b*) Understanding the problems in examining
       authority roles
       c) Understanding the effect of cognitive conflict
       on students
       d) Recognizing the limitations of verbal activity
       e) Learning to accept occasional failures

General 7. Experiencing personal cognitive conflict as the
task: teacher

THE MORAL EDUCATION MODEL IN PRACTICE

Before guiding the reader step by step through this model, we wish to convey a context for our discussion of the model. This section presents the first half of a thirty-minute moral discussion videotaped in an eighth-grade social studies classroom in Brookline, Massachusetts. The teacher, Margot Stern Strom, comments on the class at the close of the dialogue. Several major teaching strategies are noted in brackets as overall focus issues in Margot's follow-up discussion. These are (1) the importance of a trusting classroom atmosphere; (2) the identification and clarification of cognitive moral conflict; (3) focus on moral reasoning; (4) stimulation of perspective taking; and (5) development of student skills in the areas of reasoning, communicating, listening, and questioning. In addition to noting these strategies, the reader may wish to identify key characteristics of the different stages of moral reasoning used by these thirteen-year-olds.

[Asks for identification and clarification]

Teacher: Today we are going to discuss a conflict situation, too, similar to the kind of discussion we had yesterday in the library for those of you who were there, discussing the busing situation in Boston. And we talked about all kinds of reasons why people want their children bused or not bused, and we tried to figure out what makes a person a member of a mob and so on. We are going to talk about something a little different. Read it to yourselves and we will see if we can come up with some reasons as to why some action should or should not be taken. Read it to yourselves. Tell me what happens.

Boy: There is a man who is unemployed and he is dressed rather poorly and he is standing in front of a rather nice house and sees some milk that is unguarded and he is trying to figure out whether he should go get it or not.

Girl: His children are hungry. His youngest child, the baby, cries constantly from hunger, so it is not just he that is hungry, from lack of money, it is all the rest of his family.

Boy: He has no more savings.

Boy: And he has borrowed a lot of money and he was given welfare, and he still did not have enough money to support his family.

Boy: There are four quarts of milk, should he take one?

[Identifies moral conflict; focuses on reasoning; evidence of trusting atmosphere]

Teacher: Should he steal a quart of milk from the steps of the home for his children? How many of you think he should? Right now, raise your hands. One, two, three, four, five, six, seven. How many think he should not? Raise your hands. One, two, three, four, five, six. How many are undecided? I would like the undecideds to come here with me, the shoulds to come here, and figure out the very best reasons why he should steal the milk. Spend three or four minutes. And over here the should nots. (*A small group of students who think he should not steal.*)

Boy: He shouldn't because that is stealing.

Girl: Because he could be put in jail for it. [Elements of stage 1]

Boy: He shouldn't because he can find a job sooner or later, and he should because—or he shouldn't even though he is starving—

Boy: He should, because he can't afford milk himself. And he shouldn't because the other person . . .

Girl: He should just ask for a quart of milk.

Boy: That is what I think, that he should ask.

[Focuses conflict]

Teacher (*moving from group to group*): Stay with the situation, that the man is deciding whether or not he should steal it.

Boy: He should because the people are rich and he isn't. They have plenty and he doesn't.

Boy: No, they can afford milk. They can afford the four quarts, so they can afford a couple of more quarts.

Teacher: Can you get a couple of more ideas down?

Boy: They shouldn't because . . . even though he is starving he should have some friends around who are moral, but he shouldn't because . . .

Boy: It is perfectly natural . . .

(All talking. A few minutes later, whole class together again.)

[Identifies conflict; focuses on moral reasoning]

Teacher: Specifically, some of the reasons that are listed here, you go over them and read them, okay? Could we have a spokesperson for those people who think the man in this particular situation and, as Bob points out, what if we need to change the laws; but under these laws today, whatever we know them as, should this person steal the milk? These people say yes, what are the main reasons?

Boy: His children are starving and the house is nice, so the people probably have money to buy more. And the owners probably don't need it as much as the person stealing it. [Elements of stage 2]

Girl: They get four quarts a day.

Teacher (writing on the board): The owner probably does not need it as much, seeing that they get four quarts a day. The undecided people also wrote a list of shoulds and should nots that they were thinking about. What is on your list, undecided people, that is not here?

Boy: Here is one point, that it may be possible for the mother to nurse her children.

[Focuses on *moral* conflict]

Teacher: We don't know that and say it isn't.

Boy: Forget that one. This is why he shouldn't.

Teacher: Stay on the should.

Boy: We don't have anything to add, we have all that.

Teacher: Can we have somebody for the should nots? Read them to us.

Boy: First of all, he should not because if he does steal the milk, he will be in debt more. If they found out he stole it, he will still be in debt more. He will be fined or put in jail. [Elements of stage 2]

[Encourages his communi- cation; tries to understand his perspective]

Teacher: Who is "they"?

Boy: If the people who owned the milk found out, then he will be in debt to them. This is the law, and if everybody stole milk from people, there would be people running around with hoards of milk and . . . [Elements of stage 3]

Boy: If he stole it he might be put in jail and then his family would not have any way to earn money. [Elements of stage 2]

Teacher: Does anybody want to add to the *should not* list?

Boy: If there was any chance that he might find a job and later on he might find a job and then he could have paid for the milk. I am not saying that he will find it then, but he might be able to.

[Focusing on moral reasoning]

Teacher: On your main list there, what are the main reasons why he should not steal the milk?

Boy: Because he is stealing. Just for the fact you are stealing. [Elements of stage 1]

Girl: We have one, even though he is starving . . . it is immoral.

[Encourages
questioning.
Tries to under-
stand perspec-
tive]

Teacher: As a point of discussion, just to open it up, what does the comment mean it is immoral here?

Girl: He should not steal from other people. These other people worked for their stuff, they worked for their money and they are entitled to it, also, and he isn't really. And it could be thought of that though he shouldn't he really needs it. [Elements of stage 2]

Teacher: So you are still undecided?

Boy: Yes.

Teacher: What did you say?

Boy: Mike said it was immoral, and I was going to say that, too.

Teacher: (*Unintelligible.*) . . . trying to help you decide.

Girl: He is like going according to a *higher moral law,* saying he has to support these people, they are my family, they are my blood and I have to keep them alive. They are people, they were born and they have a right to survive, I've got to do this for them. [Elements of stage 3]

[Tries to
understand
perspective]

Teacher: You are saying reasons he should. The right to live and responsibility. What responsibility does this man have, what are you thinking about?

Boy: He has the responsibility that the others have the right to live. The other responsibilities are the same thing, saying it is my responsibility because they can't go out and get the stuff, I have to get it to them, it is my responsibility to do that.

Teacher: What do you have to say?

Boy: If I were him I would walk to the next store, across the street and say, I would ring the doorbell, or whatever they have and I would say, "Hi, I live across the street from you and I don't have a job, I've gone broke, I couldn't live on welfare or anything else, can I borrow some milk, or can I have some milk to keep my family alive?"

[Focuses on reasoning]

Teacher: I understand, but at this point, in this particular conflict situation we want to know, should he or should he not.

Boy: I said he should. (*Why?*) Because he has his family that is starving. They might die and he might need some, too, it doesn't say that he does. But I would want to keep my family alive, just like he would. [Elements of stage 2]

[Stimulates perspective taking]

Teacher: (*Unintelligible.*) . . . agrees with Brian, the should people. What if this man knows his family well, and knows that they would not want to steal the milk, they would not want him to break the law, what should he do then? Brian?

Brian: Then I would ask them to go across the street and ask them.

[Focuses conflict by perspective taking]

Teacher: Anybody else from the should side; you know, he should and yet the family does not want him to, what should he do then?

Boy: I still think he should. I think Brian is right. He should ask if he could borrow it. His wife wouldn't get upset; he would still have the milk. Either way he should get the milk, if he borrowed it. His wife might be stubborn and not drink it or whatever, because he took it, and if he borrowed it, his wife . . . (*unintelligible*) and she might be better off for it.

Teacher: Paul?

Paul: I am saying, some kids were saying before, he shouldn't take it. So if he did take it and got caught, then he would have less of a chance of getting a job later. But it says here that he was unemployed for some time, and if he has been unemployed for some time and *on welfare and everything, it is doubtful that he will get a job.*

[Refocuses on moral conflict]

Teacher: Do you think he should or should not steal the milk?

Paul: I think he should.

[Focuses on reasoning]

Teacher: What is the main reason you think he should?

Paul: I think he should because the children are starving and the same reason as most people because it is not that big a risk he is taking.

[Tries to understand his perspective]

Teacher: You made the statement it is not that big a risk. What do you mean?

Paul: I mean what has he got to lose really? Unless he gets caught, but still even then, it won't be against their welfare, he just won't have any milk and not much can be done for him, then he will be worse off. [Elements of stage 2]

[Stimulates conflict]

Teacher: He could be separated from his family for some time. But you still think it is more important for him to get the milk?

Boy: Yes.

Paul: I think he should not because if he takes it once and everything works out, and he gets the family the milk, and nobody notices it and he does not get caught or anything, he is going to be tempted to do it again and again. So I think he should take it, though, so that the children are not starving. [Elements of stage 2]

Teacher: Let's hear from Tom and Mark and Mary Ann, Bob, Ralph. (*Their hands are raised.*)

Tom: When he takes the stuff he will do it over and over again and then when he starts taking more stuff, he gets real . . . and gets caught and will probably be in jail for a long time. [Elements of stages 1 and 2]

Teacher: So you think he should not steal the milk.

Tom: You said he will not be able to support his family, but he is not supporting his family too well right now.

Girl: But if he steals the milk he will probably be in a long time and his family . . .

Boy: I know, I just wanted to say that.

Teacher: Do you have something else to say, Mark?

Mark: What else could he have done? It is not definite that he will go on and steal bigger things, but it is definite that if he steals milk, his kids will get milk. I changed my mind from undecided to he should, because no matter what he gets for a jail sentence, no matter what happens to him, he still has to feed his family and that's why he should steal it, because it doesn't matter if he gets caught.

Teacher: Mark changed his mind from undecided to should. Mike, have you changed your mind at all? (*Mark, Mike, and Dave were in original undecided group.*)

Mike: It is a pretty equal balance.

Teacher: Dave, have you?

Dave: No.

Teacher: You are going to add something?

Boy: He is going to steal the milk one day, right, he takes the milk. If he takes that, it is not going to last very long and he is going to go back and take some more. [Elements of stage 2]

[Focuses on moral conflict]

Teacher: So what do you think he should or should not do?

Mary Ann: I think he should not and I changed my mind, because first of all, if I was the guy and supported the family, I would think the family is dying, for one quart of milk, maybe I *will* get in trouble for this, but I will write the guy a note saying I will pay you back soon, I am broke, I can't do anything, my family is going to die, I will pay you back as soon as I get the money. [Elements of stage 2]

Teacher: So you would now, you changed your mind. Bob?

Bob: First of all, I can see that his family is dying and I know how much a quart of milk is, and I don't think a quart of milk is going to go a long way at all, really. And second of all, getting back to the responsibility that he has for his children, well, of course he has responsibility. Nobody said these are your children and your responsibility, wham bam. He made a choice to have children and he had them. So it is his problem.

[Refocuses on moral conflict]

Teacher: Bob, do you think in this situation he should or should not steal the milk?

Bob: I think he should not.

[Focuses on reasoning]

Teacher: What is the main reason in your mind that you think he should not?

Bob: Because of the law. Think about it, if everybody did it, what would it be like? First of all, the welfare laws, in this case, if they are being unfair to them, then they should be revised, looked at and changed. But right at the moment, he should not steal the milk. [Elements of stage 4]

(Discussion continues.) [2]

Before discussing this dialogue, it is important to state that this videotaped discussion represents only one circumscribed format of a moral discussion—an intense focus on the moral reasoning aspects of a moral conflict. It was intended to be a highly structured, single-issue concentration on one question, "Should the man steal the milk to feed his children?" The teacher of the class, Margot Strom, comments on the limitations of such a purpose:

> A demonstration tape like this is out of context: it's selective, done for a purpose—to demonstrate certain skills and concepts to other teachers. I made a contract with my students to do it that way. The discussion was stimulating to them, and they still say, "I remember the Milk Dilemma," and they know the vocabulary. But as far as my being comfortable I would have asked more "What if" questions. I see the difference between would and should, but I don't believe in eliminating the "would" altogether. That's a limitation in this taped discussion. I also would have probed the students' thinking more deeply, to vary the kinds of questions I asked. I would rather see the flow of the discussion come from them. You can just tell when that happens, you can just feel it. But you learn from these things too. What I did in this tape helps teachers with some of the things they want to know.[3]

Despite these limitations, we still gain valuable understanding of the basic teaching process. In the rest of this interview Margot Strom summarizes five major areas she thinks about in organizing her classroom discussions.

1. The development of a trusting classroom atmosphere:

The start of any discussion is trust. The first question we must ask ourselves is, "How do you teach without any trust?" And the answer is, "You don't." There is going to be no good teaching going on unless you can first build some kind of contract with the students. The first step before anything else is the atmosphere of the class. And that is really an adult, teacher responsibility.

The most interesting thing about this demonstration tape is that when teachers see the tape, they say, "My gosh, the kids are talking to each other. They must be special kids." They ask me, "Are these your brightest kids?" What they don't see is that we have worked hard on having discussions go on like that. They don't see a moral dilemma discussion. What they say is, "That's a great class." What is great to them is that they see kids sitting in a circle instead of in rows of chairs, actually talking together, getting up to work in groups, and following a task together; that is, doing what these teachers see as rather an orderly lesson. They're not seeing kids talk about moral dilemmas—which says that teachers want to know, "How do you build trust with students?"

What I try to do is to reaffirm a close, cooperative atmosphere. I remind the students that we're here together, we're in my class; that they've just come out of recess, for example, and we need to redefine where we are, who we are, how things have been going, any successes we've been having today. I do that. If the chairs are all scattered, we all come together; we make an atmosphere first. I'll look at a child who has glasses for the first time and say, "Gee, I notice you have glasses," and we'll talk about it. Then I remind the kids of the tasks to be done. We have only thirty minutes, and I'll say, "We have this, this, and this to accomplish today."

I work on organizational skills with them, helping to orient them to my classroom, to help the consistency from day to day. It's like renegotiating the contract a little bit everyday. They know they are going to feel secure in my classroom because there are certain things that are consistent. It's verification for them.

2. Identifying and clarifying cognitive moral conflict (through dilemmas):

The first thing you have to be able to do is to recognize dilemma situations in all materials that are raised in class. I see that in this tape I started off this dilemma reminding the kids that yesterday in the paper there was a discussion of busing, reclarifying for them that we naturally discussed that in class as a dilemma situation. Then the teacher might remind the students that they discussed "What is a dilemma?" earlier. It's very important to discuss vocabulary, since we now know that children will remember the meaning of words through their own experience. One of my key things is that you just cannot assume that the vocabulary of justice, fairness, dilemmas has been internalized by the students, although they may recognize the words. Rarely have they had the opportunity to discuss them. Recently we had a long discussion on the meaning of conscience. And the students said, "We haven't discussed conscience before. I really have to think about this!" That's because the atmosphere would allow for that child to say, "I really have to think about this."

The steps are that, first, students have to know what a dilemma means, then identify a given dilemma and clarify it. Students cannot put themselves into conflict situations unless they can do these things first—by drawing analogies, role playing, and other means.

To identify means for a child to recognize a situation as one which demands a decision of them. As the year goes on, they will constantly go back to the first time I clarified a dilemma for them. Then they will be reminded of other dilemmas which they responded to strongly at the feeling level each time a new dilemma is raised. To recognize it the second time means that they identify the situation as a dilemma. "Oh, I feel it," they say, or, "That makes me feel uncomfortable," or, "I wonder what I would do if I were in the other person's shoes."

Then next we clarify the situation. That is, I ask the students to state the dilemma in a way which says it most clearly to them. I ask students to do three things: to see, to hear, and to speak in class; to try to use all three to explain the one situation. I say to them if you're seeing a dilemma, read it again, and really see it; then listen to a classmate when he's saying what the situation is so you can hear it that way and think about how it relates to your own version; and then write it. This writing task means they are pulling together what they have seen and heard. I wait for everyone to finish. I walk around and help. Then we read them aloud, share them—all those who want to, and usually most students do. Then they are to come up with something final that they're satisfied with. We must help students to understand it's all a process.

They think the other child has the best answer. It is important to help them identify the process of thinking that people go through. I teach them note taking, word association, so that they get some control over what they can allow to go into their reasoning. All these fundamental things are what make up moral development.

3. Focus on moral reasoning:

Why do I focus on reasoning in this taped discussion? It has a lot to do with being able to accept people as different. As a teacher you try to tell students to accept differences, and it doesn't mean a thing to a youngster. You're giving them a rule: Accept another person. But if you just say, "Let's talk about us, and how we think, what's universal about us," they love it! No one's ever taken the time to do it. So then they start to contemplate, "What is this world all about?"

This in turn encourages taking the perspective of other people, while it helps children make the link between their concrete world and the beginnings of abstractions. It's a way of getting them interested in knowing, of learning, of seeing things they have in common; while at the same time they learn to see that their ways of mastering and exploring problems or questions may be different from the person next to them.

4. Stimulation of perspective taking:

Perspective taking is the basis of everything. I have to be aware of where each child is during the discussion; that is, to take the perspective of each of my students. Secondly, I have to encourage the students to take each other's perspective, as well as the perspectives of the people in the dilemma situations we are discussing. I've even done the business of standing in someone else's shoes with them, literally getting on someone else's shoes and trying to stand in them! Or I've asked kids to come to the front of the room in their stocking feet and ask how it feels without their shoes. I've also encouraged them to try out being a teacher, to put themselves in my place as I face a decision that involves the whole group in some way. I say, "I'm not sure how I'm going to handle this situation, so who will volunteer to try to solve it?" But it's important to say that we have some history in volunteering as part of our building trust together. So then a child will go to the front of the room and sit on the edge of my desk and look out at the whole group, and I'll ask, "How do you feel?" I ask them to describe what they see and to think about how they are going to make the class work at the moment. Then I say how I might feel if I were standing there instead, and encourage others to try it.

Taking the perspective of my students means having my eyes and ears open all the time. I'm so attuned now because I've had some developmental theory and I've talked to other people in this field. Now I really feel that I'm tuned in to the question that passes most people by, the one kid in class who's drifting by. I'll stop when he or she says something and let them know in some way that I really heard them, and encourage others to do so as well.

I try to model to each child that what he or she says is really important. The kids now know they have something important to say. They're viewing reality from where they are, and it makes sense. It's up to *me* to pull the thread to find out where it comes from.

We use everybody in the class. Even if a child has an unpopular argument, I'll ask, "Are you willing to argue this?" If the child says, "I'm not willing," I say, "Do you want help?" Then we discuss: "How do you get help, how do I get help?" We're in it together. My role is to see where each student is engaged, and to concentrate on that point with them. I need to let the child know, "I saw you flicker."

5. Developing student skills:

Through the vehicle of moral discussion, I am encouraging all the points I have just discussed above in my students, as well as in myself—the development of a cooperative, trusting environment, the identification and clarification of dilemma situations in and out of class, the development of moral reasoning ability and the ability to take the perspective of others—all of these.

I am also encouraging question making. I usually try to give a homework assignment which tries to strengthen the concern they have, to elaborate and clarify it further. Basic listening and communication skills are fostered as children gain control over the material. They retell what they've done to someone else, and we videotape a lot so they can see how they express themselves.

Basically, I believe I am helping them to think, to learn to make decisions for themselves. But I have tried to show how reasoning alone is not all they are learning. I am trying to involve as much of their total selves as possible.

In essence, this transcript and the follow-up discussion demonstrate that Margot Strom is translating a broad knowledge of the principles of cognitive-developmental theory into specific teaching strategies to foster her students' moral development. As an introduction to the open-ended discussion of moral issues, this dialogue reveals a high degree of student involvement in their own learning. Such an enterprise demands careful thought and planning on the teacher's part, as Margot explained in her follow-up discussion.

The first step in the development of such a teaching model takes place in the way we conceptualize the teacher's role. That is, our first question needs to be, "What does it mean to use cognitive-developmental theory as the basis for considering moral issues in the classroom?" Starting with this point, the rest of the chapter elaborates each step in the model.

THE TEACHER AS MORAL EDUCATOR

Theoretical Background

As in any area of teaching, the moral educator needs to acquire a certain body of knowledge, in this case the interactionist principles underlying Kohlberg's theory of moral development. The moral educator does not use this knowledge to become a specialist in the "subject matter" of moral development theory; instead, this knowledge is applied to stimulating a specific process of social interaction.

The teacher's task is to empower developmental theory with substantive meaning for a specific group of students at a certain period in their development. In other words, teachers need to think about the developmental characteristics of the particular group of children or adolescents with whom they are working. The more that teachers' knowledge of their students' development is specific and defined, the more likely will educational experiences designed to stimulate development be effective.

Different Moral Conflicts for Different Age Groups

Specifically, taking a developmental approach to moral education requires the understanding that what constitutes a moral problem is different for a seventeen-year-old than for a seven-year-old. In using Kohlberg's theory of moral development, teachers of primary-aged children find that young children see morality mainly in its *social* dimensions. Figuring out what is fair and learning how to cooperate and share are what interest elementary school youngsters. This is so because young children are developing the capacity to understand that other people may see the world differently from the way they see it. Children benefit from opportunities that stretch their ability to take the perspective, or role, of others. Such experiences help them develop their moral reasoning ability, since role taking is a prerequisite to the development of moral thinking. Teachers working with elementary school children therefore need to focus on activities that encourage children to expand their perspective to include others. Giving them responsibility in cooperative problem-solving activities is one way to do this.

Upper elementary and junior high school teachers find that for early adolescents, moral issues usually consist of conflicts surrounding friends, family, and other individuals or small groups close to them. These students are often in transition from stage 2 to stage 3 in their moral reasoning. This means that moral conflicts arise when a choice involving personal gain to oneself is pitted against a decision that mutually benefits one's friends or family. Trust and loyalty are primary preoccupations of early adolescents and determine the right conduct and fair decisions. As an example, the following problem was discussed by an eleven-year-old with his father and two brothers, then written out and brought to school for discussion:

It was Friday in school and this kid was in the fifth grade and that weekend was his birthday. The teacher gave tons of homework to the class 'cause some of the kids were hacking around. This kid, Joe, wasn't hacking around but he decided not to ask the teacher to excuse him from the homework.

So, even though all of his cousins came to visit that weekend, Joe had to spend most of his time up in his room doing his homework and he only got to come down for a few hours of his party.

Monday morning Joe is on his way to school with all the homework done and he meets a real good friend in his class who hasn't done the homework and is so scared she is crying. She begs Joe to let her copy his. He doesn't know what to do but he finally decides that, since she is a good friend, he should let her copy it. She does.

When they get into the classroom the teacher asks for everyone to come up to her desk with the homework. She has heard, however, that some kids cheated so she asks that anyone who either copied or let others copy from them remain in their seat. Joe feels really bad now but he decides he has to do the honest thing and so he stays in his seat and doesn't hand in the homework. While he is sitting there he sees the girl who copied from him going up to the teacher's desk to hand in the homework she copied from him!

Morally, what would you do now if you were Joe, and why would you do it? [4]

Each part of the story, of course, contains a moral conflict: Was the teacher's punishment a fair one? Was it right for Joe to decide to do the extra homework assignment even though he was not "hacking around"? Should Joe have let his classmate copy from his paper? Was it fair of her to ask him? Was it right for the girl to keep quiet about the copying? The important consideration here, however, is that from the eleven-year-old author's point of view, *the* moral issue was *whether to tell on a friend* for lying. This problem highlights the kind of moral struggle experienced by youngsters who are transitional from a "what-is-the-advantage-to-me?" perspective of stage 2 to "what-is-my-obligation-to-my-friend?" perspective, which is characteristic of stage 3. In contrast, a child even younger than the author of Joe's problem would be most concerned and probably scared, like the child crying, about disobeying the teacher.

Adolescents in junior high and high school who reason at stage 3 would see Joe's problem differently. People who use stage 3 reasoning have the ability to think with a perspective that incorporates the norms of a group. This is a cognitive giant step, since the idea of a group is an abstraction. Young adolescents' moral concerns about Joe's predicament would focus on the rights of the whole group: What should we do as a group to reach a fair solution? Should we exclude the girl who copied from "our group"? If teachers are supposed to be helping us, is it fair for our teacher to give us extra homework? Is it fair for us to have extra work if the other classes don't get extra homework for punishment? If there is no school rule that says we have to do extra work, should we have to do it? Teachers working with adolescents at this stage of moral development need to focus on such group-oriented concerns.

A teacher working with late high school students has yet a different task. Adolescents are very much interested in the generic moral dimensions of morality, that is, notions of justice. In fact, teachers often remark that late adolescents seem to be obsessed by the question of what is right. Adolescents who are at the conventional level of moral reasoning are able to think abstractly and are ready to take a legal or societal perspective in solving a moral problem. Teachers therefore need to consider moral issues from this abstract perspective. The following are common questions of concern to adolescents who reason at a conventional level:

What should I do when my friends tell me to do something that conflicts with what I have been taught?
What rules are important to have in society?
What happens when one set of rules conflicts with another?
What would happen if everyone disobeyed the laws?

A few adolescents in the last years of high school may have the ability to adopt a position which recognizes that what is right in one society may not be considered right by another society. These students, at the transition to postconventional reasoning, may take a relativistic stance on moral questions, which often results in frustration. They can see that because each society can formulate its own standards, all attempts to decide what is right for society in general are meaningless. Teachers working with these students need to help them explore possible principles that define people's rights before the establishment of specific laws for any particular society. Abstract philosophical questions may be important for teachers to pursue:

Why are laws made?

Should people obey laws under all circumstances?

Under what circumstances, if any, should a person break a law?

On what basis should one decide whether a law is just or unjust?

If one decides to break an unjust law intentionally, does a person have a responsibility to accept the consequences?

These, then, are examples of how moral problems are seen differently by students of five different age groups. They suggest that teachers need to know what constitutes a moral issue for their students. To do this, teachers need to think carefully about the developmental characteristics of the students. Trying to understand these developmental differences is fundamental to the entire teaching process.

CREATING CONFLICT AND STIMULATING PERSPECTIVE TAKING

Theoretical Background

Besides knowing about the developmental characteristics of their students, teachers need to understand what will stimulate students' growth beyond their present stage of development. That is, teachers must also consider what they actually *do* in the classroom to provide an environment which ensures that moral development will continue to occur.

Social interaction puts the individual in contact with people at different stages of moral development. In Kohlberg's interactionist model, exposure to more adequate patterns of reasoning results in cognitive disequilibrium. When trying to assimilate new information the individual may have to alter his present structure of thinking to accommodate to greater complexity. Then the building of a new structure begins. Eventually, development to the next higher stage of moral reasoning occurs.

Research has shown that the teacher can be instrumental in creating conditions to foster moral development.[5] The teacher has two principal functions in this process: (1) to *create conflict,* the kind of conflict that facilitates growth in students' patterns of thinking, and (2) to *stimulate students' ability to take the perspective of others beyond their own.*

Creating Conflict

The first principle of classroom teaching based on Kohlberg's research is that ways of thinking at each stage cannot be directly taught. Instead, a person's pattern of moral reasoning is self-generated in interaction with the social environment and changes gradually. The classroom can provide a rich environment in which cognitive conflict will arise. Four kinds of interaction may stimulate cognitive conflict: (1) student dialogue with self, (2) student dialogue with other students, (3) student dialogue with teacher, and (4) teacher dialogue with self.

STUDENT DIALOGUE WITH SELF

It is the student's internal dialogue with self that creates cognitive conflict. Students have to think through the solution to a moral problem and weigh the conflicting reasons inside their heads:

Why do I think Heinz should not steal the drug?
Do I really believe that obeying the law is more important than helping someone close to me?
Why is this moral problem so hard to solve?

The need to resolve such conflict eventually results in stage change. Ultimately, the dialogue process in the other three kinds of interaction is intended to stimulate a student's reflection in relation to his or her own thinking process. To arrive at this internal dialogue with self, however, usually requires interaction with others.

STUDENT DIALOGUE WITH OTHER STUDENTS

Interaction between students exposes them to stages of thinking above their own stage, and this stimulates them to move beyond their present way of thinking:

> Sally, why do you believe that stealing to save a person's life is more important than obeying the law?
>
> Jim, I disagree with you. You're not taking society's view into account in order to solve this dilemma.
>
> I've changed my mind. What Juan said about not wanting to hurt a friend really convinced me.

It is common to hear three contiguous stages of moral reasoning reflected in the dialogue in a given classroom. Exposure to reasoning at the next higher stage to one's own is most conducive to moral development.

STUDENT DIALOGUE WITH TEACHER

Students benefit from interaction with the teacher as well. In attempting to understand the pattern of students' reasoning, the teacher needs to respond within the framework of *their* understanding. The teacher's dialogue with students can also stimulate their thinking to the next higher stage of moral reasoning:

Student: Heinz shouldn't steal the drug. He doesn't owe his wife anything.

Adult: What do you mean, "He doesn't owe his wife anything?"

Student: Well, what if she never stole anything for him? Why should he? [Elements of stage 2]

Adult: I'm going to be the wife a minute. "Heinz, we've loved each other all these years. We have a good, strong relationship. I'm in a lot of pain. Can you put yourself in my place? I'd steal it for you if the tables were turned because I love you." Now, what would you say to me? [Elements of stage 3]

TEACHER DIALOGUE WITH SELF

The teacher has to think carefully about what conditions and behaviors are necessary for stimulating effective interaction at the three levels discussed above:

What is the best moral issue to focus on in this case?
Am I listening to the reasoning my students use? Am I encouraging them to stretch their thinking?
Am I asking effective questions that will stimulate cognitive conflict for this particular group?

The teacher initiates the conditions in which these interactions can take place. This responsibility does not mean that the teacher is the center and controlling force of moral education in the classroom. Rather, the teacher enters the classroom with deliberate and systematic pedagogical skills and acts as a catalyst whereby social interaction leading to development may take place. The process of the teacher's dialogue with self also means, of course, that the teacher grows more effective in creating cognitive conflict for students.

In summary, the creation of cognitive conflict is one of the two main roles of the moral educator. Fostering dialogue is the major vehicle for doing this. It is the teacher's role to encourage social exchanges that expose students to stages of moral reasoning above their own stage, and to stimulate them to move beyond their present patterns of reasoning.

Stimulating Social Perspective Taking

The second major function of the teacher is to stimulate students' ability to see the other person's point of view, that is, to take the role of the other person. Again, dialogue is the basic vehicle by which this role-taking process occurs. Role-taking opportunities stimulate moral development.

Theoretically, role taking is crucial to moral development because moral conflict results from being able to take the perspective of others. If we could not assume the point of view of others, we would see no conflict. In addition, as we have discussed, our capacity to assume the perspective of others changes in quality with age. We have also mentioned that a role-taking emphasis in teaching during the elementary school years is important for later moral development during adolescence. The cognitive ability to walk in another's shoes is the first step in developing from preconventional to conventional moral judgment.

In a moral education class the teacher becomes the primary role taker in the group because, as an adult, the teacher is most likely to have the capacity to take the perspective of individuals in the class and the group as a whole. The ability of the teacher to take the perspective of each student is a vital skill. This involves helping students see others as similar to themselves but different in respect to their specific thoughts, feelings, and ways of viewing the world: "So you and Polly both agree that it's wrong to shoplift; but you feel you might do it under pressure from a friend, whereas she's more concerned about what her mother might think of her if she did." Also important is the teacher's ability to encourage students to see themselves from the viewpoint of others. This, too, is an aspect of perspective taking. Not only is it important to ask such questions as "Carol, how do you think Mike would solve this problem?" but it is also necessary to encourage Carol to see herself as others see her: "Carol, how do you think Mike thinks you would solve this problem?"

Finally, a point relative to both cognitive conflict and social perspective taking needs emphasis. We cannot assume that students will "naturally" provide cognitive conflict for themselves, nor that they will "automatically" take the perspective of others. The teacher's role is to ensure that these two functions are provided. The responsibility for promoting continuing developmental opportunities lies with the teacher.

THE DEVELOPMENT OF MORAL AWARENESS

The first task of the teacher in creating classroom opportunities that stimulate cognitive conflict and social role taking is to heighten students' moral awareness. The teacher needs to help students explore the moral dimensions of their interaction together, as well as explore the content of their curriculum. To accomplish this, teachers have used a variety of approaches. The two most common are the presentation of hypothetical moral dilemmas and real moral dilemmas for student discussion.

Hypothetical Moral Dilemmas

Teachers commonly introduce moral issues in their classrooms by what has come to be known as "leading moral discussions." In the first few studies that applied Kohlberg's theory to educational practice, researchers presented "classical" moral dilemmas, such as the Heinz dilemma, to children or adolescents for discussion.[6] These dilemmas are traditionally open-ended hypothetical problems involving a conflict between the rights, responsibilities, or claims of abstract and ambiguous characters. These figures are embedded in a situational context without reference to any specific time, place, or personality. The characters are faced with a pressing decision, which the students are asked to resolve.

Although these so-called classical dilemmas are hypothetical and abstract, they do not usually lack drama and emotional appeal. They are often highly charged life-and-death situations about which we have all fantasized at some point in our lives. "The Desert" is one such hypothetical dilemma:

Two people had to cross a desert. When they started, both had equal amounts of food and water. When they were in the middle of the desert, one person's water bag broke and all his water ran out. They both knew that if they shared the water they would probably die of thirst. If one had the water, that person would survive.

What should they do? Give your reasons.[7]

We are not limiting our discussion of pedagogical techniques to the discussion of these hypothetical dilemmas. The problem with such dilemmas is their failure to engage people in the richness and ambiguity that real-life situations can offer. A variety of ways to approach and solve the moral problem is lacking. Although the questions that follow the hypothetical dilemma are open-ended, the situation itself is a tight moral package; it contains a narrow focus on the rights of the people involved and their outstanding moral obligation, duty, or responsibility to others.

Real Moral Problems

In contrast, more "naturalistic," or true-to-life, moral problems come closer to the ambiguities of daily social experience. Most important, real moral problems offer the potential for students to act on the solution to the conflict. In part, this is because discussion of real moral problems brings sustained attention to conflicts in students' lives that are often ignored. Students feel a heightened interest and keen emotional involvement as they learn that not everyone thinks as they do about how to solve the problem. In essence, real problems demand much more than the exercise of thinking, as we can judge by taking for a moment the perspective of two eighth-grade girls who wrote down the following incident:

A girl named Carol was caught throwing cheese in the cafeteria during lunch. She was already warned about this. Now all of the girls in her grade (8th grade) can't have ice cream for one week. Carol kept saying it wasn't her fault. Now all the girls are mad at her. What should she do?

1. What do Carol's friends think about her now?
2. Should they try to get the ice cream back? What would be the reasons they use in trying to do that?
3. Was it right to deprive the whole class of ice cream for a week? Why? What would be another good solution? Why? [8]

These girls obviously want action taken on this problem. They see a moral conflict and are motivated to discuss and solve it. We are suggesting, then, that teachers help students heighten their moral awareness, and therefore their opportunities to take moral action, by encouraging them to articulate, confront, and think through solutions to *real* moral problems. We add that it is important for teachers to create opportunities for students to use their own experience in solving moral problems. There are three main reasons for doing this.

First, all of us have a difficult time distinguishing between situations that involve a *moral* decision and other kinds of problem-solving issues, including questions of good and bad, praise and blame. As we have stated many times in this book, a moral problem for one age group may not be perceived as such by another. Students need opportunities to define moral problems for themselves. In trying to come to grips with this important concept for ourselves, one of the authors learned a great deal about the fine line between moral and nonmoral situations from one of her thirteen-year-old students: "Of course whether to paint your bike blue or green can be a very important moral dilemma! I'd paint my bike from green to blue any day to hide it if I stole it!"

A second reason to heighten students' moral awareness through their own experience is that children and adolescents are not used to discussing moral issues in an open-ended way. Parents, teachers, and school administrators often make students' moral decisions for them, in the form of rules to be obeyed or general beliefs to be followed. Children and adolescents may therefore doubt the sincerity of adults who present the idea that moral issues are open for discussion and thoughtful consideration together.

The third reason to expand students' moral awareness is related most integrally to cognitive developmental theory. People's understanding of moral problems differs according to their stage of moral development. Persons who reason at a preconventional level of moral reasoning are used to thinking that the solution to a moral dilemma rests in the hands of authority figures external to themselves. Moral conflict over stealing, for example, does not always exist at stage 1 because, after all, "It's wrong to steal, period." This is therefore an "easy" moral problem because there is one clear-cut moral decision to be made. This same dilemma may be a "hard" one to solve by someone who sees the conflict differently, as one between the legal rights of a store owner and a thief's right to feed a family without enough to eat. Students benefit from being exposed to the many different kinds of moral sensitivity experienced by their classmates.

Daily Opportunities to Heighten Moral Awareness

In addition to the introduction of hypothetical and real moral dilemmas, the everyday interactions of classroom life are a rich source of moral issues to discuss. Opportunities for teachers and students to develop their awareness of moral issues probably occur most intensively in the elementary school classroom. Since the same teacher and students stay together for most of the day, myriad potential moral dilemmas crop up in the course of each day:

> What should happen when a student finds property missing from desk or closet?
>
> What are fair rules for governing free time?
>
> What should happen when one group of friends refuses to share the ball with others at recess?
>
> How should students who cut in line be handled?
>
> What is a fair way to divide up materials during open activity time?
>
> How should clean-up time be divided up fairly?
>
> What should happen if a fight breaks out between the same two students several days in a row?

Obviously, this list is but a start. An important first step in generating such examples is for teachers to be able to *see* these individual situations as moral problems that affect the class as a community working together. One of the first pedagogical tasks of teachers, therefore, is to help students become aware of the moral issues in their own lives, both in and out of school. One way to do this is to ask them to keep a journal in which they record real moral problems encountered during the week. It helps for the teachers to do this too.

At first, students often do not feel that they trust other members of the class or the teacher enough to reveal their problems. It can be helpful if the teacher suggests describing a moral conflict that "happened to a friend or someone you know." Students, especially adolescents, often feel safer writing in the third person. It is crucial to respect these feelings of privacy.

Examples of such "personal moral dilemmas" written in the first few weeks of the school year, and therefore in the third person, appear below. The teacher asked the eighth-grade authors to follow up their incidents with open-ended questions to highlight the moral conflict:

Your teacher has just given you a spelling test. Beside you, you saw your best friend taking the vocabulary words out of her pocket. The teacher did not know she was cheating.

1. Should the student talk to her best friend and ask her why she cheated? Why?
2. Should the girl cheat, whether it was a good reason or not?
3. Should the student tell on her best friend? Why?
4. Should the student make believe she didn't see her best friend? Or should she bring herself to tell on her best friend? What would be a good reason for telling on her? What would be a good reason for *not* telling on her?
5. If the teacher does find out, what should she do? Why?

The principal had been going to all the classes asking the students if they had seen Cindy anywhere. She had been missing for an hour. The principal came to Betsy and asked if she had seen her, and Betsy replied, "No."

Then Betsy went to the bathroom to wash her sticky hands. When she saw Cindy there, Cindy yelled, "If you tell that I'm smoking, I'm going to get all the kids to kill you after school."

Cindy had a lot of girls who would fight for her, so Betsy was afraid. She ran out of the bathroom, frightened. Then two teachers came up to her and asked, "Did you see Cindy anywhere? She's been missing and if we don't find her, we're going to have to call the police! Her mother's terribly worried."

1. Should Betsy tell on Cindy and risk getting beat up? Why or why not?

2. Should Betsy lie and increase the worrying? Why?

3. Should Betsy say she doesn't know? What would be a good reason to do that? What would be a good reason *not* to do that?

4. From Betsy's point of view, who is more worried—Cindy's mother, her teacher, or the principal?

5. What do the police have to do with this dilemma, if anything?

Somebody stole the videotape machine from the library. The keys are hidden, and only five people know where they are: three male students and two librarians. Both librarians say that they didn't do it.

1. Should the librarians blame the three boys? Separately? Together? Why? What should the librarians say when they talk to the boys?

2. Should the principal become involved? Why?

3. If the boys did not do it, are they in any way responsible for finding out who did it? Why?

4. Whose responsibility should it be to replace the equipment? Why?

Three girls are caught smoking on school property during lunch. A teacher finds them and reports them to the office. Two of these girls have been caught smoking on school property before. The other wasn't smoking with the other girls, but is known to smoke off school property with friends.

1. Should all three girls be considered in the same manner? Why?

2. What should a fair punishment be? Why is that fair?

3. Should the principal consider their smoking habits in other situations in making his decision? Why? Should he involve the girls' parents? Why?

4. Should the principal tell the girls' teachers?

5. Would it make a difference if this incident was the first time they were caught smoking on school grounds? Why? Would the principal's decision be any different in that case? [9]

The development of moral awareness, then, depends on the active involvement of both students and teacher. Students need opportunities to explore the moral dimensions of their lives, since adults often make moral decisions for them. Teachers have a dual awareness process to consider. First, they must learn to "see" the potential moral conflicts in their own classroom and curriculum. Second, they need to conceptualize those moral issues as their students would, from the perspective of the students' level of moral development.

QUESTIONING STRATEGIES

The Importance of Questions

Once teachers begin to develop heightened moral awareness, they need specific strategies that will help facilitate moral development. The next task of the teacher, therefore, is to learn to ask effective questions. Questioning, or so-called probing, which is open-ended, is focused on moral dimensions and invites respondents to explore their reasoning. Logic is at the core of the pedagogical process that fosters structural development.

Effective questions are important because they help to stretch students' thinking. These questions invite students to explore the reasons behind their opinions and to interact with their classmates in a way that challenges their own pattern of thinking. Specifically, the "right" questions can stimulate cognitive conflict and social role taking.

There are at least two phases of questioning, initial and in-depth strategies. Initial strategies introduce teachers and students to the discussion of moral issues and continue to develop students' moral awareness. In-depth strategies focus on the elements of discussions that may lead to structural change in moral reasoning.

Initial Questioning Strategies

When teachers attempt to confront moral issues in their classrooms, they need to be very active in helping students inquire into moral problems. Teachers usually have to ask a lot of questions because (1) they must help students recognize that they are thoughtful reasoners, and (2) they need to help students articulate the elements that constitute the conflict in a given moral issue.

Examples in the previous section revealed that teachers often feel more comfortable with their first discussions if they choose a few "traditional" moral dilemmas, ones that have been tried out by other educators in the field.[10] Initially, when learning to lead effective discussions, the teacher's role includes the following main points:

1. To ensure that students understand the moral dilemma or problem in question:

Now that you have read about Heinz's dilemma, could you restate what the problem is in your own words?

Sonia gave us the facts we know in this situation. Now I'd like each of you to write down what, in your view, is the major moral conflict here.

2. To help students confront the moral components inherent in the problem:

The main question we are going to consider today is, should Heinz steal the drug?

In this dilemma, the man has to decide whether or not he should steal the milk to feed his starving family. What are the conflicts he has to face in order to decide?

3. To elicit students' reasons behind their opinions on the problem:

Why do you think Heinz should steal the drug?

Could this group get together and list the main reasons you think that the man should steal the milk? Those of you who think he should not, come over here to write your list. And those who are undecided, give your reasons as well.

4. To encourage students who give different reasons to interact with one another:

I hear two different arguments here—those who feel Heinz should not steal the drug because of the druggist's property rights, and those who feel Heinz's obligation to his wife comes first. Let's explore the differences in these arguments in more depth.

Margaret and Peter seem to have the same opinion on whether the man should steal the milk, but they have different reasons to back up their opinions. Could someone restate what those reasons are?

During this initial period the teacher has an opportunity to hear the different arguments students use to reason out their solutions. Learning to listen for the characteristics of thinking that constitute different stages of moral judgment takes time. It is important to clarify a point here. We are not asking teachers to label each response with a stage of moral reasoning. One or two statements from a student do not carve the stage in stone. In addition, students are often able to use elements of three stages of reasoning, depending on the situation.

In the beginning we suggest that teachers try to recognize the "feel" of different levels of complexity: Whose point of view is the respondent taking to arrive at a solution? How many different people's perspectives are included in trying to reason out the solution? Are any abstract considerations taken into account, such as what "the law" or "society" might think? Who does the student see as the source of moral authority in the situation?

The sequencing of qualitatively different kinds of questions and comments is important for the teacher to consider. This is necessary both because the teacher wants to stimulate moral development and because moral discussion involves risk taking. Peer pressure often discourages risk taking and therefore can run counter to the goals of moral education if group norms discourage open and honest communication. A suggested series of different kinds of questions follows.

HIGHLIGHTING THE MORAL ISSUE

These questions are usually dialogue starters that ask students to take a stand on a moral issue. They help students identify situations as dilemmas that require resolution of a conflict or choice. They usually imply a question of "should," "ought," or "right/wrong": Should Heinz steal the drug? Is it wrong to steal to save another person's life? Should people be punished for stealing under those circumstances? Such questions focus on the content of the opinion that someone wishes to back up.

The example that follows demonstrates how one of the authors began a moral discussion with a group of third graders by highlighting the moral issue. The dilemma, written by the author, was based on a class incident that had occurred four months earlier:

> *Adult:* I would like to read you a story. After the story there are questions, and I'd like each of you who would like to, to raise his or her hand, and I'll call on you. Here's the story: *Mrs. Smith is a third-grade teacher who often asks her students to work together and help one another in doing arithmetic. The students like working together because that way they can finish more work in class, and have less to do as homework. Billy and Tommy are two boys in the class who like to work together. Ruth and Sharon are two girls in the class who like to work together. Mrs. Smith usually lets friends work together. But one day Sharon is absent, and Ruth is left alone without a partner. That day Mrs. Smith asks Billy and Tommy if they wouldn't mind helping Ruth by letting her work with them. They say they don't want to.* Okay, is that clear?
>
> *Students:* Uh-huh . . . Yeah . . . I get it. . . .

[Highlights the moral Issue]
> *Adult:* Do you think it's right for Billy and Tommy to say they don't want to work with Ruth?
>
> *Students:* Yes . . . No . . . Yes . . .
>
> *Adult:* Okay, let's raise our hands.
>
> *Lana:* I think they should because she needs a friend that day.
>
> *Adult:* Okay, Donna?
>
> *Donna:* I don't think it's fair because they should

> know she needs the help. I don't think they should
> say, "I don't want to work with her!"

[Highlights   *Adult:*   What would be wrong with that?
the moral   *Donna:*   In that situation she needs the help.
issue]   *Adult:*   Uh huh. . . . Who else?

The discussion can be especially lively if class opinion is divided on what the solution should be. Teachers sometimes encounter the "dead-end" discussions in their first attempts to ask these questions, however. In that case, teachers need to remember that even in stating a one-word answer, students feel they are taking a risk. Teachers need to be patient and ask follow-up questions, such as the ones below, which help students explore and defend their position.

ASKING "WHY?" QUESTIONS

"Why?" questions ask students to give reasons for their stand on a moral issue. Reasons elicit the structure of students' thinking. These questions also give students a chance to see that they may hold the same content opinion as another classmate, but for a very different reason. These differences in thinking patterns begin to stimulate interest and dialogue. Such questions as "Why do you think your solution to the dilemma is a good one?" or "What is the main reason you decided to resolve the problem as you did?" are two examples.

The discussion of the dilemma involving Mrs. Smith's class is continued here to illustrate the adult's focus on eliciting students' reasoning.:

> *Student:*   She's the only one who doesn't
> have a partner.
> *Student:*   Yeah, but what did the teacher
> say?

[Clarifies the   *Adult:*   Well, in this case the teacher did say
dilemma]   to do it.
> *Student:*   Well, then, if the teacher said they
> have to do it, well, then, they have to. [Elements of stage 1]

[Elicits reasoning through perspective taking]

Adult: Why do you think the teacher would say for them to have Ruth work with the two boys?

Student: What I'd like to know is why she asked Ruth to work with the boys.

Student: Well, she might not have a girl who could work with Ruth.

Student: I think she should work with the boys, and then, like, if one day one of your friends didn't have anybody to work with, then you'll be used to it; you won't go, "Phew, I don't want to work with boys."

[Elicits reasoning]

Adult: Why should they get used to it?

(*Several laugh. Students pause to think.*)

Adult: Lana (*getting ready to speak*), what do you think?

Lana: I think boys and girls should learn to work together. It's nicer that way.

(*Discussion continues.*)

COMPLICATING THE CIRCUMSTANCES

Two kinds of probing questions or statements can complicate the original moral problem. The first kind adds new information or situations to the original problem to increase the complexity and cognitive conflict inherent in the original situation. In the Heinz dilemma, for example, such questions might include the following: Suppose Heinz's wife had specifically told him to (or not to) steal the drug, would that make a difference in your position? Suppose the judge who was hearing Heinz's case was a friend of Heinz, should that make a difference in his decision? Such questions stimulate greater differentiation of thinking, particularly in the area of role taking. A student is thereby urged to consider more than a single view of how to resolve the moral conflict.

A second kind of complicating question is asked to help students avoid "escape hatching" from the moral issue. Escape hatching usually occurs when students first discuss moral dilemmas. Often they feel uncomfortable taking the risk of facing squarely the question of what is right. They would rather escape from the moral problem entirely by changing the whole dilemma. Commonly they attempt to alter the facts of the dilemma, thereby effectively solving the problem by eliminating the conflict. For example, in a dilemma concerning the decision to throw certain people overboard from an overcrowded lifeboat drifting at sea, students often avoid confronting the dilemma by wanting to tie the extra people to the side of the boat with ropes. To help students face the moral question in this case, the teacher might say, "For the moment, let's assume we can't tie them to the boat" or "Suppose there were no ropes in the lifeboat." The teacher might also complicate the dilemma itself: "Suppose holding the ropes would sink the lifeboat—if you had to choose between a mother and her eighteen-year-old son, who would be cast overboard?"

Teachers must respect the fact that some students feel uncomfortable when facing moral problems head-on and discussing them directly. The practice of reasoning out moral issues is usually new, and sometimes overwhelming, to students. The teacher's role is to facilitate the process of facing the moral issue, not to "push" students to do so. Over time, the peer group helps assume the task of confronting the dilemma.

PERSONAL AND NATURALISTIC EXAMPLES

The presentation of personal and naturalistic examples continues to develop students' moral awareness while they discuss moral issues. These examples give students a realization that moral problems are a part of their daily social interaction, as well as the source of many problems and solutions in the society at large. "Personal" or "naturalistic" in this sense indicates situations within the experience of students and teacher. Questions about a dilemma in the news or on a television program may be as "personal" in this context as a personal problem.

If a dilemma is personal, there is likely to be high interest and emotional investment on the part of the students. Such situations give a person pause to think about daily problems in new ways. Questions that personalize these situations help stimulate students' thinking in many social areas: How do *you* think the principal should deal with people breaking bottles on the playground? How do *you* think the senator on the news last night should have voted?

Over time, students will initiate examples of personal experiences that remind them of the dilemma materials under discussion. These situations help students probe more deeply into the relationships among many different kinds of moral problems. Teachers need to learn to listen to these concrete cognitive connections. Such examples help illuminate the mysteries of students' thinking. We can see this in a continuation of the discussion of Mrs. Smith's dilemma with a third-grade class. The adult has just asked, "Why should boys and girls get used to working together?" The issue was raised by one of the children:

Adult: Amy, did you want to say something?

Amy: Um, mine's sort of like Justine's and Richard's: because there are other people in the class, and she could pick another person to be with if she didn't get along with them. Also, when you're grown up, you feel the same way. You have this person who's your secretary, if you're in a big business. And the man comes in and says the woman's sick and you'd have to work with the man. You'd have to get used to it. I mean you can't always be with the girls.

Adult: Laura?

Laura: Yeah, that's how I felt, 'cause when I was in the first grade I knew this lady who had her two dogs she always took to go shopping, and she said she wouldn't be back for another hour, and my mother was going to pick me up in an hour. But I had to stay there with her son. So we played records and stuff, but then he invited these three friends over who were all boys, and I had to stay in the house with three boys.

[Listens] *Adult:* How did you feel then?

Laura: Oh, I don't know.

Adult: Uh-huh.

Laura: Then he didn't talk to me anymore. He just played with his friends.

Adult: Laura, do you think that was wrong of him?

Laura: Yeah.

Adult: Yeah, okay. (*Discussion continues; adult refocuses.*) So you think the teacher ought to make Billy and Tommy work with the girl Ruth?

ALTERNATING REAL AND HYPOTHETICAL MORAL PROBLEMS

Alternating real and hypothetical moral issues serves several purposes. First, this format helps to expand the range of student's notions of what constitutes a moral problem. Second, this variation takes into account the range of student interests in the class. Third, since hypothetical dilemmas are imaginary conflict situations that highlight and often polarize the moral components of a problem, they allow more risk taking by students. The conflicts are very far removed from students' lives. When a group is building trust in one another, hypothetical dilemmas ensure that students do not feel "pushed" toward self-disclosure before the group is ready to respond at the level of personal acceptance.

For adolescents in particular, a combination of hypothetical and real dilemmas makes sense developmentally and tends to work in the classroom.[11] For those at the beginning stages of formal operational thinking, in Piaget's framework, the intriguing aspect of hypothetical dilemmas may be the abstract dimensions they entail. Part of the development of abstract intellectual thinking involves the ability to be self-reflective. Real, personal dilemmas, therefore, can complement hypothetical dilemmas, because they stimulate reasoning about the self in relation to others. Given the self-consciousness that accompanies the discovery of self, it seems important to provide a variety of opportunities for adolescents to move between the hypothetical and the real.

The five considerations presented in this section constitute the "core" of the introduction to moral discussions. For both teachers and students, they involve exposure to the *breadth* of reasoning about moral problems. The length of time that a teacher spends on these introductory efforts depends on the nature of the particular group of students and the teacher's developing ease in leading discussions.

In-Depth Questioning Strategies

The second phase of a moral discussion format involves a focus in depth. The teacher's questioning techniques parallel this change. Deepening students' exploration of a particular moral issue facilitates internal dialogue that promotes structural change. When students have to grapple with one issue from many points of view, cognitive conflict is set up. They must struggle hard with different reasons, inconsistencies, and perspectives to feel satisfied with the adequacy of a given solution to the problem.

Applying the same questions to several moral problems is not sufficient to help students move beyond using only their present pattern of reasoning. Teachers need to engage in teaching strategies that stimulate the emergence of a *new* pattern of thinking at the next higher stage. Several teacher interventions, mainly in the form of questions, can facilitate this process.

REFINING PROBING QUESTIONS

Questions should probe many sides of the same issue. A "should" or "why?" question is not sufficient to stimulate stage change. Students need to hear extended arguments from one another so they can understand the reasoning and challenge each other's logic. Five kinds of in-depth probing questions have been identified by moral educators interested in effective questioning strategies: clarifying probe, issue-specific probe, inter-issue probe; role-switch probe, and universal-consequences probe.[12]

A *clarifying probe* asks students to explain the terms they use, especially when the meaning of a statement is ambiguous or does not convey the reasoning behind the content. A clarifying probe is important if teachers are not to impart their meaning to students' words because of the differing stages of development between teacher and student.

Student: No, he shouldn't tell on his friend who cheated on the test. He might get in trouble.
Teacher: What kind of trouble?
Student: Well, his friend won't like him anymore. He might get back at him in some way. [Elements of stage 2]

An *issue-specific probe* is a question or statement that asks students to explore one moral issue related to the problem in question. "Issues" are different areas of focus in our moral judgment. We have seen how Kohlberg uses these issues in scoring a Moral Judgment Interview. A few such issues are authority, roles of affiliation and affection, contract obligations, and the value of life. By focusing on a particular issue in depth, students have the opportunity to explore fully the reasoning behind their beliefs. They apply their thinking beyond the immediate moral problem that confronts them.

Do you have any obligation to a stranger? What is the difference between one's responsibility to family or friends, and to a stranger?

Why do people have a responsibility to obey legal authority?

An *inter-issue* probe is one that seeks to stimulate the resolution of conflict between two moral issues. Often the priority of one issue over the other reflects a difference between two contiguous stages of moral reasoning (e.g., the value of friendship at stage 3 is more important than protecting one's own interest at stage 2). This kind of probe thereby causes cognitive conflict, because students have to test the adequacy of their reasons in choosing one issue over the other.

What is more important, loyalty to a friend, or obeying a law?

If it becomes necessary to steal in order to save someone's life, could you justify that decision? How?

A *role-switch probe* asks the student to assume the perspective of a different person in the conflict from the one the student has been taking. This kind of probe is important for stimulating students' role-taking ability, because it gives them practice in trying to see the same situation through another person's eyes.

(*Using the situation of whether to tell on a friend who was cheating on a test.*)

Would the friend think you were wrong to tell in this situation? Be the teacher for a minute. What would she say you ought to do in this situation. Why? What would your parents say you ought to do? What would your friend's parents say is the right thing to do?

A *universal-consequences probe* asks students to consider what would happen if they applied their reasoning so that everyone would follow it. This probe asks students to try to come up with a moral decision that would reflect fairness equally to people in general. This kind of probe tests the limits of logical adequacy behind one's moral judgment and helps stimulate moral reasoning from a preconventional, egocentric framework to a conventional level that takes into account the rights of other people as a group or society.

What would happen if everyone decided to steal from other people in order to save the life of someone they knew?

What would happen if everyone in society started to disobey the law?

How could teachers run classrooms and help children learn if everyone cheated on tests?

HIGHLIGHTING CONTIGUOUS-STAGE ARGUMENTS

A second kind of in-depth questioning involves the teacher's responsibility for highlighting arguments at contiguous stages of moral reasoning. It is the next higher stage of moral reasoning that stimulates a person's moral growth. Students at a higher stage will not "lose" that reasoning ability by interacting with people who reason at lower stages. Students at higher stages, however, also need the stimulation of a reasoning pattern more complex than their own.

There are two opportunities to highlight contiguous-stage arguments. The first occurs when students themselves use contiguous stages in dialogue. Once teachers are able to "hear" the differences in reasoning patterns, they can begin to encourage students to explore the adequacy of their thinking:

Wendy: Heinz should steal the drug because if his wife were in his shoes, she'd do it for him. [Elements of stage 3]

Peter: Yes, but why should he? She never stole anything for him! [Elements of stage 2]

Teacher: You each have very different reasons for your opinions. Wendy, suppose you wanted to help persuade Peter to change his mind. Could you role-play Heinz's wife for a minute and try to tell him why Heinz should decide to steal the drug? [Highlights stage 3]

A second occasion for highlighting contiguous-stage arguments occurs when the class is missing the perspective of a higher-stage argument. The teacher can then encourage those students whose thinking often reflects elements of a higher stage to share that perspective on a new issue:

Teacher: Carlo, you gave us an interesting solution to the problem of stealing we talked about yesterday. You said we need to think about what's good for society as well as what's good for our friends. Could you or someone else tell us how that same argument might apply to the case we are discussing today?

Sometimes, however, the whole group is unable to see a given moral conflict from more than one perspective, and no one offers a more adequate point of view. Then it is up to the *teacher* to pose arguments at the next higher stage:

(*Discussing the Heinz dilemma, the class has just considered the close relationship between husband and wife, their obligations to*

each other, and whether a "good" husband should steal for his wife.)
[Elements of stage 3]

Teacher: I notice no one has mentioned what the law argues as the right thing to do in this case. The law says that store owners have the right to protection of their property against breaking and entering. Could someone tell us why this law might have been written, and how it might make a difference in Heinz's decision? [Elements of stage 4]

CLARIFYING AND SUMMARIZING

Another in-depth teaching strategy involves a shift in the teacher's role from initiating questions to clarifying and summarizing what students say. By this phase of discussion, students have learned how to approach questions of moral conflict; *they* can ask the open-ended questions. The teacher becomes a more active listener, linking crucial elements of discussion.

The teacher needs to monitor the discussion so that students become aware of alternate reasoning patterns presented by their classmates. Although students learn to take more initiative in stimulating one another's thinking, the teacher still needs to maintain a focus that facilitates the developmental processes of cognitive conflict and role taking.

The following dialogue from an eleventh- and twelfth-grade psychology class demonstrates this shift in teacher role. The students have been discussing suicide and euthanasia. They take responsibility for addressing their comments to one another and elaborating and stimulating one another's thinking. The teacher can therefore direct attention to the group as a whole:

[Refocuses; highlights a new moral issue]

Teacher: The issue of suicide is important, but maybe for the moment we should stick to the issue of euthanasia and whether or not it's right to take someone's life or at what point could it be right.

Mike: I don't think it could be right for a doctor to, because a doctor doesn't know . . . I'm again going back to the mind thing, right? A doctor doesn't know the mind of a person as well as someone close to them. Like you come up with all these questions like, how do you know he's really gone in the mind? Well, a person's brother would know if he's gone in the mind and someone's brother could make the right decision, I think. If you really love that person you'll do what you think. . . . If the right thing to do is kill that person that's what you'll do. [Elements of stage 3]

Jim: I wouldn't want to be the guy to tell them to do it.

Mike: I'm saying in a real extreme case—like, say, he just lost his girlfriend—I wouldn't say, you know, all right, I'll kill you. He's suffering. His mind's gone. People feed him with needles. He never does anything by himself. If he asks me . . .

[Clarifies Mike's statement]

Karen: Oh, but if he didn't ask you, you wouldn't take it on yourself.

Mike: No.

[Takes the perspective of others]

Bob: That's such a personal evaluation. To you that's so much worse than losing a girlfriend like you said, but for some people it might not be.

Mike: I'm saying if there's absolutely no hope whatsoever.

[Stimulates perspective taking]

Karen: Who's to judge?

Mike: Someone who knows him extremely well is to judge.

[Complicates the circumstances]

John: What if they don't have anyone who knows them very well?

Lisa: I think if the persons themselves say they want to die.

[Highlights the moral issue]

Jim: Just because you say you want to die does that give you the right to die?

Lisa: Yeah.

[Asks a "why?" question of himself]

[Stimulates perspective taking]

[Clarifies and summarizes the reasoning of the group]

Jim: You could be wanting to die one time and another time you could be feeling a lot better. You could think to yourself, "Oh, I need to end it all now." You can think about it but I don't think a person has the right to decide "I should kill myself" when there's still a way or a reason to live.

Mike: I'm saying when there's *absolutely* no hope. You look at them and sort of brush them aside. We've got to keep them alive because that's the thing you have to do. You have to keep them alive. And why do you have to do that? Because that's what you have to do.

Karen: Who's to say you're the right person to decide?

Mike: The person who asked you to kill them.

Teacher: So you're saying a couple of things. The person has to want to die and someone who's close to him and who knows him very well has to agree that that's the best thing. [Elements of stage 3] [13]

This shift in the teaching role toward a group-oriented perspective also means that the teacher can spend more time listening carefully to the stages of reasoning that students offer, and to identify those stages that are *missing*. Listening gives the teacher greater assurance of knowing what the next higher level of cognitive complexity should be.

It is appropriate for the teacher to interject a personal opinion or moral argument once students are able to sustain the discussion. Their own interest usually diminishes the concern that the teacher has the "right answer."

ROLE-TAKING QUESTIONS AND STRATEGIES

Role-taking questions are specifically designed to stimulate students' perspective-taking ability. Role taking, of course, is part of most questioning strategies. In this section we specifically address the issue of stimulating students' perspectives from an egocentric level to a level that considers the thoughts, feelings, and rights of others.

Role-taking opportunities are not limited to discussions of moral problems. For students who are limited in their cognitive ability to take the role of others, actual experiences in assuming another person's role may be an important concrete link between their world and the world of others. We previously recommended that teachers develop cooperative activities for students at the elementary level. Role plays, debates, and student-designed plays, films, or slide tapes that center on moral conflicts also stimulate the real experience of walking in someone else's shoes.[14] As with other questioning strategies, these activities are most beneficial when students focus on the *reasoning* that the characters use as they enact the situation. This important addition to role plays (which usually stress personality and behavior) gives students a chance to "try on" another person's *thoughts* as well. This rehearsal can be a first step in moving beyond egocentric thinking. Discussing the role play afterward is also conducive to stimulating development, because this gives the whole class a chance to participate.

High school adolescents can also benefit from real role-taking experiences. Taking the role of tutor to a younger child or of peer counselor to a fellow high school student can help to develop students' perspective-taking capacity.[15] The effort to help another person encourages the adolescent to see the world through that person's eyes.

In addition, role-taking opportunities occur during discussion, when teachers ask certain questions. The following example, taken from the second half of Margot Strom's discussion of the Milk Dilemma, demonstrates how a teacher might change the focus from the perspective of one person in the dilemma to another. In this case, Margot Strom asks her students to shift their thinking from the man whose children are starving to the milkman, who might be affected by the man's decision:

[Focuses   *Teacher:* From the milkman's point of view, how
on perspec-   might he be affected if the man steals the milk?
tive taking]   *Boy:* I would say that the people would probably say

that the milkman probably gypped them and then they would have an argument or something with the milkman and there is no proof either way, so the milkman might lose his business, you know.

Boy: He might lose his job.

[Refocuses]   *Teacher:*   So does that change the situation at all for you; should you consider the milkman?

Boy: I don't know, it doesn't change the situation, I still don't know.

Teacher: Rick?

Rick: I don't know, this is what I think the milkman's position would be. "Not me," he would say. "It's not my milk, I don't care what happens to it, it is not mine, I'm delivering this to them, it has absolutely nothing to do with me. I don't care. When I put it down on the doorstep it is their concern, not mine. Get it out of my life, I don't want to hear about it." [Elements of stage 2]

Teacher: Ralph and then Dave; we have not heard Dave's voice.

Ralph: The milkman would say, "I put it down . . ."

[Listening]   *Teacher:*   That is what Irene said earlier. Do you agree with Irene?

Ralph: ". . . I left it there, I put four bottles of milk, maybe somebody else took them but I am—I am responsible for them until they get them, but I have done my job and it is not my fault and it is not theirs. Maybe my company should give them another bottle of milk, but I should not be fired."

Dave: As far as the milkman is concerned, this might cost him his job, if someone already said something to him, like maybe he would have to ring the doorbell and make sure they get it.

[Stimulates perspective taking]   *Teacher:*   Do you think this milkman if he saw this man stealing the milk. . . . The man is talking to the milkman who saw him steal it, the man says to the milkman, "My children are starving, I need this milk, I have to take it from somewhere, I am taking it from

> these steps." What do you think the milkman would
> say to him?
>
> *Girl:*   He would say, "Go ahead this time, but I don't
> think you should do it next time, because I would
> have to report you, it might cost me my job."

[Stimulates   *Teacher:*   You don't think he would tell him to take it
conflict]   back, that it's stealing? . . .

(Discussion continues.)

Leading discussions with adolescents whose role-taking ability is limited to egocentric reasoning is difficult because these
adolescents have spent many more years in this preconventional pattern than children who reason at the same level.
Egocentric role taking must give way to a concern for others if
an adolescent is to move from preconventional to conventional
moral reasoning. One way to stimulate the beginnings of appreciation of others is to appeal to family ties. Affection and
loyalty to people beyond oneself develop first in relation to the
family.

The teacher in the example that follows demonstrates the importance of focusing on role taking when adolescents are at the
preconventional level of moral reasoning. The teacher tries to
follow the students' logic at their level of reasoning and at the
same time to stimulate their ability to see beyond their own
needs. This high school social studies class is discussing the
legal and moral conflicts surrounding a gang of boys who steal
cars. The class is exploring the issue of friendship as it relates to
relationships in a gang. The dilemma and the topic of friendship are both appropriate content choices for stimulating moral
development from the preconventional to the conventional
level. One of the boys in the class has just defined a friend from
the perspective of stage 2:

> *Larry:*   A friend is a friend as far as you can see
> him. . . . You know why I say a friend is a
> friend as far as you can trust him? You can go
> around stealing stuff and all of a sudden he
> might just turn around and do it to you any-
> way. . . .

[Inter-issue
probe]

Teacher: Do you think trust is more important than staying out of jail?

Ed: Mmmm. . . . Depends on how much the other people mean to you, like whether you *want* them to trust you or not.

[Clarifying
probe]

Teacher: So it would make a difference to you if they were really your friends?

John: Of course. I'd probably tell in either situation but I'd be more reluctant if they were my friends.

David: I could give a year in jail for my friends. It would be a problem but I could give it up. [Elements of stage 3]

[Asks question
to highlight
contiguous-stage
arguments]

Teacher: Would you turn your friends in, Larry?

Larry: All depends if I like him. Or if I wanted to see him suffer. . . . [Elements of stage 2]

[Role-taking
appeal to
family ties]

Teacher: *Larry, what if the person who had to turn you in was your brother?*

Larry: I wouldn't rat on my brother.

[Issue-specific
probe]

Teacher: What is the difference?

John: Oh, I can't do that if it was my brother. I couldn't tell on my brother.

[Issue-specific
probe]

Teacher: *What makes your brother different from a friend?*

John: Blood. Blood is thicker than water. Even if I really disliked my brother or hated him I couldn't tell on him. Blood is thicker than water. [Elements of stage 3]

Paul: I'm not so sure. I wouldn't go up and tell the police if it was my brother, but if I was in a painful situation and the police were pressuring me I wouldn't think it would be wrong to tell. It's not my fault. It's my brother that got himself into trouble and it is his fault. [Elements of stage 2] [16]

In this short excerpt we see the teacher taking active responsibility for introducing a broader frame of reference *and* encouraging other students with different perspectives to interact. Theoretically, the most effective kind of cognitive stimulation from a developmental standpoint is a comment or question (by either student or teacher) that is at a *slightly* more complex level of perspective taking. The teacher did not ask the students what people in society would think if everyone thought as the students did. That question would be more stimulating to students who were already able to take the perspective of a group of friends. Rather, the adult first clarified the students' concept of friendship in order to take their perspective. Then he presented the first possible perspective available beyond their own, that of their family: "What if the person who had to turn you in was your brother? What makes your brother different from a friend?" It was equally important for the teacher to help Larry and Paul hear what John and David had to say about friendship, because they demonstrate the ability to take a perspective that incorporates notions of trust, loyalty, and obligation to others—which are characteristic of mutual role taking at stage 3.

The four kinds of in-depth questioning strategies presented in this section heighten cognitive conflict and extend students' role-taking ability. Although we stress questioning as the major skill, role play and teacher comments initiated for the same purpose also facilitate moral development. In all these ways change in the structure of students moral reasoning is likely to develop over time. Learning to ask effective questions is an art that requires patience and practice.

A Footnote: Two Cautions

Two cautionary notes need to be aired in concluding this discussion of the teacher's role in stimulating cognitive conflict and social perspective taking. Both concern the notion of stimulation.

Caution 1: Not only stimulation. The process of moral development involves both stimulation of reasoning to higher levels *and* expansion of reasoning to new areas of thought. In this chapter we have emphasized the teacher's role in exposing students to a perspective slightly more complex than their own to facilitate stage change. But equally important is the need for the teacher to provide students with new *content* situations for discussion. For example, a high school social studies class discussing moral issues and the law needs to consider moral conflicts as they affect social relationships as well. This expanded use of one's reasoning is necessary because moral growth does not occur in different areas simultaneously. We have seen, for instance, that taking the perspective of family members usually develops before one's understanding of a group of friends or neighbors, and certainly develops before taking the perspective of people in authority roles.

This horizontal stimulation recalls Piaget's theory of *décalage*, (see chapter 2), the process whereby people solidify and "spread out" their present way of seeing the world to include a greater number of activities. It is the way students' thinking matures at one stage before they can benefit from exposure to the next higher stage. Practice in applying moral judgments to many different kinds of moral conflict is crucial to the continuing growth of moral reasoning.

Caution 2: Not overstimulation. The second caution raises the question of how much stimulation facilitates moral development. Stimulation in developmental teaching can be described by such words as "challenge," "activate," "stretch one's thinking." We run the risk of overzealousness, however, in utilizing this concept in practice. *Over*stimulation can occur, changing the character of the process to mean "push," "accelerate," and "speed up."

Piaget labels the idea of accelerating development as the "American question." [17] He is opposed to the idea of trying to speed up the growth of children's reasoning abilities to progress through stages of cognitive development. Another developmentalist, William Perry of the Harvard Graduate School of Education, often draws the analogy between developmental teaching and intervening in the process of helping a plant to grow. Admittedly, he says the comparison is imperfect: a plant as an organism lacks the complexity of human developmental processes. Nevertheless, his point is a simple and important one. To ensure that your plant will continue to grow, you need to water it, provide sunlight for it, and periodically fertilize it. But tugging at the leaves and pulling up on the stem will not help it grow taller. In fact, such actions will interfere with the plant's growth. The lesson holds true for people as well. There is a significant difference between fostering students' growth and "getting them" to grow.

Just as we argue against overstimulation, we also criticize stimulation only. Both stimulation and support are necessary for effective developmental teaching. Teachers need to stimulate their students' thinking. They also need to accept them and respect them as people, whatever their thinking may be. Our students need support in their efforts to incorporate new ways of experiencing the world. The words of two high school English teachers suggest the benefit of stimulation with support:

> In a loving and supportive environment stress can actually have a positive impact by precipitating moral development as the adolescent struggles to make sense of the apparent contradictions which have confronted him. Thus we must learn to let go of our children in order that they may freely interact with the world around them; we must allow them to struggle with life's incongruities, and trust them to make their own meanings.[18]

CREATING CLASSROOM ATMOSPHERE

Rationale

Learning to develop classroom strategies that will stimulate cognitive conflict, and social role taking requires patience and experience. Effective moral education, however, is not possible without prerequisite teaching skills, because interaction in a moral education classroom requires that students go beyond merely sharing information. They must begin to reveal their thoughts and feelings about basic beliefs. Introducing moral issues from a developmental teaching perspective means that the teacher not only helps students to share their opinions about moral problems, but also asks them to share the reasons on which their opinions are based. An atmosphere is required in which self-disclosure may take place.

The journal of a social studies teacher in Albany, New York, as she reflects on her first attempts to become a moral educator, highlights the importance of fundamental teaching skills:

> As I reflect on these experiences I can see that my expectations were quite high because I believe that moral/value education is so important that I would like to see it work immediately. Since I have no criteria to judge from, not having many lessons to judge against, I felt unsuccessful. Also I skipped many preliminary steps with my classes, such as discussion skills, assuming that they knew them, or would "catch on" as we went along.
>
> I shall try again next term but in smaller doses at first and am hopeful my students will be "better people" in terms of their own lives.[19]

An important message in her comments is that "preliminary steps . . . such as discussion skills" are an essential part of moral education. An accepting classroom atmosphere in which trust, empathy, respect, and fairness are intentionally fostered is necessary if development is to occur because students need to feel they can take risks, listen to others, and be listened to in turn. Building a positive classroom climate is part of effective teaching in general and is not restricted to classrooms that provide stimulation of students' moral reasoning.[20]

The importance of a trusting and respectful classroom atmosphere is often neglected in discussions of moral education practice. Yet it is crucial to the entire process. Following are a series of five teaching strategies that may help to promote such a climate. They include the importance of physical arrangements, grouping, modeling acceptance, listening and communication skills, and encouraging student-to-student interaction. These skills go hand in hand with the other strategies discussed throughout this chapter. They should not be seen as isolated preparation exercises; they are as much the "real" curriculum as the discussion of moral issues.

Building a Facilitative Classroom Atmosphere

PHYSICAL ARRANGEMENT

Most fundamental to a positive classroom climate is a seating arrangement that is conducive to discussion among equals. Placing chairs or desks in a circle or square arrangement, with the teacher seated in the midst of the group, gives everyone a chance to see one another and address comments face to face. Whether students sit in chairs, at desks, or on the floor depends on the teacher's own ease with informality and, to some extent, the climate of the rest of the school. The important issue is not relaxation or physical comfort, but communication among students and teacher.

The advantage of a circle arrangement is that nonverbal as well as verbal contact can be developed. This is particularly important for less verbally expressive students. In schools where students are used to sitting in rows, or at isolated tables around the room, the teacher may have to work hard to encourage students to feel comfortable with the new arrangement. Our own experience with junior high school adolescents highlights the persistence a teacher needs in taking responsibility for the physical setting of the classroom:

> I found that students were not used to having discussions which centered on listening to one's another's ideas and opinions. One evidence of the novelty of this experience was that for every class session during this preliminary period, it took at least five minutes to help and encourage all students to manoeuvre their chairs so as to be seated as members of the circle (even though I had arranged the chairs in a circle *before* they came in!). In addition, students would yell out their responses and impulsively interrupt each other without realizing it.[21]

GROUPING

The importance of a physical arrangement conducive to discussion has implications for grouping students. Dividing students into pairs or small groups of from three to five students helps develop a sense of trust and cooperation. Small groups require less risk of exposure, especially when students first share their ideas about moral problems. In these groups students need specific, clearly defined tasks to accomplish if they are to feel secure with others.

Two small-group methods have been used, particularly as *beginning* strategies for teachers. They are most often practiced when teachers are learning to lead discussions, particularly of hypothetical dilemmas.[22] These strategies, however, are limited in their effectiveness over time. Initially, they can help students and teacher to begin to recognize the importance of focusing on reasoning.

Strategy 1: Students are asked to divide into three small groups according to those who agree, disagree, and cannot decide about the solution to a particular moral problem. Each group discusses and records the best reasons its members can think of for solving the conflict the way they do. The teacher then circulates among the three groups, helping students generate their reasons. At the end of this group work the teacher asks each group to report its list to the class for comparison and further discussion.

As an initial strategy this technique helps students feel comfortable with moral discussions, because they are placed in a group with people who agree with them. At the same time, they can begin to see that their classmates may hold a similar opinion, but for very different reasons. These reasons, of course, reflect different stages of moral development.

Strategy 2: The teacher organizes the class into random groups of students who have different solutions to the moral conflict. Each small group has an open-ended discussion of their differences of opinion, sharing the reasons for them.

This method is more open-ended than the first strategy. Teachers concerned that a given group of students lack prerequisite discussion skills may find these random groups too unstructured and therefore less productive than groups of strategy 1. Like the first strategy, however, this format helps teachers begin to identify the range of stages of moral reasoning used in their classroom.

Example of strategy 1: In an upper elementary or junior high classroom, a teacher might find the reports of three groups discussing the Heinz dilemma as follows:

Group A: Heinz should steal the drug because . . .

1. His wife would be so mad at him if she found out he wouldn't do that for her. She'd kill him. [Elements of stage 1]
2. After all, his wife cooks for him all those years and looks after the house. He owes it to her. [Elements of stage 2]
3. What if he gets sick sometime? If she lives, she might get back at him when he's sick and not help him out either. He wouldn't want that. [Elements of stage 2]
4. Well, a good husband would do that for his wife; they've loved each other all those years and he has an obligation to her since they have a good relationship. He knows she would do the same for him if the situation were reversed. [Elements of stage 3]

Group B: Heinz should not steal the drug because . . .

1. It's against the law. He might get caught and have to go to jail. [Elements of stage 1]
2. What if she never did anything for him? Why should he? She probably wouldn't steal for him, so he shouldn't steal it for her. [Elements of stage 2]
3. It's the druggist's fault if she dies, not Heinz's. He couldn't help it. He can just say he couldn't do it because the druggist wouldn't let him buy the drug. It's not right to steal something from someone else without paying for it. The druggist says he needs the money too. [Elements of stage 2]
4. He shouldn't do it. It's not right. If he were to talk it over with his wife, she'd say if she were in his place it wouldn't be right to take it either. If they had a good marriage, she would be able to see it from his point of view and realize he's stuck. [Elements of stage 3]

Group C: Undecided as to whether Heinz should steal the drug . . .

1. You can't decide because stealing is wrong. But then again, maybe he won't get punished as much and not have to go to jail. It depends on the judge. He might let him off easy. But he could be a mean judge too. [Ambiguous]

2. Heinz doesn't want to go to jail, but he loves his wife and she's in such pain. She's been a good wife all these years, giving him what he wants. [Elements of stage 2]

3. It's so hard to decide. He knows the druggist is at fault, but he's caught in the middle of everybody. He loves his wife and she's in so much pain. Anyway, a good husband would do it for his wife. But she knows it is against the law too, and he realizes she wouldn't want him to disobey the law. He respects her point of view. [Elements of stage 3]

MODELING ACCEPTANCE

A third vital teacher skill is the ability to model behavior that communicates acceptance and respect, both for the person and for his or her thoughts and feelings. Counselors often call this attitude "unconditional positive regard."

A nonjudgmental atmosphere is critical if students are to feel they can share their ideas about moral issues openly. The teacher is a model-setting participant who sets the standard for the classroom attitude toward learning, as well as for students' attitudes toward one another's ideas.

It is difficult to avoid sending judgmental messages to students. As teachers we cannot shun our own emotional responses to moral conflict. Nor would we want to do this. Even if we worked hard to eliminate verbal style and vocabulary that communicate praise or blame, we still have a vast repertoire of gestures, facial expressions, and tones of voice that convey our personal reactions to what students say.

As suggested in the discussion of questioning strategies, the practice of moral education straddles a fine line. We are asking the teacher to model behavior that helps each student feel accepted as a unique person and at the same time to set a model for the development of a wider repertoire of responses to other people's ideas. That is, we need to accept the *person* while stimulating his or her *thinking*. The variations of teacher response range from supporting, agreeing with, and encouraging elaboration of students' ideas to challenging, questioning, and taking an adversary (devil's advocate) position.

Often, students need to have their feelings accepted *before* their thoughts are challenged. This is particularly true when the moral issue arouses intense emotion. Exploring students' reactions is then necessary because they are too involved in their own point of view to consider anyone else's. The example that follows demonstrates this point in an eighth-grade health education class. As part of their curriculum, the students are discussing medical ethics with a local pediatrician. The physician has just asked, "If your best friend had leukemia and your parents told you that your friend did not know, should you tell him?"

> *Angela:* No, definitely not.
>
> *Sarah:* No, I personally wouldn't because it would be hard to sit there and not tell him.
>
> *Angela:* First of all, he didn't ask me to. It's not up to *us* to tell him how long his life span's going to be.

[Tries to stimulate a different opinion, a "yes" or "don't know"]

> *Adult:* But you're one of the most important people in his life.
>
> *Angela:* If someone's going to tell him, it ought to be his parents.
>
> *(Silence.)*
>
> *Peter (with emotion):* I wouldn't even see him!
>
> *Ramon:* I wouldn't see him either. I'd be afraid I'd tell him.
>
> *(Several argue loudly.)*

[Accepts their feelings]

> *Adult:* You'd have trouble facing it.
>
> *Maria:* It would bother me. I'd just stand there and start to cry if I saw him. Maybe you can't hold it in any longer.

[Accepts their feelings]

> *Adult (warmly):* Yeah, you might cry if you're with him, and he might see you crying. Yeah, that's hard.[23]

In a second example, a high school teacher models a nonjudgmental stance toward a student, and at the same time challenges his ideas. The teacher becomes an open-ended questioner, bordering on a devil's advocate, or cognitive gadfly. The context of this short dialogue is a high school psychology class discussion of the film clip "When Parents Grow Old" from the feature-length film *I Never Sang for My Father*." [24] The grown son in the film, Gene, is trying to decide whether to place his aging father in a nursing home:

[Complicates the circumstances and highlights the moral issue]	*Teacher:* Suppose Gene's father got worse and was severely incapacitated and he asked Gene to kill him as an act of mercy. Should Gene do that?
	Bob: I can't answer that because I don't think I could ask someone else to do it for me.
["Why?" question]	*Teacher:* Why not?
	Bob: I knew you were going to ask that. Why should you put that weight on someone else's shoulders? If you have enough courage to ask someone else to do it, it shouldn't take a great deal more to do it yourself.
[Role-taking question]	*Teacher:* It would be all right if the father did it himself?
	Bob: I'm not saying it would be all right. I'm just saying I can't see asking someone else to dispose of you.
[Personalizes the moral conflict]	*Teacher:* Would it be all right to do it to yourself?
	Bob: I think that ultimately it's up to him. But the hard question is whether or not he's well enough to decide this or not.
[Poses argument at stage 4 to elicit a decision]	*Teacher:* What about the argument that the value of human life is sacred and that no one should take a human life in any case? [25]

Bob is confused here about his position on the question. The teacher is patient with the adolescent's confusion, maintaining a dialogue with him in his confused state. At the same time, though, the teacher stimulates Bob's thinking by asking him to personalize the dilemma and to role-take. The teacher eventually presents an argument at stage 4, a level of complexity he thinks will stretch Bob's thinking.

LISTENING AND COMMUNICATION SKILLS

A fourth necessary teaching skill is the ability to listen and communicate effectively with one's students *and* the ability to foster those same skills in students. The teacher and students need effective communication skills because, as in any thoughtful discussion, (1) people need to be able to follow the flow of topics and to feel that they can make a pertinent contribution; and most germane to Kohlberg's framework, (2) participants in a moral discussion hear and respond to issues with various thinking patterns because of their developmental differences.

If teachers are to help students hear these differences, the teachers must take the principal responsibility for learning to listen carefully to what students say. It is all too common to hear from students what we want to hear from our own framework of reasoning. That is, our preconceived idea of what is the "right answer" stops us short of truly understanding the way students see the same situation. There are at least two major steps in learning to listen—learning to communicate listening and remembering dialogue over time.

Learning to communicate listening. The teacher needs to be active in setting the model as listener when the class begins discussing moral issues. Communicating that one has heard correctly what the other person has said often takes three forms: checking for comprehension, asking for clarification, and encouraging elaboration.

1. Checking for comprehension:
   Did you mean _____ ? or are you saying _____ ?
   Let me see if I can repeat what you just said.
   Could someone else tell us in your own words what _____ just said?

2. Asking for clarification:

Several people look confused (responding to nonverbal cues). Could you say what you're confused about?

I think I understand the first part of your statement. But I lost you when you began to say _____. Could you say it again in another way?

I'm not sure I understand what was just said. Could someone help me out?

3. Encouraging elaboration:

Could you give us an example of what you just explained?

Can you think of a time when the situation we have been talking about happened to you or someone you know?

Could you tell us some more about what you just said?

Sometimes people talk about _____ to describe what you are saying. How is that similar (or different) from what you just said?

We have pointed out that words are used differently at different stages of moral reasoning. The moral educator who asks, "What do you mean, 'You'll get into trouble'?" raises a genuine question. The teacher truly does not know, except by *asking*, which of the following notions a given student may mean:

Getting into trouble means . . .

1. Getting caught by your father and being punished. [Elements of stage 1]
2. Going to jail [Elements of stage 1]
3. Having your friend get back at you for doing something to him. [Elements of stage 2]
4. That your friend will get mad at you and not trust you anymore, and that might destroy the good relationship you have. [Elements of stage 3]
5. Doing something wrong so that the other kids won't think you're a nice kid and won't like you anymore. [Elements of stage 3]
6. Disobeying the law that society has set up to keep order and prevent chaos. [Elements of stage 4]

There is another reason to be clear about the meaning of words students use. If we are unclear about meaning, we can rightly be accused of putting words that students neither intended or understood into their mouths. In both cases, students soon understand the message that the teacher has the "right answer" and that their own opinions matter little.

Finally, we need to be aware that moral educators are in a complicated position regarding what constitutes "good" listening. Taking the role of *only* acknowledging and reflecting back to students what they say will not, over time, expose them to a higher stage of moral reasoning. Still, we cannot stimulate students' thinking *until* we listen well enough to understand what it is we are stimulating. Without listening and communicating skills, cognitive stimulation cannot be accurately practiced by the teacher. In this sense, listening and communication skills are prerequisites to any specific questioning techniques.

Remembering dialogue over time. The second kind of listening skill for teachers to develop is the ability to remember what students say over time. The teacher has a responsibility to be the group historian for three main reasons: (1) a teacher who remembers accurately what students say from one day and one week to the next acts as a model for students to do likewise; (2) the teacher demonstrates interest in students as valuable contributors to what the class learns; and particularly important in Kohlberg's model, (3) students learn to understand the pattern of their own thinking and to differentiate among the kinds of reasoning in the class:

I knew you'd say that, Susan. That's the same argument you gave yesterday when we talked about whether you should shoplift.

I guess I haven't changed my mind very much. I still think going against the law is wrong.

Gee, I don't know what I think now. Mike just said something that changed my mind.

This kind of recognition, the refining of one's ability to hear different reasoning styles, is crucial to students' moral development. They need to hear the differences in one another's arguments to be stimulated by what others have to say. For this reason, the teacher needs to encourage individuals and the group as a whole to remember previous relevant comments. It helps, therefore, if the teacher takes notes on the class over time.

In the following dialogue from a junior high class, the teacher demonstrates the role of group historian. Students are discussing their role play of whether a policeman should arrest his good friend for drunken driving:

[Asks "why?" question]

Teacher: Brian, what do you think is the best reason to arrest him?

Brian: 'Cause the chief told him to arrest drunken drivers. [Elements of stage 1]

[Encourages elaboration]

Teacher: And if you don't?

Brian: Because they told you to and if you don't—

(*Police siren sounds loudly outside classroom. Lots of comments: "There is the policeman now! There they go!" Laughter.*)

[Repeats]

Teacher: Okay, now what were you saying about if he doesn't?

Brian: The policeman could get in trouble. [Elements of stage 1]

Sarah: He won't get into trouble if he doesn't follow the car, but still, if you get the job as policeman, you're still expected to. [Elements of stage 3]

Mei-ling: If he gets into an accident or something, it's kind of his responsibility for not stopping him.

[Asking for clarification]

Teacher: Responsibility in what way?

Mei-ling: It's kinda like if a bartender kept giving someone a drink when he's drunk, it's *his* responsibility. [Elements of stage 3]

["Group historian" role in referring to Luther's previous comment, at same stage as Mei-ling's]

Teacher: I'm kind of thinking, too, of a comment Luther made the first week when we talked about pulling a chair out from somebody, and you said, Luther, it was the responsibility of the *group*, not just the teacher and the two students who were fighting. Is this sort of similar, Mei-ling? [Elements of state 3]

(*Silence; everyone listening closely.*)

Mei-ling: Yeah—.

[Highlights differences in stage arguments]

Teacher: Would it be a different kind of responsibility than being in trouble with the police chief? [26]

ENCOURAGING STUDENT-TO-STUDENT INTERACTION

A fifth prerequisite teaching skill involves combining the previous four skills into an interaction style that encourages student dialogue with one another. Most of our discussion has centered on the teacher's importance as an active model-setting figure in the classroom. It may sound as if the teacher is the controlling force of the moral education classroom. The main purpose, however, of modeling all these attitudes and skills is *to help students interact with one another*. In essence, the teacher is trying to foster these same skills in students.

Two outcomes may occur when the teacher systematically builds experiences of student-to-student interaction into the classroom. First, students benefit from the cognitive conflict and different perspectives generated by their fellow classmates as much as, if not more than, those offered by the teacher. Second, when encouraged to do so, students begin to initiate the learning process for themselves. That is, they learn to confront and stimulate one another's thinking.

The following example illustrates the first point. In this fifth-grade class, children are in the middle of small-group discussions about a moral problem that Carl, a member of the class, brought to school for discussion:

You know the ticket for the free ice cream you get from Baskin-Robbins (an ice-cream chain in the Boston area) for your birthday?

Well, I wrote my name down just once to get one and I got three in the mail. The moral problem is, should I keep them or should I bring the two extra ones back? This is a real one. It happened to me. I have them at home.[27]

One boy, David, became agitated by the argument of one of his classmates over the dilemma and decided that he wanted to switch groups:

Leader: Why switch? You liked your reason a minute ago.
David: I still like my reason but I like her reason more.
Leader: Why?
David: Her reason is bigger and so it includes my reason.[28]

This is a dramatic example in which a child experienced cognitive disequilibrium as a result of listening to a classmate's reason at the next higher stage to his own. The teacher worked hard to encourage this kind of listening.

A second example demonstrates the impact of student-to-student interaction on a high school adolescent. The dialogue, part of a junior-senior psychology class, highlights that students both benefit from one another's arguments and learn to "take over" the teaching role for themselves. The teacher intervenes very little. Students are discussing a film segment from *Abandon Ship*, in which Captain Holmes, commander of an overcrowded lifeboat adrift at sea, decides to order several people overboard to avoid sinking everyone: [29]

[Highlights the moral issue]

Teacher: The last thing that Holmes says in the movie is, "You're alive. It was right." Certainly one question would be, was it right?

George: I don't think it was because he was putting himself in the place of God.

[Stimulates opposite opinion for George]

Joan: But didn't somebody have to?

[Highlights the moral issue for Joan]

Jim: Do you think he was right, Joan?

> *Joan:* I'm not going to give my opinion. (*Laughter.*) I'm tired of giving my opinion. I'm not going to give my opinion until the end because it always changes from the beginning to the end of the class. So I'm going to wait until the end this time. (*More laughter.*)

In reflecting on the class, the teacher comments about this dialogue:

> Joan had been a very active participant in class discussions and this statement seemed to indicate she was experiencing cognitive conflict as she gave her reasoning and was heard by others. This, of course, is one of the prime objectives of moral discussions. Joan did in fact take an active part in the discussion of this film. Again, as the discussion proceeded Joan found her ideas changing. She at first defended Holmes on the grounds that someone had to assume authority and make a decision.

Joan continues to participate in the discussion, despite her protests to the contrary:

> *Joan:* I think his timing was off but someone had to take the authority. The authority had to be taken and the only reason I would say it wasn't right is the very idea of taking that much responsibility is sort of hideous. But I'm saying he had to take it.

[Stimulates his own thinking]
> *Bob:* When I watched the film it bothered me that it was happening but at the same time it had to happen because everyone would die or twelve or fourteen or whatever would live and he had to decide it was worth it. Should everyone die or should twelve people live, especially when you know which twelve people will live. I guess I kept feeling he shouldn't be doing it but I began to realize I think that what was bothering me was that the people weren't doing anything on their own. He had to do it for them.

[Reflects on her
own cognitive
conflict]

Joan: The whole idea (*pause*), I think (*pause*), again my opinion is changing but I'd say maybe he really could have left it up to God. When the storm comes and the boat goes over, whoever is supposed to hang on will hang on and whoever doesn't, doesn't. But the captain took that responsibility (*pause*) okay (*pause*)? It's sort of— that's why it's so hard for me. If he really was going to take the authority of doing that and the people let him, in a way they really let him do that.

Again the teacher remarks on the dialogue after the class:

Joan clearly was in conflict about her judgment of Mr. Holmes's decision. At first she was fairly sure of her judgment of the situation. But as the discussion proceeded she began to question her initial reasoning as a result of the various arguments raised.[30]

Clearly, Joan gives us evidence that students are affected by others' comments and questions when they learn to listen and communicate.

In summary, the five skills described in this section constitute the beginnings of classroom atmosphere in which moral development can occur. It is important to reiterate that these skills are not necessarily developed separate from, or before, teachers' attempts to lead moral discussions. The fostering of moral awareness, effective questioning strategies, and prerequisite teaching skills all need to be integrated into the moral educator's teaching behavior.

Two caveats hold true. First, teachers need to work systematically at building a facilitative classroom environment. An atmosphere of trust and acceptance does not simply happen as a result of students and teacher being together over time. The teacher, we have pointed out, is instrumental in creating an accepting atmosphere by modeling specific behaviors from the first teacher-student interaction that takes place. Students are often not accustomed to participating in discussions that center on listening to others' opinions. It is the teacher's role to help them learn to talk to one another and to respond to one another's ideas and feelings. Planning must be directed as part of the core of the moral education classroom to teach discussion skills.

Second, it takes time to develop an environment of trust, respect, empathy, and fairness. This is especially true when students are at the preconventional level of moral reasoning. These students perceive obligations to other people as stemming from people in authority, as is characteristic of stage 1 reasoning; or as a means of "getting something" from others through cooperating with them, as at stage 2 thinking. Teachers who understand their students' level of moral development tend to be more patient when students do not respond to adults' "perfectly reasonable" arguments. Moral development takes time. We cannot expect instant trust and empathy to spring up overnight.

DIFFICULTIES OF PRACTICE

Throughout this chapter we have asked the reader to think about the teaching role in new ways, to develop new interaction strategies, and to reintegrate current teaching skills into a new framework. In asking this, we realize that we ascribe the role of juggler to the teacher. One problem in embarking on this new role is a lack of awareness of what to expect. For this reason, we wish to highlight certain assumptions inherent in the moral education process that, when unrecognized, may make practice difficult.

Peer pressure often discourages open and honest communication. Peer-group norms of conformity run counter to the atmosphere needed for effective moral education. Since the discussion of moral issues involves self-disclosure, students take a risk when they state a deeply felt conviction. Teachers interested in the moral development of their students are asking them to engage in behavior that is the opposite of what peer pressure dictates: "Take your own stand on this issue, back your opinion with your own reasons, and feel free to disagree with what others in the class believe."

The norms of the peer group, particularly among adolescents, affect the attitudes and behavior of students even before they enter the classroom. When youngsters of the same age are confronted by one another in large numbers, they feel nervous and threatened. Extreme pressure mounts to conform to an expected code of behavior, one that reduces the possibility that individuals will be placed on "public display" in front of their peers. An adolescent wishes to avoid standing out like a sore thumb. If adults demonstrate their sincerity and willingness to accept all opinions, including "unpopular" ones, however, students often lose their self-consciousness and feelings of exposure before a jury of peers. Instead, they become interested in issues for their own sake. This motivates them to say what they really think, even at the risk of disagreeing with friends. With the loss of self-consciousness they can begin to hear, and benefit from, the differences in reasoning.

An additional variable, most frequent at the upper elementary and junior high levels, is the effect of subgroupings. Cliques within the class hierarchy indirectly wage war with one another through the vehicle of discussion. All members of one group take pride in taking a stand in opposition to a rival group. Rival phalanxes of opinion are hard to penetrate even by the most experienced teacher. Teachers in these circumstances have a difficult time and need all the patience and perseverance they can muster. Encouraging students to write down their opinions and reasons before discussion is helpful, as is organizing the class into small groups of three or four students.

Moral issues often involve the examination of authority roles. Classroom discussions of what is right and fair inevitably turn to a questioning of authority relationships in class, school, and family. This is so because our beliefs about authority figures are a vital part of our moral judgment.

Teachers who have been used to operating as the sole authority in the classroom, not sharing their beliefs or reasons for beliefs openly, might find it painful to accept an atmosphere in which authority roles and responsibility are examined. Such a classroom might seem no less threatening to students who are oriented toward teacher-approved behavior, and who in the process also worry about their classmates' opinion.

The authority question also relates to the school as a whole. When schools demand adherence to external authority as the sole arbiter of moral decision making, they thwart movement to postconventional moral development.[31] In fact, teachers and administrators frequently rely on their authority for the very purpose of avoiding risk taking, which would expose their vulnerability and loss of control. All of us have experienced this use of authority.

Teachers need to consider the degree and amount of authority-related discussion that they and their school environment are willing to confront. Conducted in the spirit of inquiry, these discussions are useful to both students and teacher, because they create greater understanding of the reasons behind classroom rules and guidelines. Considered in the spirit of social action, such discussions lead to a more democratic sharing of the governance process, and the building of Kohlberg's so-called just community.

Cognitive conflict can be painful for students. Dialogue with self and others means that students often go through a period of personal doubting and confusion when their thinking has been taxed. For new patterns to develop, old patterns have to be challenged. The experience of having one's accustomed way of thinking challenged can be painful. It is helpful to students if teachers take time to have them discuss these feelings, as in this example where a high school junior confronts her personal moral philosophy:

> *Lisa:* The only thing—I tell you I'm really confused because I, since this class, I've had to consider an awful lot more than I ever would. And I'm so confused as to what is really right and what is really wrong. I feel like in a sense that I know so little about what is right and what's wrong that I can't really say that Hitler was even bad. Or that we all have a right to our own lives. I don't know.

[Clarifies]   *Teacher:* One thing, we are making a distinction between whether Hitler was bad or whether he was wrong.

Lisa: I don't really know whether he was wrong. Just because I don't want to say anything definite. I'm afraid of, somebody could prove me wrong in a different way.

If I was to be selfish, if I was to really think to myself and be selfish about the whole thing I'd say Hitler was wrong. I would say that we all have a right to our own lives. As a matter of fact last week when you asked about how we would consider, how we would judge things morally right or wrong the first thing that occurred to me was whatever pleased myself, whatever I thought was good for myself. That's how I decided what was right or wrong. Then I thought about it a little while and I thought, "Gee, I wouldn't feel very good about myself unless other people felt good about it too." And then I could keep going on and on and on, just keep enlarging on it really. And then I just really didn't know how to go about judging things.

[Communicates listening]

Teacher: In other words you were judging on an egotistical basis, what was good for you?

Lisa: Yeah, and then I just decided that wasn't right either but I couldn't find anything better.

[Communicates listening; remembers her comments over time]

Rich: And then you went beyond to larger and larger numbers of people beyond yourself.

Lisa: Right. So I'm going to stay up in the air.

[Links to future curriculum]

Teacher: You may find the idea of justice which we've been talking about and will talk about next time helpful in finding a way of deciding what's right and wrong.

Lisa: Maybe we should talk about this some more then. I'm doing a lot of thinking.[32]

Lisa's questioning is characteristic of people who are transitional in their thinking from one stage to another. It was important to Lisa that the teacher and her classmates take her doubting seriously, and that the teacher listen to her concerns.

Moral development does not necessarily result from verbal activity. Active thinking is not equated with a high quantity of verbal activity. Internal dialogue is the crucial factor leading to cognitive disequilibrium. It helps, of course, for students to articulate their internal conflict aloud. Nevertheless, the so-called quiet student is as likely to experience development in moral reasoning as the more active one. Conversely, students who voice their opinions frequently do not always change their pattern of reasoning over time. Talking by itself does not necessarily challenge a person's thinking.[33]

The vignette that follows demonstrates the importance of students' internal dialogue, whether they share their thoughts aloud or not. As part of their curriculum, eighth-grade health education students were discussing medical ethics with a local pediatrician. When the class was over, the doctor remarked that "the most active participant of all, a student who didn't say a word during the entire discussion" intrigued him the most. The physician continued:

> I kept watching his face during the discussion. His mind was working too hard on what was being said to be able to contribute anything out loud to the discussion. He didn't have time to talk. He was too busy thinking.[34]

Some moral dilemmas fail to generate discussion. Sometimes a given moral problem does not "work" with a certain group of students. The dilemma may not be appropriate for their developmental level. As discussed earlier in this chapter, it is important for a teacher to anticipate the reactions and reasonings of the class *before* presenting the dilemma to them.

Another reason why a dilemma may lead to a dead-end discussion is that students sometimes agree on a single solution to the problem in a few minutes. The teacher may then have to take a devil's advocate stance or change the circumstances to elicit disagreement.

A third reason why certain dilemmas fail is that the content is too emotionally charged for a given group, which often happens when a dilemma is too personalized or not age-appropriate. Then teachers may find that students "regress," both in their ability to listen and communicate and in their willingness to reason through the problems in depth.

Finally, sometimes we must realize that even the best planning on the teacher's part may result in a "flat" discussion. Experienced moral educators are not immune to this problem, as teacher Paul Sullivan attests after one such discussion that he recalls in his doctoral dissertation:

> There is nothing quite so disconcerting to a teacher as to see his discussion go down the drain before his eyes. It is exceedingly difficult to discuss an issue when the discussants do not see it as an issue . . . . The teacher must be flexible. Materials will fail at times and the teacher must be able to switch from these specific stimuli to other materials or to questions which will produce conflict and discussion.[35]

In summary, then, teachers can anticipate some difficulties in practicing moral education for the first time. The five assumptions above need to be considered inherent in the process of fostering moral development. In addition, evaluation and analysis of each class can benefit teachers as they learn to predict other pitfalls that might arise.

CONCLUSION: COGNITIVE DISEQUILIBRIUM FOR TEACHERS

In closing this chapter we return to the experience of teachers as they begin to practice moral education. Just as children and adolescents must be exposed to cognitive conflict and new perspectives, so must teachers. These moments of new awareness and insight are what help teachers integrate the inevitable and necessary frustrations that accompany teacher growth. We believe that conflicting feelings and seesaw experiences are a necessary part of embarking on something new, including moral education. Teacher Joan Ripps of Schenectady, New York, describes her feelings in her classroom journal as she "takes the plunge" to begin her first moral discussions:

I knew that I had to take the plunge and begin practicing what I had learned. Where to begin? That was the question that really plagued me and was at the bottom of my procrastination. Well, *Man: A Course of Study* had many dilemmas such as the theory of dominance or wife-swapping. Then again there was the field of law education. That was really the safer and more appealing area to begin, I rationalized. Should we discuss the dilemma of "Justice for all with more for the wealthy?" How about the dilemma of "Justice is blind but not color blind"? So many places to take the plunge, but I was still afraid of the water. Then I realized that my stage fright was due to my lack of experience. We had had so much theory, so much stimulation but not enough of the nuts and bolts. We had everything one needed to be convinced of the need to use moral dilemmas, but no practical experience in actual classroom use. So I played safe. I decided to use the Heinz dilemma. It did not really fit into my curriculum, but then again I could defend it if needed with the statement that I was teaching the concept of law and order. This facet did not disturb me too much and so I drew up the lesson plans. By this time we had received additional literature and I had found some good hints for running discussions to follow in my preparation. I did it according to the book. Five minutes for this, and ten for that, and was pleased with the early stages of the lesson. Large group work went well, small group work went well, and then it was time for the opposing groups to present their ideas to each other and "expose themselves to the levels of moral reasoning." I eagerly convened them into the large circle, and with probing questions asked for their group reasons. Thirty seconds later it was all over. The shouting, in some cases screaming, of the kids made my classroom seem like the tower of Babel. I quickly called them to order, but they were not discussing their positions.

I took the class again, and nothing that I did could establish the warm trusting atmosphere for an interchange of moral reasoning. I ended the class by "leading" the discussion or as is often found in a traditional classroom, directing the discussion. But I became the focal point of the class. I knew that I had failed! Then to top it off, one of my students asked me what I would have done in that dilemma situation. I was not prepared for the question. While I knew what I would do if I were presented with such a dilemma I feared public announcement. I was afraid to publicly say that I favored the theft of the drug. I had not informed my administrator of the lesson plan and I had visions of the kids going home to their parents "translating" the lesson and messing up the situation in such a way that it would cause waves, a serious infraction of the unstated rules of the school. And so to my embarrassment, I told the kids the opposite of my moral choice and faked the reasoning behind such a choice!

After class I sat with my head in my hands, a pounding headache from the noise and commotion during the attempted discussion. Also, there was the result of my failure to be honest with the kids. Where had I gone wrong? I had carefully set the stage, chairs in a circle, a fairly even split on the dilemma, a large paper and marking pens to record the ideas of the groups, and had kept well within the suggested time limits for each stage of lesson. Then it dawned on me. I had never had an open discussion in the classroom. My class discussions had all been teacher directed with some but very little free discussion of a really controversial subject. The kids had no experience in a large group discussion and had no skills in listening as well as talking. They all could talk, but very few could listen and respond to their fellow students. I had not failed, I had revealed a major weak point in my education. I also realized that the kids were unsure of my position, that they needed to know what the "right answer" was. . . . I needed teaching strategies for group discussions on moral issues, and the ability to create a classroom climate that made the student feel safe enough to voice his/her opinion without the need of my approval.[36]

For Joan, a "pounding headache" was the result of a lack of "strategies for group discussions" and an inability "to create a classroom climate that made the student feel safe enough." The next sentence of her journal, however, begins with optimism:

If the above makes you think I quit using moral dilemmas in the classroom, or that I am not among its advocates, let me assure you that it did not.[37]

Beginning moral educators have their ups and downs, but Joan's commitment is a common thread among teachers wishing to become moral educators.

At least six elements underlie this willingness to work hard at moral education: (1) genuine concern for the moral dimensions of teaching, (2) enthusiasm for testing new ideas, (3) willingness to be self-reflective, (4) flexibility· in trying new approaches, (5) willingness to learn and even fail in public view, and (6) commitment to continue over time.

Teachers react to different aspects of the learning process according to their individual needs, teaching style, and philosophy. This is only natural; the moral education teaching process is not intended to "change" teachers to adapt to one certain method. Rather, we ask teachers to integrate their current teaching interests and talents into an educational rationale that fosters moral awareness and moral development. For Sharon Wilkins, this philsophical examination was more critical than building classroom climate or trying out new strategies:

> After an initial exposure to moral education theory at a workshop, I thought of myself as an "instant convert." "Instant conversions" are generally suspect to me and I was uncomfortable with my own enthusiasm. Some of my colleagues were skeptical or taking a conservative "wait and see" attitude toward what might prove to be just another educational fad. After an intense internal dialogue (to extend the analogy, a "soul-search"), I realized that I wasn't a convert at all. I had always been a "believer," but thought of it as my personal philosophy toward classroom teaching. It now had a label of sorts. I could be a moral educator or humanist teacher or whatever I chose to call myself while espousing this philosophy, with its attendant theory and techniques in the classroom. The acceptance, resolution, and subsequent integration of a moral education philosophy into my personal approach as a teacher was the most important step. Without that personal dialogue and integration, the workshop would have simply meant three Fridays away from my classes and three Saturdays away from my family. I could introduce a dilemma once in a while as a relief from content presentation as many would do, or I could incorporate a moral awareness into every part of my teaching. There was really no choice.
>
> Because I was a "disciple" of sorts (unbeknownst to myself) the classroom atmosphere was already there.[38]

Each teacher finds different sources of excitement and frustration in learning to become a moral educator. The important thing is for individuals, teachers and students, to find meaning in the experience.

To conclude this chapter, let us look at individual experiences of three teachers in the Brookline, Massachusetts, public schools who have been involved for at least three years in the classroom application of Kohlberg's theory.[39] Each teacher, working with a different age group, describes two basic issues: (1) the personal meaning of integrating Kohlberg's theory into their ten or more years of teaching experience and (2) their individual approach to adapting the general moral education model to accommodate their own needs.

First, elementary school art teacher Barbara Traietti describes how knowledge of moral development helps her explore her teaching role in new ways:

I have gained a great deal of insight in dealing with students since my involvement in moral development workshops. Previously, I had felt obligated to be the sole provider of morality or law in the art room when situations arose concerning a behavior code. I now feel more comfortable in questioning the class or a group of students regarding what they think the appropriate action or behavior might be.

When fourth graders start to draw pictures of people they "don't like, in horrible situations," for example, I can engage them in a discussion. When I ask them whether it is all right to make pictures like that, I can gain a better understanding of how they are apt to reason about and make sense of their world and their place in it. From there I can relate what they are doing to the concepts in art that I am trying to teach.

In this statement, teacher Traietti basically underscores two important changes in her teaching derived from moral development theory: (1) a movement from adult authority over classroom behavior to a shared responsibility and (2) increased perspective taking of her students' points of view. She has also developed ways to highlight moral issues that confront art and society by eliciting a concrete link between the moral reasoning of the artist in each child and the artists of the world:

Recently my upper graders were looking at examples of art from different periods. When confronted with a nonobjective painting by William DeKooning, they started laughing and questioned how it could be a legitimate work of art: "My three-year-old sister could do better!" and "Imagine, some jerk paying money for that junk." I asked them to give the reasons behind their reactions. They felt that a good artist should be skillful in drawing things as realistically as possible. This is a very understandable response from youngsters who are at the point of struggling to achieve realism in their own art work. I then questioned the group further, asking if they felt comfortable making a decree that all art should be realistic in order to be considered "good" art: Did they think it fair that all artists should paint or draw in certain ways to fulfill such a law or decree? Suppose one of them were an artist that could draw everything with a great deal of skill in making everything look quite real, but that they were tired of drawing that way? Is it fair that he or she could not try another way, through color and form?

I was aware in raising these questions that the students were dealing with concepts of law, justice, and power in their social studies classes, specifically in regard to Hitler's rise to power as a dictator. The discussion went back and forth between different students as to what was right and wrong. They soon forgot the problem of personally liking or disliking a certain painting, and were instead deeply concerned about artistic freedom versus dictatorial decree.

I don't think for a minute that I have developed a class full of DeKooning lovers, but I do believe they have gotten a sense of the role freedom and art can play in their lives. I now have a vehicle to carry the questioning further, to complicate an issue for them so they do not become "stuck" with their first assessment of a situation. Rather, I try to help them see it from different viewpoints. In the past I would probably have tried to justify DeKooning's painting to them. This would not have gotten to any issues they could use or with which they could identify.

In this example, the elementary teacher also shows us her commitment to linking the curriculum in one classroom to that of another. That is, being aware of moral issues inherent in the students' social studies curriculum helped her to formulate meaningful and stimulating questions in her art class. Such continuity enhances the possibilities for growth in students' moral reasoning.

The second teacher, Margot Strom, who teaches at the junior high level, discusses how knowledge of moral development has helped her teaching to become more stimulating to herself and her students:

Learning about moral development came at a time in my life when teaching was becoming routine, when my teaching practices were successful, and when students went away saying, "I've learned a lot in her class, and she's a good teacher." But I didn't trust that. It wasn't until I began to discover moral development and ego development—development—that I began to feel challenged; that I began to see new dimensions in my classroom with my students and myself. I knew instinctively that there was something missing. For nine years kids were saying, "You're a good teacher." But inside I was feeling, "You're not quite." I don't trust that.

I found a real interest in theory and development. I found that this learning allowed what people were saying to come up close to what I thought was good and fair. This body of knowledge expanded my horizons, helped me realize that educating is more than teaching. It really feels good to hear kids say at the end of the year, not, "I learned *Lord of the Flies*," or this or that, but that, "I enjoyed those discussions; this was meaningful to me. This was interesting." I say,

"Terrific!" It is interesting to me too. The class is still interesting to me.

Focusing on moral development has taught me that skills are related; that it is not just a moral dilemma discussion that fosters development. It is not only posing a conflict situation. It's realizing what grade you're teaching, what age you're teaching, pulling together all the skills, and calling those the developmental basis—vocabulary, writing, listening, and all the group process skills. These are also development, not just discussing a moral dilemma.

You see, I now have the confidence to be critical. When you first learn a new theory, you are intimidated. And you say, "Everybody else understands it." But the writing is difficult, the language and vocabulary are difficult; it's a new educational theory, it's a philosophical theory. And finally, you tackle it, and you begin to draw parallels. You begin to use it a little and feel comfortable with it. And finally, you're able to say, "*I* know what works; *I* can be critical." And when you're more critical of something, what's there is more useful.

Here we see that Margot Strom has the ability to be critical of her own teaching and to take a thoughtful, inquiring attitude toward Kohlberg's theory as it relates to her own classroom needs. This attitude enables her to create, from existing theory and practice, new directions in her teaching:

I have had to learn how to really listen, to relate to what each child says, to hear what they are saying, to respect them. My students have started to evaluate their own work with me, to learn ways to share the power. We have discussions of fairness. I think the teacher must find places to do that, no matter what the curriculum. The teacher has to struggle constantly with the question of what the relationship between student and teacher means. What are my obligations and responsibilities to the class and the school?

One of my concerns is that a moral dilemma discussion doesn't allow enough time for students to practice being moral or fair or caring, except that they're building up trust listening to one another. Children need the chance to be proud of themselves, to master something so they can feel good. What have you done with a dilemma discussion a week? You're just talking a lot in the class. The next step is to bring these dilemmas alive in the class, to give students more situations to practice what they say or find. Bringing analogies in is very important, if you are unable to get to it outside the classroom.

Students now tell me that they go away with skills they did not have before, that help them recognize conflict situations. They also realize that conflict situations are full of frustration. Moral education gives them tools to face life, as well as classes in school. And in the end, when they evaluate themselves, they say, "This meant something to *me*." They're at that point in their lives when they are moving from the concrete to the abstract, so everything I do with them is an eyeopener. You have the chance at this age to turn them off or to make cynics of them. You also have the chance to help them ask questions, to sparkle; to see that the world is interesting and exciting, and full of conflict, but that we can move on.

Margot realizes the limitations of seeing moral education as defined by the discussion of moral dilemmas. Her growing interest concerns the expansion of moral awareness to the governance process of her classroom, by involving her students in their own evaluation, discussing injustices as they arise in the classroom, and helping students find opportunities to act on their moral reasoning.

Yet another way of integrating Kohlberg's theory and educational strategies is reflected in the work of high school social studies teacher Thomas Ladenburg, also of Brookline, Massachusetts. He describes how he has enhanced his twenty years of teaching American history through writing and teaching curriculum within a cognitive developmental framework:

After being introduced to Kohlberg's work in a series of four intensive workshops in Brookline, I discovered that I had indeed been doing moral education, although in a somewhat clumsy and haphazard way. It suddenly struck me that all of the times I had had some very good discussions in my class, the students were talking about moral issues—such as whether Truman should have dropped the bomb on Hiroshima, whether the passengers and crew on the *Lusitania* were adequately warned, or whether landlord or tenants should be responsible for repairing broken windows or clearing litter in the halls.

Kohlberg had said somewhere that each child is his own moral philosopher. That idea really hit home. Even my own children have very definite ideas of what behavior on my part is fair and what types of punishment are not. What struck me with increasing clarity was that these conceptions were indeed reasoned at different levels, that Kohlberg did not make up the stages, but that they existed in that invariant, sequential order that he claimed. That helped me understand why my ten-year-old would respond much more quickly to the threat of losing money from his allowance if his room were not clean, than my sermon on the virtues of neatness.

It was also soon clear to me that my students were capable of understanding, participating in, and discussing issues which involved stages of reasoning within their developmental levels, while they were bored to tears with questions that raised issues too far above their own competence. This does not mean, however, that we should forego asking meaningful questions about the nature and structure of our society. This in fact has been my own personal commitment in teaching and curriculum writing—to raise the substantial issues and more difficult questions in our history within the range of the students' moral reasoning ability. Once they are "hooked" into the curriculum in this way, I can begin to stimulate their capacity to think beyond that starting point. With this perspective I have learned that a fifth-grade class can discuss the merits of federalism versus anti-federalism. The difference is in the way the adolescent and child understand the nature of the conflict. The fifth grader needs a concrete reference point from his or her own immediate experience. The right to secede, for example, is in the words of my fifth-grade son, "like quitting the club and taking the clubhouse with you." Most eleventh graders, on the other hand, can begin with the abstract notion of secession itself.

The most reassuring knowledge to me, however, is that all the exercises that have traditionally been seen as ways to interest and involve students—role plays, mock trials, small group discussions, simulations, and so on—have a developmental benefit. Educators have always stressed the importance of that nebulous and indefinable goal of teaching: to help students to think. Now we not only know more about what we are doing and have ways to measure our success, but we know enough to know how to do it better.

Thomas Ladenburg sees the importance of using Kohlberg's approach to enhance his teaching in two ways: (1) to heighten the moral awareness of students in relation to the most fundamental ethical decisions we have had to face throughout our history; and (2) to take the cognitive perspective of his students in order to understand their current pattern of thinking, with the goal of stimulating their reasoning to more sophisticated understanding.

In this chapter we described a model of moral education that begins with the teacher's own awareness of self as a moral philosopher and facilitator of moral growth in students. This framework delineates the importance of helping students become more aware of moral issues in their lives, as teachers develop open-ended discussion strategies to stimulate cognitive conflict and perspective-taking ability. A major foundation underlying this entire moral education process is the development of a trusting and respectful classroom atmosphere.

In addition, the voices of practicing teachers have communicated the importance of curiosity, sensitivity, and self-examination as basic to developmental moral education. These qualities, together with a clarity about one's own personal teaching goals, help educators develop the self-confidence to take the next step toward curriculum reconstruction.

6

Curriculum Construction for Moral Education

The aim of this chapter is to provide a rationale for, and some examples of, the integration of moral development theory with the process of curriculum construction. Because teachers should be concerned with teaching specific content, this chapter explains how a concern for content need not exclude a concern for promoting moral reasoning.

CONTENT AND STRUCTURE AS TEACHING OBJECTIVES

Although moral development theory focuses on the way we structure our thoughts about moral issues, the substance or content embodied within that structure is clearly important and should continue to be a primary focus for teachers. It is a misinterpretation of Kohlberg's work to say that *what* we teach should be ignored in favor of putting all our energy into promoting stage change through moral discussion. This misconception may have been formed because so much *research* has emphasized results of the technique called moral discussion. The fact that these discussions have substance is equally important.

Analyses of moral issues may result from an examination of three types of data—hypothetical, content specific, and real or practical concerns. Hypothetical dilemmas, such as the Heinz dilemma, are not based on fact, but they are believable. The major value of hypothetical issues is that students have less personal involvement in them; thus, they are more willing to risk public discussion of them and to generalize the principles involved. Content-based dilemmas are found in a particular discipline of study, such as President Truman's World War II decision to drop the atom bomb, found in the study of American history. Content-based dilemmas can demonstrate to students moral dimensions of the lives of people they are studying, and the fact that issues of morality transcend time and place. Real or practical dilemmas, such as "Should I tell the teacher that my friend is cheating on the test?" maximize emotional involvement and thus personal interest in the topic.

Each kind of moral dilemma is substantive and involves the use of particular data, concepts, generalizations, and principles. Consequently, what is normally referred to as "substance," "knowledge," "content," "subject matter," or "material" plays an important role in moral education. This chapter examines how the objectives of moral development may be met while adhering to the legitimate content demands of schools.

WHAT IS A MORAL DEVELOPMENT CURRICULUM?

By moral development curriculum we mean a curriculum based on the moral dimensions of life that arise from two information sources common to schooling: (1) the subject matter and (2) the interaction among teachers and students, which is often referred to as the "hidden curriculum." Space limitations prevent us from elaborating on all aspects of curriculum development. But we wish to emphasize how moral development theory can become part of the existing school curriculum by using content-based and reality data. This integration is more difficult than using only hypothetical issues, but it is also more authentic.

This point is illustrated by Joan Ripps, who first attempted moral discussions using hypothetical dilemmas in her law and society class. She used a dilemma that portrayed a teen-ager, Sharon, trying to decide whether to reveal her best friend Jill's identity to the police. Jill was suspected of shoplifting. The use of such hypothetical dilemmas, although they gave Joan Ripps a chance to practice moral development teaching strategies, seemed too contrived to her students.

> It soon became apparent that the Moral Dilemma approach to teaching moral reasoning could only be vital if it could be incorporated into the curriculum. The Sharon dilemmas and the others were all fine exercises but *unless it was part of your curriculum,* it lost its meaning. It became artificial.[1]

Joan began to think about her law curriculum. In what ways, she wondered, could usual content mesh with her concern for moral development. Outside resources helped.

> I sought ways to make it a natural outgrowth of the curriculum. I had a Family Court Judge come to the classroom. One of the questions asked of him by a student presented the perfect situation for a discussion: "Is a public defender for juveniles as good as a lawyer that another juvenile's parents are able to afford to hire?"

As Joan provided her students with additional contacts with legal realities, she noted their increased interest in questioning. After a visit to the county jail, the students asked, "Does jail teach you not to break the law?" Joan also improved her own sensitivity to, and ability to ask, moral questions.

> I found many areas that could launch a discussion. "If you saw a crime being committed, would you report it?" "Knowing what serving on a jury entails, would you accept jury duty if you could legally avoid it?"

One benefit of the integration of reality into the curriculum is that students begin to see the curriculum as relevant to their lives. It is no longer something simply to be tolerated on school time. Joan concludes:

I used the lesson plans, curriculum and what the students brought to the classroom to involve the students in moral discussion. And it worked, it worked very well. Especially when it was not artificial but revolved around them. The discussions were great, and more times than not, organized and productive. One of the important side effects was the student eagerness to begin and to carry the discussion over class time and/or into the end of the day after school.

CURRICULUM DEVELOPMENT

We have asked teachers with whom we have worked to describe the process they use to develop a curriculum incorporating moral development theory. From their responses we have gleaned a pattern. Although we list the activities they found most useful in a logical order, we do not wish to have the list read as if codified in stone. We are fully aware that logic is often the least relevant variable in the psychology of planning a curriculum.

The first five planning procedures listed below are concerned with learning how to structure a curriculum and choose materials that will engage students in thinking about moral issues. Activities 6–10 are concerned with conditions that support the teacher's effort in the development of moral education competence. These procedures suggest that teachers look beyond themselves for help in curriculum development and broaden the opportunities for students to act on their reasoning.

Planning a Moral Development Curriculum

1. *Develop a rationale.* An understanding of the theoretical constructs embodied in the first four chapters of this book is essential in building a moral development curriculum. Because initial practice will be frustrating, one needs to be clear about curricular goals. The rationale is a personal translation of the theory and is required for enhancing clarity in the curriculum-building process.

2. *Identify moral issues in the curriculum.* Moral issues can be found by examining curricular materials (e.g., in literature, history, art) for relationships among persons or be-

tween persons and institutions. Or these issues may center on events in the home, classroom, school, or society. One must assess the issues in relation to the level of reasoning and social role-taking perspective required of the students.

3. *Relate the moral issues to students' lives.* Students should be able to respond to such questions as: Have any of you faced this type of conflict? What would (could, did, should) you do? What other examples of this conflict can you tell us about from your own experience? Have you encountered a similar dilemma in other areas—movies, other classes, your own life?

4. *Use material that promotes role taking.* Role taking means taking another's perspective. Perspective taking helps clarify conflicting issues and makes moral questions more real. Moral development requires that a person realize that people are different with respect to attitudes, thoughts, abilities, feelings, and viewpoints. By role taking, the students can move from a self-centered view of the world to the point where they can see themselves from an external perspective. Role taking is critical to development because it enables individuals to experience moral viewpoints that conflict with their own. Cognitive conflict promotes the development of moral reasoning.

5. *Expose students to more adequate reasoning structures.* The structure of reasoning provided in the curriculum should be slightly higher than the reasoning level of the students. For most people, reasoning one stage above their own creates cognitive disequilibrium and initiates developing a new reasoning structure. Whether this structure is created through reading character dialogue, debating, role plays, interviews, drama or film making, it should stretch the mind.

6. *Encourage students to be curriculum developers.* Opportunities for students to ferret out any moral issues *they* find in content are essential. Once students become aware of moral issues, they will be quick to point them out. Also, students are perceptive evaluators of what

works and what fails and will be willing to share their perceptions with the teacher in initiating curriculum change.

7. *Work with another colleague.* Often we will find that another colleague's thinking out loud jogs our own thinking; the result is greater than the sum of two separate individual's thoughts. This may take only minutes of conversation, but teachers need support and dialogue even as students do. Moral education is a risk-taking enterprise. Being able to share doubts, questions, and successes with a colleague will help create a supportive environment.

8. *Do a pilot test of material.* The use of mini-units may provide a good test of one's first efforts. By asking a colleague to observe, and asking students for their reactions, such changes can be made as utilizing smaller discussion groups or finding a more relevant set of issues. Were the issues too hypothetical? too real? Were the probing questions sufficient to cause disequilibrium? Was enough time provided for students to think about their answers? Was the physical arrangement conducive to discussion?

9. *Examine materials beyond textbook data.* Teachers can utilize movies (including commercial movies), television, records, novels, poetry, art, and newspapers. Once their moral awareness is heightened, they will recognize moral issues everywhere. Examples abound. At this point teachers and students will have to discard some of the available material.

10. *Develop experiences in which students can act on their reasoning.* The opportunity to *act* provides a test of reasoning. Other activities in school life—clubs, athletics, student government—provide opportunities to transfer moral reasoning to moral action. It is crucial to encourage this behavior and provide time to discuss such events. Having students act on their reasoning is an important ingredient in helping them move from moral reasoning to moral behavior.

Taking the Perspective of Students

An important ingredient in selecting relevant moral issues is the teacher's ability to take the social perspective of students. The more teachers can understand the moral viewpoint of their students, the easier the task of curriculum development. As we have discussed previously, teachers' level of moral development may enable them to comprehend the reasoning structure of students.

In designing a curriculum, teachers might ask such questions as: How would my students feel if they were faced with this dilemma? Are these enough facts to make the issue comprehensible and believable? Is there too much information, which will cause confusion? What questions might I ask to help my students see the point of view of _____? In what way is this material connected to previous and future subject matter? Can my students relate these events to their own lives? If I were in their shoes, how might I respond?

These questions are not easily answered. The purpose of the questioning is to create a sensitivity to student reasoning. This sensitivity helps when observing students. Evidence of thinking not only is verbal but also can be inferred from such non-verbal cues as frowns, raised eyebrows, stares at ceilings, hands in hair. Listening to student responses carefully reveals additional clues. Patterns of interactions develop between some students, whereas other students remain consistently silent. Autobiographies, informal chats, written assignments, and careful listening to student dialogue provide numerous clues to what students value and how they think. Taking these data into account provides a context for the discussion of moral issues.

Curriculum Development in Practice

There is no one moral development curriculum, no "teacher-proof" package. Teachers must reconstruct their content and use school life as the bases for promoting moral development. Our faith in this perception emanates from our observation of elementary and secondary teachers and our reading of materials developed by teachers in our workshops and university courses. The examples that follow are from some of these teachers. These examples are not provided as complete renditions of curriculum material; rather, they illustrate the thinking and behavior of teachers that we believe represent the essence of curriculum construction.

Two kinds of examples follow. The first kind illustrates how one might tap the content of literature, history, and reading as sources for moral issues. The second kind demonstrates how the content and process of classroom reality ("hidden curriculum") can be used as a vehicle for moral education. Both kinds of examples illustrate the curriculum-building process. As such, they focus on the first five suggestions for curriculum development: (1) develop a rationale, (2) identify moral issues, (3) relate the moral issues to students' lives, (4) use material that promotes role taking, (5) expose students to more adequate reasoning structures.

THE USE OF LITERATURE

Literature is rich with potential for promoting moral development as part of the traditional school curriculum. In this section we cite examples from three teachers with whom we are acquainted. Guy Bramble teaches in Massachusetts and Andrew Garrod teaches in New Brunswick, Ontario. As graduate students, they developed a literature course employing moral development concepts; we have chosen from their curriculum the example of *Huckleberry Finn*. Muriel Ladenburg of Arlington, Massachusetts, is an English teacher who is fully committed to her content discipline. More recently, she has become interested in a synthesis of the development of moral reasoning and the teaching of literature.

Developing a Rationale

Bramble and Garrod are enthusiastic about teaching literature and see in that endeavor an opportunity to enrich the analysis of selected works by taking into account the moral perspective of both the characters in the narratives and their ninth- and tenth-grade students. The teachers' rationale shows a recognition of their responsibility as moral educators.[2]

> The following curriculum has evolved from our shared conviction that literature offers a rich, and largely unmined, source for moral discussion in the high school classroom. Because our own academic training and interest lie in the field of literature, we have generated a curriculum which seeks to use literature as a vehicle for the stimulation of moral development. This strategy reflects our belief that—in terms of human growth—moral learning is the most meaningful kind of learning that can occur in the classroom; yet, because of our affection for literature, we should be heartily sorry if moral learning came at the expense of, *rather than in conjunction with*, other kinds of learning. Morality is not, after all, a system of abstract ideas which can be learned in a vacuum; it's a perspective on life—a set of principles which, applied to given circumstances, helps to guide one's actions. Far from being exclusive of life and learning, morality is, at least implicitly, an integral part of most of what we do, say and read.

Bramble and Garrod recognize the tension created by multiple teaching objectives. They reiterate the need for fusion and define the role of teacher in a more expansive mode.

> We should make it clear that this curriculum is *not* intended to replace a standard English curriculum. We are English teachers, and we believe in the importance of fostering sensitive and sophisticated readers, just as we try to teach good writing skills (grammar, syntax, spelling, etc.). Nevertheless, we wonder whether these skills and attitudes represent the full extent of our obligation to students. In wrestling with this question, we have gone right to the heart of educational philosophy and the conclusion we have drawn—which is manifest in this curriculum—is that our obligation goes well beyond the teaching of reading, writing and literature. When we consider the world as it exists today, overflowing with greed, hypocrisy, hatred and the power to destroy life itself, we see only too clearly the pressing need to develop a heightened sense of morality in men everywhere—among national leaders, and especially among ordinary citizens.

Muriel Ladenburg also shows that an understanding of moral development theory can help provide a rationale for moral development curriculum: [3] "The premise for such a course rests on generalized knowledge from my professional experience and the distillation of what I have learned about moral development." Ladenburg allows for her students' being high school juniors and seniors. The reality of adolescents' lives and the knowledge of moral development theory help Ladenburg define her rationale.

> It comes as no surprise to most high school teachers, even those with little knowledge of developmental psychology, to see the period of adolescence depicted as one of turbulence, conflict, inconsistency, frustration—an aberration of growth, experienced with peculiar ferocity in our culture. Yet, in his article on "Conflict and Transition in Adolescent Moral Development," Elliot Turiel suggests that it is exactly under stressful interactions young people gain access to the conditions promoting them to more advanced levels of human conduct, attainments unknown in cultures that have no adolescence.

All three teachers created a rationale informed by theory. Selecting content begins in earnest, however, when deciding which of the moral issues embedded in the content are appropriate for analysis.

Identifying Moral Issues

Kohlberg's research indicates that the movement from conventional to postconventional thought rarely occurs before late adolescence. Whereas Bramble and Garrod structured their curriculum with a concern for helping younger students grow into conventional thinking, Muriel Ladenburg developed a literature course that she hoped would challenge the deeply rooted conventional thought of older high school students. To do this she divided her course into two sections. The first section, she says, "presents literature of relativism and rejection, where individuals call into question many central aspects of conventional thought represented by their society." A sense of moral relativity and a rejection of convention are typical of the transition from conventional to postconventional thinking. To help students understand this perspective, Ladenburg chose to use

The Stranger by Albert Camus, *The Conversion of the Jews* by Phillip Roth, *A & P* by John Updike, and *The Loneliness of the Long Distance Runner* by Alan Sillitoe.

In choosing these works she paid attention not only to the usual criteria for good literature but also to a content that would allow students to explore their own values through the characters' lives. Choosing to begin her course with Camus was more than a choice of selecting a book from the usual list of acceptable high school texts. The particular perspective portrayed by the characters in *The Stranger* seemed appropriate to the level of her particular students. Assuming her students to be operating at the conventional level of reasoning, it seemed necessary to find literature that confronted the students not only with similar conventional points of view but also with a perspective beginning to move beyond such convention.

> Camus seeks to jolt the reader from complacent acceptance of conventional morality, and he does so first by attacking the least questioned obligation—that we love our mothers. Tied to this central event, the death of Meursault's mother, are numerous other jabs at the conventional responses that relate to many aspects of the adolescent's life.

Ladenburg focuses on such important adolescent issues as friendship, authority, and self-identity. The treatment of the novel now takes on the potential for exploring the relativity between the moral issues within the novel and those same moral concerns of most adolescents.

> Meursault's behavior at the funeral, his date with Marie, his attitude toward their relationship, his friendship with Raymond all raise questions about Meursault, the main one being is he normal? This kind of question solicits discussion of many generally accepted modes of behavior that students subscribe to and allows them to begin questioning conventionally held views about social conduct, marriage, honor, and friendship.

Guy Bramble and Andrew Garrod also sought relevant moral issues. Although their process of identifying relevant moral issues was like that engaged in by Muriel Ladenburg, the task in their case was to find issues at a level more suitable for younger adolescents, usually moving from preconventional to conventional thinking. They chose Twain's *Huckleberry Finn.*

> We have selected *Huckleberry Finn* because it's familiar to most English teachers as a book which is rich in issues involving friendship. As Huck's relationship with Jim begins to blossom, we see the boy grow increasingly more concerned with Jim's welfare at the expense of his own; some of the *explicit* reasons for this concern reflect a rejection of self-interest as a moral principle (Stage 2) in favor of trust, respect, loyalty, and gratitude—qualities which are characteristically embedded in Stage 3 moral reasoning.

Both examples provide a guideline for selecting moral issues. Not only are the issues themselves important but the level of reasoning about those issues is important. In both examples the issue of friendship is mentioned. Ladenburg asks her students to consider the meaning of friendship as it might be understood by a conventional-thinking adolescent confronted by postconventional reasoning. Bramble and Garrod understand the saliency of the same issue but ask their younger students to consider the issue from an earlier-stage perspective, recognizing that issues become most relevant when the level of reasoning exhibited by the characters is appropriate to the students' level of understanding.

Relating Content Moral Issues to Students' Lives

In part, because of different levels of moral reasoning, particular pieces of literature appeal to some students and not to others. Guy Bramble and Andrew Garrod, in analyzing the potential use of *Huckleberry Finn* for moral development, illustrate the understanding that relevancy is partially defined by structure of reasoning. As teachers, they are thus attempting to relate to their students' lives.

> It has often been remarked that some novels, like *Huckleberry Finn*, seem to grow richer in meaning with each successive reading: the ten-year-old sees only an adventurous yarn, while the fifteen-year-old discerns a tale of friendship in addition. But the twenty-five-

year-old sees all of this and also begins to detect the satiric humor which characterizes Twain's burlesque of the values and customs of the "genteel tradition" in the antebellum South. Yet it's obviously not the book which changes every few years—it's the reader; so when high-school sophomores claim to have read *Huckleberry Finn* already (as they inevitably do), we shall encourage them to reconsider the story and characters from the more mature point of view which they have reached as 10th-graders.

In identifying possible relevant moral issues in the literature, Bramble and Garrod, like Ladenburg, take into account the age and experience of their students.

In aiming at an audience of sophomores, we designed our curriculum for readers who will understand the story of Huck and Jim to be primarily a tale of friendship. This is not to suggest, of course, that 10th-graders will be oblivious to all other issues; but Kolhberg's research supports our own classroom observations that 15–16 year-olds are particularly responsive to considerations of friendship because they are themselves in the midst of the transition from Stage 2 to Stage 3. No group of students will develop at a uniform rate, so we can expect that some will shoot ahead of the pack while others lag behind; but friendship will typically be a matter of deep concern to most 10th-graders, and they will usually be quite receptive to discussions which explore friendship issues (i.e., trust, respect, loyalty and gratitude). This is why we have included *Huckleberry Finn* in our curriculum, and it's why Twain's greatest novel rarely fails to capture the interest—and stimulate the thinking—of its adolescent readers.

Moral development theory requires that students confront alternative realities. Only by constructing a new way of thinking is growth promoted. The search for appropriate content involves more than identifying relevant issues. It also requires the possibility for conceiving of a different reality.

Muriel Ladenburg's use of *A & P* to help students confront the conventional concerns for appearance, security, and authority exemplifies the teacher's need to see within a piece of literature an opportunity to help students explore the alternative meanings of their own lives.

John Updike's story *A & P* is more impersonal and explores more the quarrel between adolescent and adult institutional authority, making the conflict more directly relevant to the present lives of the students. Sammy is a check-out clerk at the local A & P. Through his eyes we perceive the sterile, ugly, routinized adult world of aisles with stacked cans and sheep-like people pushing carts up and down with grim seriousness. Suddenly a nubile young girl and her two friends enter the store wearing their bathing suits. The aura of their audacity, in contrast to the dismal atmosphere of the store, makes Sammy nearly swoon. He follows the first girl, the leader of the trio whom he dubs Queenie, up and down aisles with his eyes and his heart, endowing her with all the qualities of "class" painfully absent from his own life. When Langly, the martinet manager, criticizes and tries to humiliate the girls for their inappropriate attire, Sammy spontaneously rises to their defense and quits his job. He does so in spite of Langly's warnings about his future and his parents, and ironically, he does so without reward, for it is doubtful that the girls ever noticed his heroic stance, let alone appreciated his sacrifice.

Confronted with Sammy's rebellion, Ladenburg's students relate the ensuing discussion to their own lives.

This story stimulates discussion about everyday rules and regulations regarding things like dress codes and respect for adult authority. Students will debate the advisability of Sammy's bravado, and many will have their own work-related stories to tell. Discussion should center on their own needs to get out from under and express, really or symbolically, their own feelings and sense of right and wrong.

Opportunity for Role Taking

Guaranteeing that content and reasoning level relate to the lives of one's students is insufficient to the task of promoting the growth of moral reasoning. Engaging students in role taking and exposing them to slightly more adequate modes of reasoning provide additional catalysts for growth. In the taking of another's perspective one becomes aware of the inadequacy of one's own reasoning. Confronting a more adequate stage of reasoning begins the search for a new balance of thought. Literature may serve as a powerful vehicle for the stimulation of this process, as Bramble and Garrod explain.

Normally, student role-taking in a moral discussion is confined to the members of the immediate group, but our curriculum invites students to assume the perspective of fictional characters as well as that of their peers. We have attempted to promote this sort of role-taking by posing questions which are designed to elicit *value-identification* as well as moral reasoning. By value-identification we refer to that role-taking process by which students attempt to *isolate* and *identify* specific attitudes and values which they perceive to be held by others. When a member of the discussion group is the subject of this process, verification can always be obtained by asking for "feedback" from the subject; but when the process is directed toward a fictional character direct feedback is no longer possible and the discussion participants must identify the character's values by a collective role-taking process in which each student compares his impressions of the fictional character with the impressions of his peers.

Bramble and Garrod add a new dimension to the function of the role-taking process. Not only do they encourage the process for its facilitation of moral development but they also find that role-taking the lives of characters is a means of enriching the literary experience.

Applying this role-taking process to the values and attitudes of fictional characters (which many experienced English teachers do as a matter of course) may impose stringent demands upon the empathic powers of the discussion participants; but only in this manner can these characters be brought to life for students. Only thus can the phantoms of a creative literary imagination escape the two-dimensional world of an hypothetical Heinz to become realistic three-dimensional figures.

In addition, the literary characters themselves may model the role-taking process for students. Twain oftens portrays Huck in a state of cognitive and moral conflict, and one such example of the role-taking process comes from the novel itself. Huck, in a quandary, thinks:

Conscience says to me, "What had poor Miss Watson done to you that you could see her nigger go off right under your eyes and never say one single word? What did that poor old woman do to you that you could treat her so mean? . . . She tried to be good to you every way she knowed how. That's what she done." [4]

Because Huck can take the perspective of another person, he is caught between conflicting personal loyalties—to Miss Watson and to Jim. Confronted with such a dilemma involving friendship, what ought one to do? In the story Huck vacillates between his concern for his friend Jim and his own personal needs and desires. This is nowhere more clearly seen than when Huck articulates a principle by which he intends to resolve all future moral dilemmas.

> They went off and I got aboard the raft, feeling bad and low, because I knowed very well I had done wrong, and I see it warn't no use for me to try and learn to do right. . . . Then I thought a minute, and says to myself, hold on; s'pose you'd 'a done right and give Jim up, would you felt better than what you do now? No, says I, I'd feel bad—I'd feel just the same way I feel now. Well, then, says I, what's the use you learning to do right when it's troublesome to do right and ain't no trouble to do wrong, and the wages is just the same? I was stuck. I couldn't answer that. So I reckoned I wouldn't bother no more about it, but after this always do whichever come handiest at the time.[5]

So Huck's moral principle seems to be that what defines the "right" is whatever most conveniently meets his immediate personal needs. Shades of stage 2 thinking.

Muriel Ladenburg also employs various teaching strategies to facilitate the role-taking process. For example, she asks her students first to role play the major event in Camus' novel.

> A role play of the trial (before this part of the book is read) is a particularly effective means of getting students directly involved with these issues. Here students as Meursault, lawyers, judge, and jury members get to articulate the pros and cons of his alleged guilt, and to consider a just response. If only one or two students can identify with Meursault's existential rejection of conventional morality and articulate their feelings, debate will be heated.

Role taking is a vehicle for producing cognitive conflict. Such conflict occurs when people become aware that their own point of view has been confronted by another, which seems more satisfying. Hence there is a need to expose students to reasoning structures more adequate than their own.

Exposing Students to More Adequate Reasoning Structures

Muriel Ladenburg's choice of literature takes into account the need to provide students with reasoning beyond each student's current level. An example of this can be found in the literature selected for the second section of her course, which was chosen for the issues of principle inherent in the plots. Concern for principled reasoning is the beginning of the developmental dialogue required for movement from conventional reasoning. For this purpose Muriel chose *The Crucible* by Arthur Miller, where the resolution of a moral dilemma is the central theme. A concern for principle is also evident in her choice of Alan Paton's *Cry the Beloved Country*. Both novels provide an opportunity for historical analysis and an extrapolation of the characters' moral concerns to the reality of the students' lives. In both, students begin to confront the anomalies arising out of the interaction of conventional and postconventional reasoning. Muriel's use of Paton's novel allows for such questions as: What moral principle may be used to solve the black-white conflict? What moral principles motivate persons exemplified by the central character? Is morality situational? What is the basis for justice?

> Reverend Kumalo's prostitute sister, his militant and corrupt union leader brother, the near saintly white minister who is his friend, and the murdered man's heart-broken father all raise many issues of trust, duty, fairness, love, anger, but it is Absalom's crime and its punishment that demand that each reader exercise fully his own concept of justice. Is the law of the white man who invaded, exploited, and brutalized the natives to have final dominion over the black African? Is murder and violence to be judged in accordance with its heritage or on an absolute basis? More particularly, students should be asked whether Absalom received justice; how one fights injustice; and if they feel it would have been better to punish the cousin too. Finally, the students must answer for themselves whether the frail bridge of hope wrought by the two grieving fathers can sustain pressures of the past injustices and all the sorrows to come.

Commitment to Moral Development

If placing students in contact with more adequate reasoning levels promotes growth, it is also painful. Frustration results as one lets go of an old world of meaning not easily or soon to be replaced. Teachers who become aware of this process and see it happening in their students find it painful and often wish to retreat to the usual curriculum. Yet the theory requires that we respect the process of development and the belief that meaning is defined ultimately by one's students. Bramble and Garrod best sum up the process.

> At the opening of the novel, Huck's moral development has been checked due to the smothering effects of the Widow's motherly re- forming, Pap's bullying, and Tom's domination; but Jim seems to intuit that caring for human beings often necessitates letting go of them—that showing respect for the dignity of the individual means honoring his right to make autonomous decisions. This is perhaps the most valuable lesson to be gleaned from the application of Kohlberg's theory to Twain's novel: adolescents—and people in general—develop most fully in an environment which is supportive without being repressive. Children learn to cope with the world by living in it; thus we dare not become so over-protective in attempt- ing to shield our children from pain and harm that we indiscrimi- nately wall them off from experience. Naturally we hate to see our loved ones in distress, but we couldn't adequately insulate them even if we wanted to; and the fact is that *in a loving and supportive environment stress can actually have a positive impact* by precipitating moral development as the adolescent struggles to make sense out of the apparent contradictions which have confronted him. Thus we must learn to let go of our children in order that they may freely interact with the world around them; we must allow them to struggle with life's incongruities, and trust them to make their own mean- ings.

This use of literature illustrates the conceptual process of in- fusing content with moral development concerns. The process is common to all content areas, although not all content areas are as easily adaptable. The following section on the use of history content exemplifies how a teacher might begin to create a continuum of units of work within a specific course.

THE USE OF HISTORY

The teaching of history affords the teacher the same opportunities for integrating moral development concerns with content as does the teaching of literature. At any grade level of history one encounters content rich in moral problems: Galileo rejecting church authority, a father and son having to decide whether to join the Union or Confederate armies, Gandhi rebelling against a colonial force, Constitutional-era farmers deciding to count slaves as three fifths of a person. All are examples of moral issues often treated as no more than historical happenings, names, dates, events, and places.

Thomas Ladenburg, shares with his wife, Muriel, a recognition of the connection between traditional content teaching concerns and the opportunity such instruction provides for moral development. The analysis of decision making as a major purpose of historical study provides opportunity for such integration.

> Man operates within a time frame or context. He perceives problems and makes decisions from alternatives open to him. At some future moment he may look back and more clearly analyze the reasons for his decisions. The model of man as a decision maker operating within the context of time, and of man standing apart from the decision, reflecting back on it, helps us to understand the many and diverse activities of the historian, as well as the nature of the discipline and the four types of questions historians try to answer. These questions are: What was the historical context in which the dilemma occurred? What sequence of events preceded the decision? Was the decision that was reached a correct one? Why was the particular decision made at that time? [6]

By combining a search for answers with the historian's questions, and by involving students in moral discussions arising out of such inquiry, the student not only must grasp factual events but also must help resolve the decision maker's dilemmas by reconstructing the decision maker's *reasoning* process. Such, we may recall, was the case in Mr. Hake's class in the second episode in chapter 1. Developmentally the student is confronted with the need to integrate historical facts, particular social role perspectives, and his own and others' level of moral reasoning. Doing so sparks student interest.

> Besides linking the "what" and the "why" questions, moral dilemmas also have the unique quality of "turning students on." The query, What should _____ do? Was _____ justified? or Who was right? whether asked in the context of the Stamp Act, the Tea Party, or the Battle of Lexington, has always been in my experience the question that elicited the most interest, discussion, and debate.[7]

Thomas Ladenburg explains this phenomenon in Kohlbergian theory.

> The reasons for its power to elicit a response are partially a matter of speculation, but seem closely connected to Piagetian and Kohlbergian theories. Every student has formulated a mental construct, uniquely his own, concerning issues of justice, fairness, or right and wrong. A contrary opinion, or one argued at a higher stage that serves to jar this construct or attack the structure of the reasoning, is opposed as long as there are intellectually valid grounds to combat it. In defending their views against alien ideas, students are forced to dig deeply into their own resources and ultimately modify their own structure of moral thought. Facts become weapons that are used to reinforce their own ideas or eventually to batter down their citadels. As the mind is exposed to reasoning which it recognizes as more complex or complete, it alters or modifies its views, incorporating these newer and more adequate concepts. Thus dilemma discussions are the means by which we encourage students to deal with new ideas and to modify their own patterns of thought. Moral dilemmas have more power to accomplish this change than abstract discussions of causality because they summon immediate feelings of right and wrong which are always with us.[8]

A major point made by Ladenburg is the use of history content in defining moral dilemmas. He agrees with the literature teachers' views, which see hypothetical dilemmas as having limited value. With regard to history, hypothetical dilemmas are devoid of historical time or place. As such, they function as appendages to the curriculum and do not readily serve the dual objectives of development and the teaching of history. Thus Ladenburg opts for using historical dilemmas as the vehicle for curriculum building and discussion.

. . . with the wealth that historical events afford, there is ample reason to require that the dilemma be real rather than hypothetical. The case of the slave mother who kills her child rather than permit the master to sell it as he has the other three is one example. So, too, is the case of Johnathan Harrington who must choose between his loyalty to family and his allegiance to friends and the Revolution, when he decides whether or not to stand with the Lexington militia in the face of superior British forces. Both of these dilemmas are real and reveal something of the nature of the conditions surrounding them.

More complex historical dilemmas can be drawn from cases of actual decision makers faced with crucial decisions that affect the lives of others. Several examples easily come to mind: Abraham Lincoln agonizing over the Emancipation Proclamation, Harry Truman debating whether to drop the atomic bomb on Hiroshima, or a juror at the trial of the soldiers involved in the Boston Massacre. The reasoning needed to engage in these dilemmas must of necessity become interlaced with a consideration of the historical factors which played a role in the decision.[9]

Continuum of Curriculum Development

Using historical dilemmas as a vehicle for integrating content and process, Ladenburg provides examples of how a teacher may develop a curriculum starting with a single historical moral dilemma, such as the trial of the soldiers in the Boston Massacre, and eventually moving to a full history course consistently integrating moral questions within a historical context.

Broader than a single dilemma is the mini-unit. As an example of a mini-unit, Ladenburg uses the parallel between the Boston Massacre and the Kent State incident. Who were the people to blame, British soldiers or National Guardsmen? He suggests that such discussion can be extended to include the Battle of Lexington with its shot from an unknown source. Using these three examples provides a small unit from which students might begin to formulate general principles regarding dissent and protest and at the same time learn about particular historical events.

Ladenburg hopes that teachers will not end their curriculum development with mini-units but will consider broader units of work. He has developed, for example, a major unit of work revolving around the writing of the U.S. Constitution. In this unit students engage in simulation and assume the roles of the Founding Fathers while resolving five major issues before the Constitutional Convention. Later, students read the Constitution and see how the issues were actually resolved.

> The exercise of writing a constitution is really an experience in arriving at a social contract. Students are required to go beyond simple obedience to the law; they must decide what the fundamental arrangements governing our political institutions should be. This would obviously require some application of what Professor Kohlberg labeled as stage five reasoning, the "official morality of the American government." However, in arriving at this stage many lower stage arguments are used.[10]

The simulation of the Constitutional Convention provided Ladenburg's students with an opportunity for role taking, a chance to become acquainted with the reality of historical moral issues and come in contact with various levels of reasoning. The following is an excerpt from that mock convention:

> *Luther Martin:* The purpose of these United States was because we needed to protect the state government from bigger powers. Before they were the United States they had to be protected from the British Power and now you want to just impose the power of the national government on each state. The state of Massuchusetts should have the right to take care of any law itself. . . .
>
> *Gouverneur Morris:* Do you realize what might have happened if Shays' rebellion had occurred in another state? It might have been taken care of in a completely different way. They might all have been executed—maybe they would have been tarred and feathered. We don't know. We can't have that type of disorder going around. We have to have a unified type of law that will affect everyone in every state; that they will get the same punishment no matter what state the rebellion took place in.
>
> *John Lansing:* I really disagree with that statement. That is saying that each person's feelings and each person's ideas are the same throughout the whole country and people in New Hampshire, say, are going to have different issues and are going to feel differently about things than people in Georgia which is about 900 miles away—so you can't say that in one country each person is going to

> feel the same way and going to want to react the same way; so you
> can't have one law govern all those people.
>
> *Charles Pinckney:* What has been stated as an idea is that all men are
> equal. If all men are equal they deserve to have the same rights,
> the same laws governing them . . .
>
> *John Lansing:* You are saying that all men are robots—that's what
> you're saying.
>
> *Charles Pinckney:* I'm not saying that; I'm saying they deserve to
> have equal rights; they deserve to be treated equally; which means
> they must have equal laws.[11]

Ladenburg sees such simulation as an excellent opportunity
for role taking while partaking in a re-creation of the nation's
political historical culture.

> By playing the roles assigned them in the convention, students not
> only partake in their nation's political-historical culture, they gain
> the ability to see a situation from another point of view which is an
> essential factor in cognitive development. Perceiving problems from
> a responsible adult perspective also provides the adolescent with
> conditions that promote the confidence, self-esteem, and sense of
> mastery so important to psychological development. Thus, the
> young man who argues against the national government on the basis
> that its power may be excessive learns something for himself about
> the relationship between authority and freedom. So does the young
> woman who, as Gouverneur Morris, tells the Convention that be-
> cause of Shays Rebellion "we obviously need a stronger federal gov-
> ernment." [12]

Finally, one can see the logical extension of curriculum from
the unit to a full course in history. Ladenburg, for instance,
extrapolates the moral dimension of American history to include the Federalist era, the establishment of the National Bank,
the suppression of the Whiskey Rebellion, the Alien and Sedi-
tion Acts, the Dred Scott decision, and on through our history,
including the more recent concerns for racial and sexual
equality—issues like those discussed earlier in the Constitutional Convention.

The creation of a history curriculum is thus not simply the
finding of moral issues for discussion; it is the integration of
moral questions and discussion *within* the context of the historical data. Rather than sacrifice the time spent on teaching histor-

ical content, this strategy, as demonstrated above, attempts to enrich such study with greater historical meaning *and* promote moral development. This process is not unique to high school teachers. Gail McIntyre, a fourth-grade teacher in California, provides an example of how social studies content in the elementary school may serve as a springboard for moral development.

McIntyre planned a "moral education" lesson to teach the concept of conservation. Previously she had taught a lesson centering on the concept of scarcity. In that lesson Gail had initiated a discussion about values and how our values may contribute to a condition of scarcity. The scarcity of certain kinds of fish, buffalo, lumber, water, and oil were all mentioned by students as examples of how things that society values have become more and more scarce.

In her conservation lesson McIntyre planned to extend the previous values discussion and have students generate reasons for people to live with the problem of scarcity and ways this could be accomplished. She carefully planned to discuss examples immediate to her children, such as too few books in her reading series, not enough instruments for a class band, and only two paddles for the Ping-Pong table. She hoped to move on to examples outside the school, examples that she knew her students were aware of from their previous discussion. What follows are excerpts from that lesson.

The students quickly recognized that their solution to scarcity problems in their classroom had been properly solved by sharing or by taking turns in using the materials. McIntyre asked how the class had resolved the Ping-Pong paddle problem. Vance, sounding like the class historian, pronounced, "A few boys pushed the rest away when we wanted to play." The class laughed, remembering Vance was the biggest offender.

"And then what did we do to solve that problem?" asked McIntyre. One girl answered, "The first week we agreed to draw numbers from the hat and people took turns in order." Another girl added, "Then we invented a new game where more than two people played at one time."

Some time later, the discussion turned to water conservation, something that California children had been experiencing in their lives. McIntyre asked what would be the fairest way to conserve water. Someone flippantly yelled out, "Take turns using it." As the laughter subsided, Benjamin said he didn't think that answer was so funny because his mother had made him use the same bath water his baby brother had been washed in. Jessica said, "I can't take turns using the shower anymore—now I have to shower with my mother."

The discussion continued. The next day, McIntyre asked students to talk about the problem of some people living in the community who did not try to conserve water while others were indeed sacrificing. Some students were clearly punitive: "Put them in jail." "Turn off their water." Others echoed the reality of current practices: "Fine them." Lonnie suggested that these people be punished in such a way that they would understand the problem of using up the water: "Don't let them drink anything for a while until they understand how thirsty we would all get if we didn't save the water."

Gail McIntyre's lesson was a well-conducted integration of content and moral development concerns. Building a lesson around a substantial and important concept, she was able to engage her students in the consideration of the moral dimensions of the societal problem of conservation.

The development of single lessons, mini-units, or courses to accommodate a concern for moral development is equally applicable to other areas, such as the content usually found in elementary reading instruction. Although many teachers focus their concern for teaching reading on the *process* of reading, the content need not be ignored for its moral dimensions. The example that follows, which is from a Canadian elementary classroom, illustrates this point.

THE HOLE IN THE FENCE [13]

The Hole in the Fence is a set of materials prepared by the Canadian Health Ministry as a reader in values education. The authors did not have Kohlberg's moral development theory in mind. In the reader, vegetables are portrayed as people, each with a specific set of valued (or devalued) attributes: Carrot, an "insecure person," feels the need to cheat in a race against Radish, the best runner in the garden; Pumpkin, fat and slow, envies slim Asparagus and feels hurt because his friends call him "chunky"; Eggplant is purple and suffers prejudice because of his color; Chinese Cabbage is strange to this garden because his ways are different; and Little Green Tomato is slighted by others because of her youth and immaturity. There are also other vegetables in the garden, and as a potential community they must learn to live together. Inevitably there is conflict, and issues of fairness pervade the story. Children's discussion of this story often centers on the obligations of friendship, the value of honesty, the consequences of cheating, and the rights of others who may look or sound different.

The use of vegetables engages the interest of beginning readers and at the same time forces confrontation with moral issues, as in the problem with Eggplant. Eggplant arrives at a party in the garden. Upon his entering, Cauliflower exclaims, "But he's purple."

"He *is* purple," the rest exclaim. "What does that mean?" asks Beet, thinking she has asked a stupid question. "It means we can't have anything to do with him," Cauliflower says. "Just because he's purple, Cauliflower?" asks Corn. "Yes!"

Children reading this story are provided with an opportunity to engage in role taking: "What must it be like to be treated like Eggplant?" asks a teacher.

"I wouldn't like it," answers one little girl at the back of the room.

"Why not?" the teacher asks.

"Because it isn't nice to treat people that way," the girl answers.

And so the dialogue begins. Other students chime in. Eventually the discussion and probing relate to their own reality and to a variety of values issues. Children have an opportunity to role-take, ask questions, reason out loud, hear different points of view, and relate their reading to their own emotional and thinking lives. And they have enjoyed themselves. They have been engaged in listening and talking. They have engaged in moral discussion.

This is but one example of reading instruction that has potential for integration with moral development objectives. Children's literature is replete with stories demanding social role taking, the resolution of competing value claims, and an excitement that promotes discussion far beyond the content or skills derived from the literal reading of the material.

CLASSROOM LIFE AS CONTENT FOR MORAL DEVELOPMENT

In addition to using the usual academic content in a moral development curriculum, a teacher may also focus on the moral issues raised by daily classroom living. During the normal course of any school day, at any level of schooling, students are confronted with moral issues—cheating, lying, stealing, friendship, obedience to authority. The process of living in the social environment of a school provides another kind of content for use in a moral development curriculum.

The Bulldozer Affair

A moral issue arose in one elementary school in which the students had been planning to build a creative playground. The teacher in this case had been using the design of the playground as a springboard for teaching measurement skills, design and drawing techniques, and ecology concepts. At the same time she wanted her students to learn how to cooperate on a project that would have tangible and practical benefits, both for her class and for the entire school.

The students began to gather such materials as old tires and scrap wood for their new playground, only to realize that the terrain they had chosen as the playground site needed leveling. They began a group problem-solving session around this issue. The teacher saw an opportunity to engage her students in a moral discussion and wrote up the dilemma in capsulated form.

A sixth-grade class, planning their own creative playground, needed outside help to bulldoze the land. The students were able to enlist the services of one of the fathers in the community to work on his own time on the weekend to prepare their site.

On Saturday the man began to bulldoze as the students watched with eager anticipation. At noon the man told the students that he was going to lunch and that it was important that no person go near or on the bulldozer because it was dangerous to do so and also because this was not an insured operation since it was not a contract. He explained to the students that if anyone violated the agreement and did get on the equipment he would have to end the bulldozing and could not finish what he had started.

While he was gone two of the boys did go on the bulldozer and managed to start the machine. They then turned off the engine and left the grounds.

Should the remaining students tell the bulldozer driver what happened?

The class was divided into five groups of six students and asked to perform two major tasks. The first was to discuss what possible alternative actions there could be, and to list those alternatives. The second task was to choose the one alternative which that group felt was what students in the dilemma *should* do, and to provide reasons for their choice. Below is one group's list.

What the Students Could Do!

1. Be honest and tell the bulldozer driver.
2. Walk away like nothing happened.
3. Tell the operator nothing happened.
4. Tell the operator after he gave them a ride on the bulldozer.
5. Tell the operator some teen-agers messed around on it.
6. The two boys could confess and apologize.

What We Picked and Why

One person wanted to go away. The rest of us would be honest because maybe he (the operator) might forgive the children and because they were honest and told the truth he might finish the job.

After each group completed its list and chose a solution from the alternatives, the lists were taped on the wall, and the students engaged in a full class discussion of the problem. They probed one another's reasons to some degree, but the most consistent strategy was "escape hatching," that is, solving the dilemma by making it a nondilemma. This can be seen in the list of the group above, who believed that being honest would result in the bulldozer driver's compassionate reply that he would finish the job.

The debate became heated as students attempted to balance their potential individual loss of the playground and the loss to the whole school. One boy, a strong leader in this discussion, continued to figure out ingenious escape hatches. "If the bulldozer driver quits, we will find another father in the school to do it." Others nodded in agreement. The teacher, playing devil's advocate, said, "Look, I'm the bulldozer driver and I'm a man of my word. If you tell me that someone got on the bulldozer, then I am absolutely going to stop the project!"

The issues were now clear, either tell the truth and lose the services of the bulldozer driver or lie and have the project completed. Given those two options, what should this student do? The student, thus confronted and confused, thought for a while, rose up in the silence of the class, and exclaimed, "Now that's a dilemma!" This illustrates the beginning of cognitive disequilibrium.

This, then, is an example of a teacher making use of a classroom project not only to teach the usual academic content but to probe the students' thinking about moral issues. Her willingness to listen and her use of appropriate small-group settings helped the students to brainstorm before reaching closure. The teacher's probing and the resulting student awareness of the meaning of the dilemma is an example of what is required in helping students to deal with the difficult task of engaging in dialogue about moral issues.

This teaching episode was a planned moral development lesson. At times, however, a teacher may recognize a classroom event that lends itself to spontaneous moral education. The junior high school example that follows is one such incident.

Girls and Cars

In planning an art lesson for her class, Peggy Gaston, a junior high school teacher, decided to ask her students to draw three sketches of a car of the future. In this particular class Peggy knew from previous projects that although some of her students were keenly interested in cars, many were not, so she decided to supply them with a number of auto magazines to provide ideas for design. Her only admonition was that no drawing could be a copy of a magazine picture.

Peggy placed the pile of ten magazines on a table in the center of the room. She suggested to her twenty-seven students that they might begin sketching at any time. "I'm sure most of you have wonderful ideas already, so you won't need any help. Those who get stuck may want to look through a magazine." Instantly a conglomeration of boys hurdled desks and chairs to reach the magazine table first. The onslaught left three magazines torn and every girl in the class empty-handed. The boys gathered in small groups, leafing through magazines and talking car talk; the girls sat and watched.

Recovering from her shock and naiveté, Peggy abandoned her planned lesson and asked the students to participate in a class meeting. She expressed to the group her surprise and concern over what had happened and asked if they recognized what they had done. After some silence, one boy said, "We didn't do anything wrong." This broke the ice. Others mentioned "not sharing," "not fair to the dumb girls," "it was a stupid assignment anyway," and "we can bring in more magazines from home."

Peggy asked the students to consider a more general issue, the issue of how to decide what is fair when there isn't enough of something to share equally. One girl asked the boys how they would have felt if the situation had been reversed, if the girls had taken all the magazines (role taking). One boy replied that the boys would have beaten up the girls. Another girl retorted, "But suppose *we* had been given the magazines by Miss Gaston, would that be fair?" The discussion continued with the class ultimately agreeing to formulate rules for sharing materials in future art projects.

The examples above provide evidence that it is quite possible to integrate traditional school content with moral development objectives. It is also possible to utilize the process of learning and interaction in the classroom as "content" for furthering the growth of moral reasoning. The foregoing examples relate to specific classrooms that are but a microcosm of the school as a larger community. Kohlberg recognizes that classrooms are not isolated entities but share social space within the institution called school. He thus proposes the creation of a "just community" as the social vehicle for maximizing moral development within a school setting. The school, in a sense, thus also becomes part of the curriculum. This dimension of the theory and practice is explained and illustrated in the following chapter.

7

The Just-Community Approach

In the preceding chapters we have been suggesting a progression in the implementation of developmental moral education. A conducive classroom atmosphere should be set up. Moral issues should be raised to awareness and considered in classroom discussions. Single discussions should be woven into the curriculum and used as a means for resolving conflicts. Although it is difficult to achieve all these things in a classroom, we believe it is both possible and worthwhile.

Moral issues do not end at the classroom door, however. They often involve the school as a whole or larger units within the school. If there are racial or social-class tensions, incidents of stealing and vandalism, people who are dissatisfied with the academic policy or with the way the lunchroom is run, the source of the problems lies not in single classrooms but in the school. Schools as well as classrooms have moral atmospheres, and although it is much harder to change whole schools, some problems can be dealt with only on a school-wide level.

We do not know of any large school that has attempted to alter its structure in the light of Kohlberg's theory. Efforts have been made to create several alternative "schools-within-a-school" that incorporate aspects of the theory. Kohlberg himself has been involved with one such alternative high school in Cambridge, Massachusetts. He and his colleagues are attempting to implement a "just-community" approach to moral education. Because this approach may provide promising contributions to the field, in this chapter we describe this latest step in developmental moral education.

THE ALTERNATIVE SCHOOL IN CAMBRIDGE [1]

Although Cambridge, Massachusetts, is known for its universities, as a city of more than one hundred thousand residents, Cambridge is made up largely of working-class people from different ethnic backgrounds. The city high school is filled not with the children of university professors but with the children of the working class.

In 1969 a group of professors and students from the Harvard Graduate School of Education convinced the Cambridge public school system to set aside space in the high school for a small, informal, and culturally diverse alternative school. That school took root and succeeded so well that by 1974 there was a waiting list to get in.

A parent of one student on the waiting list polled parents whose children were in the same situation and ascertained that there was a strong desire on their part to start a second alternative program within Cambridge High School. They petitioned the superintendent of schools, who gave his permission for the second program. The school committee approved a summer-planning workshop composed of parents, students, and resource persons. Kohlberg was one of the resource persons.

Kohlberg had been working with his colleagues for several years, implementing a just-community approach to prisons. By 1974 that effort was well established, and he was eager to begin working in a high school setting. The invitation to meet with the Cambridge group led to an active partnership; he committed himself to working as a consultant to the new alternative program, and the group committed itself to trying to implement a just-community approach in its school.

Initially the just-community approach entailed the following: (1) the school would be run democratically, with staff and students each having one vote in the making of school decisions; (2) the school would remain small enough (about seventy students and eight staff members) so that it could meet in a face-to-face community meeting once a week; (3) the staff and students would work together to build a spirit of community within the school; and (4) the staff members would learn about the theory of moral development so that they could apply it to classes and community meetings.

The school began in September 1974 with sixty students (ninth- through twelfth-graders) and six staff members, who had volunteered in order to participate in the program. The school met in two adjacent classrooms within Cambridge High School. Students were required to take a daily two-hour core course in English and social studies. Elective courses were also offered, but students continued to take many of their courses in the regular school. The staff also divided its teaching time between the alternative and the regular school. Thus, both staff and students retained dual status as members of both schools.

DEMOCRATIC GOVERNANCE

Democratic governance stands at the heart of the just-community approach. For students and teachers to overcome their reliance on traditional authority patterns, they have to learn to share democratically the responsibility for decision making.

Traditionally, teachers and administrators make the decisions in the school. They claim the power for themselves and are left with the responsibility for enforcing their decisions and rules. They may or may not take time to explain to students the rationale for these decisions but, in either case, expect students to abide by the rules whether or not they understand or agree with their rationale. Students are left with a choice of passively obeying, actively rejecting, or subtly undermining the staff's decisions.

Even though this traditional authority pattern may prove relatively effective from a managerial perspective, from the perspective of moral development theory there is little to recommend it. Passive acceptance and negative rejection are not stances likely to promote students' moral development. Insofar as students stand outside the decision-making process, they will not feel responsible for decisions that are made. They will not see themselves as *morally* bound to uphold the rules, but as *pragmatically* bound either to conform or to avoid punishment.

The Cambridge alternative school is run as a direct democracy. Everyone in the school meets once a week for a two-hour community meeting at which basic decisions about how to run the school are made. Although the rules of the larger school are in effect, the community exercises the right to interpret these rules and enforce them in its own way. Thus, while cutting classes or using drugs is outlawed in the larger school, in the alternative school these rules were adopted by the community only after intensive discussion when a majority agreed to their necessity. Initially the community voted a liberal policy of allowing everyone ten legal cuts, far more than the number allowed in Cambridge High School. When that policy interfered with the running of classes, the community altered its course and did away with all legal cuts. That, too, proved unenforceable, and a compromise of four cuts was adopted. At meetings, the teachers favored fewer than four cuts, but it was the majority of students who made the decision.

Students also enforce these decisions. No one gets sent to the headmaster or has to see the teacher after class. Violators of rules are responsible to the community. At first the students were reluctant to discipline one another, but when it became clear to them that classes could not be conducted smoothly if too many students were disruptive or absent, they began disciplining those guilty of excessive behavior. Students' investment in their own learning and in the maintenance of the school overcame the reluctance to punish peers.

A democratically based community meeting for seventy or eighty people is a hard show to run. It requires several conditions: (1) student interest must be maintained; (2) there must be a clear but flexible procedural order; (3) issues must be raised clearly so that the pros and cons of concrete proposals can be discussed; (4) students and staff must discuss issues by voicing reasons for their stands and not by attacking one another on personal grounds; (5) everyone has to feel that the decisions of the community will be carried out and will not be subverted by higher authorities or dissenting minorities.

In the Cambridge school, none of these conditions was present in the fall of 1974. There was no established procedural order, and the staff ran the meetings. Students spoke up far less than staff, and when students did speak, it was to voice an opinion unsupported by any stated reasons. Votes were taken before issues were thoroughly discussed. Students were distrustful of the faculty and used their majority to vote for unwise decisions (e.g., dismissing school early). Only gradually, over a period of a year, did the democratic conditions listed above come into existence.

Student interest was the exception in the overall picture. Interest was high from the start because students sensed that real issues affecting them were being discussed. Maintaining interest was more difficult; adolescents (and adults) can quickly tire of the task of self-governance. This is especially true when discussions get bogged down in details.

To offset this tendency, the Cambridge staff has adapted a strategy from the theory of leading moral discussions. Interest in moral discussions is raised by posing a hard-to-resolve dilemma that engages the discussants' social and moral reasoning. Similarly, the staff, who meet once a week to plan an agenda for the community meeting, try to pick topics that are currently "hot" and to plan a strategy for discussion that will highlight any moral or fairness issues involved. For example, a discussion about using drugs will focus on whether it is fair for some people to come in "high" when others are trying to conduct a serious class session.

The day before the community meeting, each staff member meets with a different small group of students to discuss the topics of the week. Each student in each group has an opportunity to express opinions and to work with others at arriving at the group's positions. The staff member moderates the discussion, highlighting fairness issues and contributing opinions and reasoning. The next day, the general meeting opens with representatives from each group reporting on their group's positions on the topics at hand.

Each week a different group of students is responsible for leading the community meeting. One member of the group is selected to chair the meeting. This person sits at the front of the large classroom, flanked by the group members. The faculty adviser stands by for assistance. The chairperson opens the meeting by announcing the first item on the agenda and then calls for small-group reports. One or several representatives of each group usually make a proposal for action. Discussion commences. As the participants raise their hands, a member of the group in charge records their names on the board and calls off their names to allow them to speak in turn. At the most productive meetings there is healthy debate, with an even balance between the number of student and staff remarks. People listen to one another and address themselves to supporting or refuting the opinions and reasoning offered by others.

Upon sensing that the first round of discussion has concluded, the chairperson calls for a straw vote. That vote is followed by further discussion in which the minority get a second chance to win over votes to their side. Having heard the pros and cons, the members (at least the majority who have been listening) are ready to take a real vote and make a communal decision.

In this process great stress is placed on the discussion itself. As mentioned, initially the students were not accustomed to discussing issues and tended simply to state their opinions and quickly call for a vote. The staff had to work hard at modeling discussion techniques. They would ask people why they held the positions they articulated. They would raise issues of fairness and ask how a given proposal would look from the perspective of the group's welfare. They encouraged diversity of opinion, insisted that everyone have the right to dissent, and protected individuals from being personally attacked by those who disagreed with them. The staff put off the vote until reasoning for both sides of an issue had been heard and some consensus or compromise had developed. They accepted the majority's decisions even when it went against their opinions. With time, the students followed suit.

As an aid to this learning experience, an elective course in democratic process was offered during the first year. Class members reviewed with the teachers community meetings that had recently taken place and discussed more efficient ways for running the meetings. They also visited other communities and were taught more explicitly about moral development theory and its goals. Out of this original class came some of the suggestions for running meetings that were later adopted and have been described above. In addition, several of the most effective chairpersons came from this class. After the first year, the democracy class was incorporated into the orientation sessions for incoming students.

Once the community started making decisions and adopting rules, it was expected that both staff and students would adhere to them. Adherence, however, has not always been forthcoming. To deal with violations of its rules, the community has set up a rotating discipline committee made up of one student representative from each small group and two staff members. If, for example, a student disrupts a class or is caught using drugs, or if a faculty member is accused of acting abusively to a student, the case comes before the committee at its weekly meeting. If the person involved is a first-time offender, the committee tries to effect a reconciliation between the parties. If there has been a history of offense, the committee recommends a punishment to the community. The community hears the case, allows the parties to present their sides, discusses the issues, and makes its decision. Offenders are given every chance to make amends and change their ways; but when that route has been exhausted, parents are called and students are expelled from the school.

Kohlberg considers this way of running a school "just," not only because it is directly democratic but also because the community's decisions can be made at the highest level of moral reasoning available to its student members. That is not to say at a principled level, for no student in this school has developed beyond stage 4, and most students reason at a stage 3 level. The staff's task is not to impose higher-stage reasoning but to offer the soundest reasoning the students are capable of understanding and to encourage students to exercise the best of their moral reasoning in arriving at communal decisions. When that is achieved, and when the students stand behind their decisions and enforce them, the school can be said to be operating as a just community.

THE CAMBRIDGE SCHOOL IN ACTION

To give a more concrete sense of this school in operation, let us consider how the community dealt with the problem of stealing in its first two years of operation.

Students' stealing property from others is a common problem in Cambridge, as in other high schools. In December of the first year of the first community, an intern working at the alternative school invited a group of students to her home to make candles. The next day, her roommate told the intern that five pairs of earrings were missing. Because there had been no other guests or intruders, they suspected that a student had taken the earrings. But when the intern raised the issue at school, no one would volunteer any information.

A month later, a student brought to school a box of silver rings, which he showed around. During a class one of the rings "disappeared." All anyone would suggest was that the ring had been pushed out the window.

As a result of these incidents, the issue of stealing was raised at a January community meeting. The meeting opened with a proposal from one group that "the people who stole should go to the discipline committee and the property should be returned or paid for." There was some discussion of what the punishment would be, but nothing more happened until the staff interceded.

Kohlberg, who participated regularly in these meetings, asked: "Maybe someone can explain why the stealing has been going on. Don't people think stealing is wrong and a violation of the community?"

Student reaction was subdued. One student responded: "I don't think you should worry about that. The fact is it happened, and to worry about why it happened isn't worth it."

One of the staff persisted: "I think that ripping off is not an individual business; it is a community business. It is not a discipline issue as much as it is some feeling by the community that people have to have a level of trust which is inconsistent with anybody ripping off from anybody else in the community."

Only one student picked up the issue of level of trust. The sentiment of the majority was expressed by a frank girl who said: "This is a bunch of bull. You can make a rule [about stealing], but everyone doesn't have to get upset. . . . Someone is always on your back in this school."

The discussion returned to the question of making a rule about stealing. Although no one was sure such a rule would work, they agreed that making a rule and stipulating a punishment for its violation was a first step. As one student argued: "If they call his parents about it, next time he will think about it and it will cut down on it."

With that argument the meeting ended, but the problem persisted. Stealing continued throughout the first and partway through the school's second year.

In October of the second year, nine dollars were taken from the purse of one of the female students. She was sure that a student in the community had taken the money, but no one would admit to it. A community meeting was called to discuss the incident.

Reports from the small groups opening the meeting reflected a concern on the students' part that acts such as stealing were disruptive to their sense of community: "We said that everybody give fifteen cents because fifteen cents isn't going to hurt you." That is, they suggested that if every member gave fifteen cents, the nine dollars could be returned to the student from whom it was stolen.

The rationale for this collective reimbursement was interesting: "Everyone, some fifty people, should put in fifteen cents to give her back her money because it is not her fault. It is everybody's fault, because people just don't care about the community. [They think] they are all individuals and don't have to be involved in the community. [But] everybody should care that she got her money stolen."

From our point of view, this statement by a student and the support it received from other students marked a turning point in the school's development toward a just community. For the first time, students articulated a sense that they were responsible for what went on in the school. If someone's money was stolen, it was everyone's fault for not caring enough about the community. To be sure, the statement was challenged by other students who felt that the theft was the responsibility of either the girl who allowed her money to be stolen or the individual who stole the money. Nevertheless, the majority agreed to a compromise proposal that if the money was not returned by a certain date, every member would pay fifteen cents to replace it.

That this was a turning point was borne out by events that followed the meeting. For a week there was no confession, and it seemed everyone would have to pay. Then some students admitted they knew who had stolen the money and agreed to speak to the person privately. When this proved unsuccessful, they grew impatient with the guilty person and revealed her name to the group. Eventually she was expelled by her peers from the school. What's more, no further incidents of stealing occurred in the school. Students did not swear off stealing entirely but came to an agreement that was articulated by one student: "If you want to rip off, rip off on your own time and not in school."

The progress from the first to the second year, as reflected in these meetings, was modest but significant. We can understand it in the following terms:

1. Students took a more active role in the second year in dealing with stealing as a community problem. They made the connection that they could not have a community if people could not trust one another with their property.
2. The quality of the meetings improved, for students not only proposed different actions but also backed up their

proposals with reasons why they should be adopted. Students addressed one another's positions and reasons.

3. A decision was made that led from judgment to action. Whereas in the first year the rule and possible punishment for its infraction did not deter stealing, in the second year a norm evolved among students that stealing was not to take place in the school. Their revealing the name of the person who stole meant they would be willing to enforce this norm.

The progress was modest. In a neighborhood where there is a lot of street theft, one cannot expect to eliminate all stealing at once. Still, an important inroad was made, not only because in one area of life they all agreed not to steal but also because they became attached enough to an institution to care about upholding its norms. We believe that their active role in forming the norm was essential to their committing themselves to its enforcement.

CONCLUSION

As argued at the beginning of this chapter, issues that can be dealt with on a school-wide level (even in a small alternative school) are harder to deal with than issues that arise in a single classroom. Nevertheless, we believe that elements of the just-community approach have applicability to the life of classrooms. We also see no reason why building a community or democratizing decision making cannot begin on an elementary level.[2]

Perhaps most important, we see developmental moral education as moving into a second phase, one in which emphasis will be placed on integrating moral discussions with other educational goals. These may be learning subject matter through revitalized curricula or learning how to assume responsibility as a member-citizen of a democratic community. Both aspects of this second phase are still tentative, for details of them are only now being worked out. Their fate, we believe, will depend on administrators and teachers willing to adapt them to their own quests for establishing more just schools.

Epilogue: All's Well That Begins Well

The end of this book marks the beginning of the reader's practice of moral education. Given the apparently overwhelming nature of the theory and practice of moral education, it might be only natural to ask, "Can I really do this?" The answer, and we hope we have adequately conveyed this answer throughout this book, is an enthusiastic "Yes." Nevertheless, we wish to leave the reader with the simple but important truth that time, commitment, and patience with self and others are required for successful integration of theory and experience. The moral education practitioner must be willing to struggle with complexity.

We began writing this book with the conviction that we would need to take the perspective of our readers if we were to communicate effectively the complex philosophy, psychology, and pedagogy of Kohlberg's work. With this in mind, we have tried to engage in a hypothetical dialogue with our readers. One problem that naturally arises if we concern ourselves with what and how teachers learn is our neglecting to discuss the impact of this same process on students. Briefly, let us address this important concern.

WHAT DO STUDENTS LEARN?

There are three main ways by which teachers can expect, over time, to facilitate student learning: (1) heightening moral awareness, (2) developing more adequate moral reasoning, and (3) affecting moral behavior.

Increasing students' moral awareness includes recognizing the rights and claims of others, as well as one's responsibilities and obligations to them. Identifying conflict over what is fair may begin with the curriculum content presented by the teacher. Heightened moral awareness eventually extends to involvement in classroom rules and the treatment of others, and to the awareness of moral issues in the school, family, peer group, community, and society at large. Increased empathy for others is also part of a broadened moral awareness, as one sees the need to consider the points of view of others.

The second effect of moral education on students is the development of more adequate moral reasoning. In a broad sense this involves effective discussion skills and more critical thinking ability. Specifically, group moral discussions require the practice of both self-expression and listening to others. The focus on reasoning adds the important notions of elaborating, clarifying, modifying, and differentiating one's thinking. These opportunities can result in growth in students' moral judgment. The moral decision-making process also means that through challenging and being challenged, persuading and being persuaded, students learn that they can indeed be their own decision makers and moral agents.

The third effect of moral education on students, that of affecting moral behavior, is the most problematic area and also the area that interests teachers most. It is important to reiterate that the same behavior can result from many different ways of reasoning about a given action. We need to be careful not to equate more moral behavior with "better discipline" or with the virtuous-deeds approach criticized by Kohlberg.

Instead, we must look at the moral components of the behavior we are considering—evidence of fairness, concern for others, cooperation, empathy, shared responsibility, mutual obligation, and democratic participation. The goal of moral behavior change through moral education also needs to be considered carefully in the light of the stages of moral reasoning possible within students' thinking capacities. What is the capacity of the students to take the perspective of other students? the teacher? a small group? the class as a whole? the school as an institution? Understanding students' perspective-taking ability enables us to get at the meaning behind their behavior.

WHERE SHALL WE BEGIN?

The major task of the book has been to articulate a sequence of the steps we consider necessary to understand the role of the moral educator. Let us restate our position. We have endeavored to weave three main themes into the fabric of each chapter of this book. Certainly the most basic is that moral issues are a part of all educational experience—content, process, and the nature of institutional life itself—whether we choose to confront these issues or not.

A second and closely related theme is that once we decide to embrace the moral domain as part of our classroom inquiry, we deepen our own moral awareness. In detailing moral development theory and practice we have emphasized the steps in the process of facilitating moral growth in children and adolescents. It is equally important that these steps, reflected in the chronological organization of the book's chapters, represent the sequence of the teacher's internal development as moral educator.

This process of inquiry into moral issues begins with understanding the importance of Socratic dialogue and developmental principles. For this reason, we presented a detailed discussion of theoretical issues in the first part of the book. The teacher's inquiry progresses gradually toward mastering discussion strategies, reconstructing curriculum to incorporate moral issues, and eventually recognizing the implications of sharing responsibility and authority in building a more just community. The progression reflects the chronological development of Kohlberg's own thinking as a psychologist and educator. This body of work is still being reworked, as Kohlberg mentions in the Foreword.

On completing the chapter on the just-community approach, the reader may have noticed that there is within Kohlberg's approach to educational practice, as well as in his developmental stage theory, an inherent thrust toward greater equality and shared responsibility. We would agree that a teacher's decision to become a moral educator by leading moral dilemma discussions may resemble the opening of Pandora's box. This is the risk inherent in any philosophical inquiry. Nevertheless, it remains each teacher's unique choice as to which aspect(s) of moral education to embrace. Our respect for the integrity and creativity of each teacher remains paramount.

This brings us to the third major theme of this book. We opened this work with a skeptical view of bandwagon phenomena. We wish to close our writing with a restatement of this stance, with the knowledge that the reader now may join us in this skepticism. It is our firm belief that Kohlberg's approach cannot succeed as an additive approach to everything else that goes on in a given teacher's classroom. We have tried to describe the process of becoming a moral educator as an integrative one, wherein the teacher's own educational goals and pedagogical style and competence can be uniquely meshed with the principles of Kohlberg's philosophy of educational practice.

Indeed, Kohlberg's theory of moral education is not a fixed system. The theory is a changing and growing one, nourished by the critical stance of questioning researchers and practitioners. Such criticism involves risk. We invite our readers to share the risk of moving from theory to practice in the same spirit that they ask their students to take risks in dialogue. We hope this book is the beginning of that effort.

Notes

CHAPTER 1

1. See Louis E. Raths, Merrill Harmin, and Sidney Simon, *Values and Teaching* (Columbus: Charles E. Merrill, 1966); and Sidney Simon, Leland W. Howe, and Howard Kerschenbaum, *Values Clarification: A Handbook of Practical Strategies for Teachers and students* (New York: Hart, 1972).
2. For a more adequate critique of values clarification, see John S. Stewart, "Clarifying Values Clarification: A Critique," *Phi Delta Kappan* 56 (1975): 684–88; and Anne Colby's critique of values clarification in *Harvard Educational Review*, February 1975, pp. 134–43.
3. Raths, Harmin, and Simon, *Values and Teaching*.
4. William K. Frankena, *Ethics* (Englewood Cliffs, N.J.: Prentice-Hall, 1963), p. 47.
5. Raths, Harmin, and Simon, *Values and Teaching*, pp. 114, 115.

CHAPTER 2

1. Jerome Bruner, *The Process of Education* (New York: Vintage Books, 1963).
2. As examples, see Herbert Ginsburg and Sylvia Opper, *Piaget's Theory of Intellectual Development* (Englewood Cliffs, N.J.: Prentice-Hall, 1969); and Barry J. Wadsworth, *Piaget's Theory of Cognitive Development* (New York: David McKay, 1971).
3. Ginsburg and Opper, *Piaget's Theory of Intellectual Development*, p. 3.
4. The next two sections owe much of their conception to Herbert Ginsburg and Sylvia Opper.
5. Sidra Ezrahi, "The Yom Kippur War—A Personal Diary," *World View* 17 (1974): 13.
6. Although it may be helpful for the reader to get a sense of the approximate age of development of these stages in children in our society, it must be stressed that the age differs among individual

children and among children in different societies and sub-societies.

7. Jean Piaget, *The Origins of Intelligence in Children* (New York: International Universities Press, 1952).

8. Jerome Bruner, *Beyond the Information Given* (New York: W. W. Norton, 1973).

9. Jean Piaget, *The Child's Conception of the World* (Paterson, N.J.: Littlefield, Adams, 1963).

10. Barbel Inhelder and Jean Piaget, *The Growth of Logical Thinking from Childhood to Adolescence* (New York: Basic Books, 1958).

11. Anne Colby and Lawrence Kohlberg, "The Relation between Logical and Moral Development," in *Cognitive Development and Social Development: Relationships and Implications* (New York: Lawrence Erlbaum Associates, in press).

12. Deanna Kuhn et al., "The Development of Formal Operations in Logical and Moral Judgment," *Genetic Psychology Monographs* 95 (1977): 115.

13. Jean Piaget, *Six Psychological Studies* (New York: Vintage Books, 1967), pp. 33–38.

14. Kohlberg and Gilligan, "The Adolescent as a Philosopher," *Daedalus* 100 (1971): 1062.

15. Jean Piaget, *The Moral Judgment of the Child* (New York: Free Press, 1965). [Originally published in 1932.]

16. Emile Durkheim, *Moral Education* (New York: Free Press, 1961). [Originally published in 1925.]

17. Piaget uses the games of marbles. We have adapted his observations to baseball.

CHAPTER 3

1. Lawrence Kohlberg, "Stages of Moral Development as a Basis for Moral Education," in *Moral Education*, ed. C. M. Beck, B. S. Crittenden, and E. V. Sullivan (New York: Newman Press, 1971), p. 42.

2. For a review of psychologists who have followed up on Piaget's research, see Thomas Lickona, "Research on Piaget's Theory of Moral Development," in Lickona, *Moral Development and Behavior* (New York: Holt, Rinehart and Winston, 1976), pp. 219–40.

3. David Riesman, *The Lonely Crowd* (New Haven: Yale University Press, 1950).

4. Erik H. Erikson, *Identity: Youth and Crisis* (New York: W. W. Norton 1955).

5. Erich Fromm, *Man for Himself* (New York: Rinehart, 1955).

6. For a treatment of women's moral reasoning in actual cases of abortion, see Carol Gilligan, "In a Different Voice: Women's Conceptions of the Self and of Morality," *Harvard Educational Review* 49 (1977): 481–517.

7. Lawrence Kohlberg, "Stage and Sequence: The Cognitive-Developmental Approach to Socialization," in *Handbook of Socialization Theory and Research*, ed. David A. Goslin (Chicago: Rand McNally, 1969), p. 398.

8. See Robert L. Selman, "Social-Cognitive Understanding: A Guide to Educational and Clinical Practice," in Lickona, *Moral Development and Behavior*, pp. 299–316.
9. Ibid.
10. Kohlberg, "Stage and Sequence," pp. 352–53.
11. The dilemmas are not usually used for children under the age of nine. For younger children, see William Damon, note 16.
12. More exact data on the ages at which stages of moral judgment develop appear in chapter 4.
13. All comparisons in this chapter between cognitive and moral stages are based on Anne Colby and Lawrence Kohlberg, "The Relation between Logical and Moral Development," in *Cognitive Development and Social Development: Relationships and Implications* (New York: Lawrence Erlbaum Associates, in press).
14. Lawrence Kohlberg, "The Development of Modes of Moral Thinking and Choice in the Years Ten to Sixteen" (Ph.D. dissertation, University of Chicago, 1958).
15. Robert L. Selman, "Taking Another's Perspective: Role-Taking Development in Early Childhood," *Child Development* 42 (1971): 1721–34.
16. William Damon, "Early Conceptions of Positive Justice as Related to the Development of Logical Operations," *Child Development* 46 (1975): 301–12.
17. Selman, "Social-Cognitive Understanding," pp. 314–15.
18. Ibid. All further references in this chapter to development of role-taking stages will be based on Selman's article.
19. The stereotyped "law and order" argument, in which the person reasons that breaking any law will cause society to fall apart, has been recently analyzed as being a stage 3A judgment. See Lawrence Kohlberg, "Moral Stages and Moralization, The Cognitive and Developmental Approach," in Thomas Lickona, ed., *Moral Development and Behavior: Theory, Research and Social Issues* (New York: Holt, Rinehart and Winston, 1976), p. 41.
20. Lawrence Kohlberg, "Development of Moral Character and Moral Ideology," in *Review of Child Development Research*, ed. M. L. Hoffman and L. W. Hoffman (New York: Russell Sage Foundation, 1964), p. 403.
21. Lawrence Kohlberg, "From Is to Ought: How to Commit the Naturalistic Fallacy and Get Away With It," in *Cognitive Development and Epistemology*, ed. T. Mischel (New York: Academic Press, 1971), pp. 131–235.
22. Lawrence Kohlberg, "Continuities in Childhood and Adult Moral Development Revisited," in *Lifespan Developmental Psychology*, ed. P. B. Baltes and L. R. Goulet (2nd ed.; New York: Academic Press, 1973).
23. Ibid. Kohlberg has suggested that this type of relativistic thinking may be a substage between stages 4 and 5. He calls it stage 4½. Also see chapter 4, note 16.
24. Lawrence Kohlberg, "The Claim to Moral Adequacy of a Highest

Stage of Moral Judgment," *Journal of Philosophy* 40 (1973): 63ᶜ

25. John Rawls, *A Theory of Justice* (Cambridge, Mass.: Harvard Uni versity Press, 1971).

26. Kohlberg, "The Claim to Moral Adequacy of a Highest Stage ᴏ Moral Judgment," pp. 641–45.

CHAPTER 4

1. Lawrence Kohlberg, "Stages of Moral Development as a Basis fo Moral Education," in *Moral Education*, ed. C. M. Beck, B. S. Crit tenden, and E. V. Sullivan (New York: Newman Press, 1971), pp 30–41.

2. Lawrence Kohlberg, "Stage and Sequence: The Cognitive Developmental Approach to Socialization," in *Handbook of Socialization Theory and Research*, ed. David A. Goslin (Chicago: Ranc McNally, 1969), pp. 397–401.

3. For an articulate expression of this critique, see Elizabeth L Simpson, "Moral Development Research: A Case of Scientific Cultural Bias," *Human Development* 17 (1974): 81–106.

4. Carolyn Edwards, "Societal Complexity and Moral Development: A Kenyan Study," *Ethos* 3 (1975): 505–27.

5. Kohlberg, "Stages of Moral Development as a Basis for Moral Education," p. 55.

6. For the two claims, see ibid., pp. 46–54.

7. Ibid., p. 58.

8. This is but one of several possible formulations of a principled stance in relation to abortion.

9. See Richard S. Peters, "A Reply to Kohlberg," *Phi Delta Kappan* 56 (1975): 78.

10. Kohlberg, "Stages of Moral Development as a Basis for Moral Education," p. 54.

11. Kohlberg, "Stage and Sequence," pp. 362–68.

12. Richard Krebs and Lawrence Kohlberg, "Moral Judgment and Ego Controls as Determinants of Resistance to Cheating" (manuscript, Harvard University, 1973).

13. Kohlberg, "Stage and Sequence," p. 395.

14. Norma Haan, Brewster Smith, and Jean Block, "Moral Reasoning of Young Adults," *Journal of Personality and Social Psychology* 10 (1968): 183–201. Also see review of this article in Roger Brown and Richard J. Herrnstein, *Psychology* (Boston: Little, Brown, 1975), pp. 326–38.

15. By the latest standards of scoring Moral Judgment Interviews, it is unclear whether what in 1968 was called "stage 6" reasoning would still be so considered. To avoid confusion, we will therefore refer to these students simply as "principled," assuming they are at stage 5, if not stage 6.

16. See Elliot Turiel, "Conflict and Transition in Adolescent Moral Development," *Child Development* 45 (1974): 14–29.

17. See Marvin Bressler, "Kohlberg and the Resolution of Moral Conflict," *New York University Education Quarterly* 7 (1976): 2–8.

18. Lawrence Kohlberg, "Development of Moral Character and Moral Ideology," in *Review of Child Development Research*, ed. M. L. Hoffman and L. W. Hoffman (New York: Russell Sage Foundation, 1964), pp. 400–404.

19. Kohlberg, "Stage and Sequence," p. 388.

20. Ibid., pp. 384–85.

21. John Gibbs, "Kohlberg's Stages of Moral Judgment: A Constructive Critique," *Harvard Educational Review* 47 (1977): 50.

22. Joseph Reimer, "A Study in the Moral Development of Kibbutz Adolescents" (Ph.D. dissertation, Harvard University, 1977).

23. Deanna Kuhn et al., "The Development of Formal Operations in Logical and Moral Judgment," *Genetic Psychology Monographs* 95 (1977): 115.

24. Brown and Herrnstein, *Psychology*, pp. 325–26; Gibbs, "Kohlberg's Stages of Moral Judgment," pp. 43–61.

25. William Kurtines and Esther B. Greif, "The Development of Moral Thought: Review and Evaluation of Kohlberg's Approach," *Psychological Bulletin* 81 (1974): 453–70.

26. See Kohlberg, "Stage and Sequence," p. 384; Kuhn et al., "The Development of Formal Operations in Logical and Moral Judgment," pp. 147–48.

27. Moshe Blatt and Lawrence Kohlberg, "The Effects of Classroom Moral Discussion on Children's Levels of Moral Judgment," *Journal of Moral Education* 4 (1975): 147.

28. Elliot Turiel, "An Experimental Test of the Sequentiality of Developmental Stages in the Child's Moral Judgments," *Journal of Personality and Social Psychology* 3 (1966): 611–18.

29. James Rest, Elliot Turiel, and Lawrence Kohlberg, "Level of Moral Development as a Determinant of Preference and Comprehension of Moral Judgments," *Journal of Personality* 37 (1968): 225–52.

30. William Damon, *The Social World of the Child* (San Francisco: Jossey-Bass, 1977).

31. Carol Gilligan, "In a Different Voice: Women's Conceptions of the Self and of Morality," *Harvard Educational Review* 49 (1977): 481–517.

32. Gibbs, "Kohlberg's Stages of Moral Judgment."

33. Charles B. White, Nancy Bushnell, and Judy L. Regnemer, "Moral Development in Bahamian School Children: A Three Year Examination of Kohlberg's Stages of Moral Development," *Developmental Psychology* 14 (1978): 58–65; and Elliot Turiel, Carolyn P. Edwards, and Lawrence Kohlberg, "Moral Development in Turkish Children, Adolescents and Young Adults," *Journal of Cross Cultural Psychology* (in press).

34. Susan L. DeMersseman, "A Developmental Investigation of Children's Moral Reasoning and Behavior in Hypothetical and Practical Situations" (Ph.D. dissertation, University of California, Berkeley, 1976).

35. Robert L. Selman and Dan Jaquette, "Stability and Oscillation in Interpersonal Awareness: A Clinical-Developmental Analysis," in

The XXV Nebraska Symposium on Motivation, ed. C. B. Keasey, 1977.

36. Lawrence Kohlberg, "The Moral Atmosphere of the School," in *Unstudied Curriculum,* ed. N. Overley (Washington, D.C.: Association for Supervision and Curriculum Department, 1970).

37. Lawrence Kohlberg and Rochelle Mayer, "Development as the Aim of Education," *Harvard Educational Review* 42 (1972): 449–96.

38. Blatt and Kohlberg, "Effects of Classroom Discussion on Children's Levels of Moral Judgment," p. 133.

39. James R. Rest, "The Research Base of the Cognitive Developmental Approach to Moral Education," in *Values and Moral Development,* ed. Thomas Hennessy (New York: Paulist Press, 1976), p. 118.

40. Blatt and Kohlberg, "Effects of Classroom Discussion on Children's Levels of Moral Judgment," p. 153.

41. Ralph Mosher, "Theory and Practice: A New E.R.A.?" *Theory Into Practice* 16 (1977): 81–88.

42. Philip Jackson, *Life in the Classroom* (New York: Holt, Rinehart and Winston, 1968).

43. Lawrence Kohlberg, Peter Scharf, and Joseph Hickey, "The Just Community Approach to Corrections: The Niantic Experiment," in *Collected Papers on Moral Development and Moral Education,* ed. L. Kohlberg (Cambridge, Mass.: Center for Moral Education, Harvard University, 1975).

44. See chapter 7.

CHAPTER 5

1. Thomas Lickona, "Creating the Just Community with Children," *Theory Into Practice* 16 (April 1977): 97–98.

2. This unedited transcript, from a social studies class in October 1974, is used with permission of Margot Stern Strom. The source of the Milk Dilemma is "The Teacher's Guide," *Comparative Political Systems: An Inquiry Approach,* ed. Edwin Fenton (New York: Holt, Rinehart and Winston, 1973).

3. Margot Stern Strom's commentary, and the ones that follow on the next few pages, is quoted from an interview with the authors, January 1978.

4. P. M. Grimes, "Teaching Moral Reasoning to Eleven Year Olds and Their Mothers: A Means of Promoting Moral Development" (Ph.D. dissertation, Boston University, 1974), pp. 63–64.

5. See, for example, Robert L. Selman and Marcus Lieberman, "Moral Education in the Primary Grades: An Evaluation of a Developmental Curriculum," *Journal of Educational Psychology* 67 (1975); or Moshe M. Blatt and Lawrence Kohlberg, "The Effects of Classroom Moral Discussion upon Children's Level of Moral Judgment," *Journal of Moral Education* 4 (1975). The variety of doctoral dissertations noted throughout this chapter also explicate the teacher's crucial role in fostering moral development.

6. Moshe Blatt, "Studies on the Effects of Classroom Discussion Upon

Children's Moral Development" (Ph.D dissertation, University of Chicago, 1970), was the first researcher to use such dilemmas to stimulate moral reasoning. Joseph Hickey, "The Effects of Guided Moral Discussion Upon Youthful Offenders' Level of Moral Judgment" (Ph.D. dissertation, Boston University, 1972), was another pioneer, who used hypothetical dilemmas with young adult prison inmates.

7. Moshe Blatt, Anne Colby, and Betsy Speicher, *Hypothetical Dilemmas for Use in Moral Discussions* (Cambridge, Mass.: Moral Education and Research Foundation, 1974).

8. D. P. Paolitto, "Role-taking Opportunities for Early Adolescents: A Program in Moral Education" (Ph.D. dissertation, Boston University, 1975), p. 363.

9. Ibid., pp. 356–59.

10. Sources of such hypothetical dilemmas include Blatt, Colby, and Speicher, *Hypothetical Dilemmas for Use in Moral Discussions;* and Ronald E. Galbraith and Thomas M. Jones, *Moral Reasoning* (Anoka, Minn.: Greenhaven Press, 1976).

11. See, for example, R. C. Alexander, "A Moral Education Curriculum on Prejudice" (Ph.D. dissertation, Boston University, 1977); A. M. DiStefano, "Adolescent Moral Reasoning After a Curriculum in Sexual and Interpersonal Dilemmas" (Ph.D. dissertation, Boston University, 1977); and P. J. Sullivan, "A Curriculum for Stimulating Moral Reasoning and Ego Development in Adolescents" (Ph.D. dissertation, Boston University, 1975).

12. See Barry K. Beyer, "Conducting Moral Discussions in the Classroom," *Social Education* 40 (April 1976): 194–202; Edwin Fenton, Anne Colby, and Betsy Speicher-Dubin, "Developing Moral Dilemmas for Social Studies Classes" (manuscript, Center for Moral Education, Harvard University, 1974); Ronald E. Galbraith and Thomas M. Jones, "Teaching Strategies for Moral Dilemmas," *Social Education* 39 (January 1975): 16–22.

13. Sullivan, "A Curriculum for Stimulating Moral Reasoning and Ego Development in Adolescents," pp. 113–14.

14. See, for example, Grimes, "Teaching Moral Reasoning to Eleven Year Olds and Their Mothers," for a detailed description of how to develop "morality plays" with fifth- and sixth-graders.

15. On cross-age tutoring, see V. S. Atkins, "High School Students Who Teach: An Approach to Personal Learning" (Ph.D. dissertation, Harvard University, 1972). On peer counseling, see R. C. Dowell, "Adolescents as Peer Counselors: A Program for Psychological Growth" (Ph.D. dissertation, Harvard University, 1971); and P. Mackie, "Teaching Counseling Skills to Low Achieving High School Students" (Ph.D. dissertation, Boston University, 1974).

16. Diane Tabor et al., "A Report to the Staff of the Law in a Free Society Project" (paper, Harvard University Graduate School of Education, Center for Moral Education, 30 June 1976), pp. 26–28.

17. See, for example, Jean Piaget, "Equilibration and the Development

of Logical Structures," in *Discussions on Child Development*, vol. 4, ed. J. M. Tanner and B. Inhelder (London: Tavistock, 1960). Also see Jean Piaget, "Piaget's Theory," in *Carmichael's Manual of Child Psychology*, ed. P. H. Mussen (New York: John Wiley, 1970).

18. Guy Bramble and Andrew Garrod, "Ethics I, Friendship: An Experimental Curriculum in Moral Development Which Uses Literary Works as Vehicles for Moral Discussion" (paper, 1976), p. 34.

19. Richard H. Hersh and Janet M. Johnson, eds., "Values and Moral Education in Schools" (manuscript, Schenectady City School District, State University of New York at Albany, and United States Teachers Corps, June 1977), pp. 10–11.

20. See, for example, Maurice P. Hunt and Lawrence E. Metcalf, *Teaching High School Social Studies* (New York: Harper & Row, 1968), and Kurt Lewin, *Resolving Social Conflicts* (New York: Harper & Bros., 1948).

21. Paolitto, "Role-taking Opportunities for Early Adolescents," p. 116.

22. See Beyer, "Conducting Moral Discussions in the Classroom"; or Lawrence Kohlberg, Anne Colby, Edwin Fenton, Betsy Speicher-Dubin, and Marc Lieberman, "Secondary School Moral Discussion Programs Led by Social Studies Teachers," in *Collected Papers on Moral Development and Moral Education*, vol. 2 (Cambridge, Mass.: Moral Education and Research Foundation, 1975).

23. Paolitto, "Role-taking Opportunities for Early Adolescents," p. 376.

24. This is one of a series of films entitled Searching for Values: A Film Anthology, which is available from Learning Corporation of America (New York). These short film segments from feature-length films highlight open-ended moral conflicts.

25. Sullivan, "A Curriculum for Stimulating Moral Reasoning and Ego Development in Adolescents," p. 111.

26. Paolitto, "Role-taking Opportunities for Early Adolescents," pp. 238–39.

27. Grimes, "Teaching Moral Reasoning to Eleven Year Olds and Their Mothers," p. 63.

28. Ibid., p. 65.

29. This film segment, entitled "The Right to Live: Who Decides?" is another film in the Searching for Values series.

30. All portions of dialogue and teacher commentary on these pages are from Sullivan, "A Curriculum for Stimulating Moral Reasoning and Ego Development in Adolescents," pp. 116–17.

31. See John P. Miller, "Schooling and Self-Alienation: A Conceptual View," *Journal of Educational Thought* 7 (1973): 105–20.

32. Sullivan, "A Curriculum for Stimulating Moral Reasoning and Ego Development in Adolescents," pp. 147–48.

33. Several doctoral dissertations have demonstrated that both so-called quiet and active students develop in their moral reasoning over time as a result of moral discussion. See, for example, Blatt, "Studies on the Effects of Classroom Discussion upon Children's

Moral Development," and Paolitto, "Role-taking Opportunities for
Early Adolescents." These researchers also suggest that high interest in the class is a factor common to students whose moral reasoning develops through moral education.

34. Paolitto, "Role-taking Opportunities for Early Adolescents," p.
274.
35. Sullivan, "A Curriculum for Stimulating Moral Reasoning and Ego
Development in Adolescents," pp. 126–27.
36. Hersh and Johnson, "Values and Moral Education in Schools," pp.
12–14.
37. Ibid., p. 14.
38. Ibid., p. 4.
39. The statements of these three teachers were obtained especially for
this book in private communication with the authors, February
1978.

CHAPTER 6

1. Excerpted from Richard H. Hersh and Janet M. Johnson, eds.,
"Values and Moral Education in Schools" (manuscript, Schenectady City School District, State University of New York at Albany,
and United States Teachers Corps, June 1977), pp. 10–11. All
quotes attributed to Joan Ripps are taken from this source.
2. Quotes from Guy Bramble and Andrew Garrod are excerpted from
their "Ethics I, Friendship: An Experimental Curriculum in Moral
Development Which Uses Literary Works as Vehicles for Moral
Discussion" (paper, 1976).
3. Quotes from Muriel Ladenburg are taken from her "The Individual
and Society: A High School English Course Designed to Promote
Post-Conventional Reasoning" (paper, n.d.).
4. Mark Twain, *The Adventures of Huckleberry Finn*, ed. Ralph Cohen
(New York: Bantam, 1965), p. 85.
5. Ibid., p. 89.
6. Thomas J. Ladenburg, "Cognitive Development and Moral Reasoning in the Teaching of History," *History Teacher*, March 1977, p.
187. An additional explanation may be found in Muriel Ladenburg
and Thomas Ladenburg, "Moral Reasoning and Social Studies,"
Theory Into Practice, April 1977, pp. 112–17.
7. Ibid., p. 189.
8. Ibid.
9. Ibid., pp. 190–91.
10. Ibid., p. 193.
11. Ibid.
12. Ibid., p. 194.
13. *The Hole in the Fence* (Ottawa, Canada: Department of Health and
Welfare, 1976). Material excerpted here is taken from the teacher's
guide, "Hole in the Fence: A Living Skills Program."

CHAPTER 7

1. An extensive treatment of the history of the alternative school in Cambridge can be found in Elsa R. Wasserman, "The Development of an Alternative High School Based on Kohlberg's Just Community Approach to Education" (Ph.D. dissertation, Boston University School of Education, 1977). See also her "Implementing Kohlberg's 'Just Community Concept' in an Alternative High School," *Social Education* 16 (1976): 203–7.
2. See Thomas Lickona, "Creating the Just Community with Children," *Theory into Practice* 16 (1977): 97–104.

Index